ALSO BY MARK NEPO

NONFICTION

Things That Join the Sea and the Sky
The One Life We're Given
The Endless Practice
Seven Thousand Ways to Listen
Finding Inner Courage
Unlearning Back to God
The Exquisite Risk
The Book of Awakening

FICTION

As Far As the Heart Can See

POETRY

The Way Under the Way
Inside the Miracle
Reduced to Joy
Surviving Has Made Me Crazy
Suite for the Living
Inhabiting Wonder
Acre of Light
Fire Without Witness
God, the Maker of the Bed, and the Painter

EDITOR

Deepening the American Dream

RECORDINGS

More Together Than Alone
Flames that Light the Heart (video course)
The One Life We're Given
Inside the Miracle (expanded, 2015)
Reduced to Joy
The Endless Practice
Seven Thousand Ways to Listen
Staying Awake
Holding Nothing Back
As Far As the Heart Can See
The Book of Awakening
Finding Inner Courage
Finding Our Way in the World
Inside the Miracle (1996)

"*More Together Than Alone* is not a business book, but any person, in any business, can heed Mark Nepo's call."

—Anthony Salvanto, author of *Where Did You Get This Number?*

"What an amazing book this is! Mark is writing at the height of his powers here. I have found myself deeply moved time and again while turning the pages."

—Jeff Zaleski, editor and publisher of *Parabola*

"In an age of racial divisions, school shootings, and international conflict, this book's message about the necessity of coming together is timely, and its examples of human compassion and unity often comforting."

—*Publishers Weekly*

"A series of short, optimistic pep talks with a collective message: We *can* all get along.... Readers feeling a need for an inspirational kick in the pants will enjoy this book."

—*Kirkus Reviews*

"A poignant and timely meditation on the importance of community, and demonstrates how we live more enriching lives by cultivating connectedness."

—*Elevated Existence* magazine

"Poet and spiritual writer Mark Nepo, one of our 'Living Spiritual Teachers,' brings to this masterwork on community his skills of observation, his ability to reflect in universal terms, and his personal openness to the many ways people approach their life together."

—*Spirituality & Practice*

"A timely reflection on the importance of community and how we can deepen our sense of togetherness to improve both our individual lives and the world."

—Thrive Global

"Mark Nepo has written a guidebook for our complicated, polarized time, with his poet's heart and compassion.... The combination of practicality and inspiration leaves readers with hope for our world, and gratitude for this beautiful book."

—*Light of Consciousness: Journal of Spiritual Awakening*

MORE TOGETHER
THAN ALONE

Discovering the Power and Spirit
of Community in Our Lives
and in the World

MARK NEPO

ATRIA PAPERBACK
NEW YORK   LONDON   TORONTO   SYDNEY   NEW DELHI

An Imprint of Simon & Schuster, Inc.
1230 Avenue of the Americas
New York, NY 10020

First Atria Paperback edition July 2019

ATRIA PAPERBACK and colophon are trademarks of Simon & Schuster, Inc.

For information about special discounts for bulk purchases, please
contact Simon & Schuster Special Sales at 1-866-506-1949 or
business@simonandschuster.com.

Interior design by Kyoko Watanabe

Manufactured in the United States of America

10   9   8   7   6   5   4   3   2

The Library of Congress has cataloged the hardcover edition as follows:

Names: Nepo, Mark, author.
Title: More together than alone : discovering the power and spirit of
  community in our lives and in the world / Mark Nepo.
Description: New York : Atria Books, [2018] | Includes bibliographical
  references and index.
Identifiers: LCCN 2017043772 (print) | LCCN 2017051433 (ebook) | ISBN
  9781501167850 (Ebook) | ISBN 9781501167836 (hardcover)
Subjects: LCSH: Communities. | Communities—Philosophy. |
  Communities—Religious aspects.
Classification: LCC HM756 (ebook) | LCC HM756 .N47 2018 (print) | DDC
  307—dc23
LC record available at https://lccn.loc.gov/2017043772

ISBN 978-1-5011-6783-6
ISBN 978-1-5011-6784-3 (pbk)
ISBN 978-1-5011-6785-0 (ebook)

This book is dedicated to Howard Zinn (1922–2010), who was not only a rare historian but an extraordinary teacher and an actively engaged citizen of the world. He repeatedly pulled open events, past and present, with such honesty and integrity that we have been forced to reassess who we are and where we come from, all in the service of the common good. Personally, I am deeply grateful to have been in his presence for a short time and to have learned from him. Being with Howard always felt cleansing. And reading his unwavering sense of history is an affirmation in truth-telling and of the community that lives within us all. Like many others, I miss him and draw strength from his voice.

When you have models of how people can come together, even for a brief period, it suggests that it could happen for a longer period. When you think of it, that's the way things operate in the scientific world, so why not socially? As soon as the Wright brothers could keep a plane aloft for 27 seconds, everyone knew from that point on that a plane might be kept aloft for hours. It's the same socially and culturally.

We've had countless incidents in history where people have joined together in social movements and created a spirit of camaraderie or a spirit of sharing and togetherness which have absented them, even momentarily, from the world of greed and domination. If true community can stay aloft for 27 seconds, it is only a matter of time before such a community can last for hours. Only a matter of time before a beloved community, as Martin Luther King, Jr. spoke of, can come into being.

—HOWARD ZINN

CONTENTS

FROM I TO WE

ISLANDS IN TIME

ix

CENTERS OF LIGHT

WITH AND AGAINST COMMUNITY

How We Meet Adversity

Our Interests Are the Same

We Can Find Each Other

In the Hindu Upanishads, there's a passage that speaks to how those who become wise lose their names in the Great Oneness, the way rivers lose their names when they flow into the sea. In this transformation from the solitary to the communal, there's a mysterious physics that each generation has to relearn regarding what is possible when we can work together.

Time and again, we're asked to discover, through love and suffering, that we are at heart the same. How do we come to this knowledge in our lives, in our families, and in our communities? What brings us together and what throws us apart? How do we inhabit what we have in common as well as what makes us unique in ways that deepen our daily practice of service and compassion?

To explore these questions, I have gathered stories and lessons from across cultures and history, which reveal moments of community and the qualities of being and relationship that bring people together. My aim is to affirm that, despite the hardships always present, we are more together than alone.

The back-and-forth struggle between solitude and community is an archetypal passage. Being alone and being together each has its lineage. There are countless stories of those who have shunned the world for the depth of their own journey—be they contemplatives, monks, hermits, or misanthropes. And countless stories of those who have given up who they are for the common good.

The word *community* derives from the Latin, *commun*, meaning "common." The same root informs the word *communicate* (to share our understanding, to have understanding in common) and *communion* (to share our experience, to have experience in common). It's not by chance that the word *community* contains *unity*. Our possibility is rooted in the very word. For community is an ever-potent seed waiting for our effort and care to animate what we have in common, so we can share our understanding and experience in our time on Earth.

I offer these moments of community, not as utopias or models, but as sunspots of human behavior that bear looking into, hard as that may be. These flashpoints of relationship and community arise from time to time when we're inspired, and forced, to care for each other.

For years, I've been a student of Japanese woodblock printmaking (*moku hanga*). Early on, my teacher, Mary Brodbeck, outlined the difference in seeing between the West and the East. If I'm trying to draw or carve a portrait of you, the Western approach will have me capture every line and wrinkle and mole. Trained in the West, I aim to draw and include everything to evoke a complete view. The Eastern approach has me look at your face till I can see the four or five lines that will bring the essence of who you are into view. In Eastern training, the heart of the artistic process is to be present enough till I can surface the handful of details that reveal who you are and how you are connected to everything.

In writing this book over the past twelve years, my aim has been to be present enough to the history of community, large and small, that a portrait might surface of what it means to live together and care for each other, to bring into view the essential lines in our human face and lift up a set of stories and insights that confirm the truth that we are more together than alone. It's my hope that, by understanding authentic moments of community, we can affirm that community is real and possible—beyond any illusion or deception. For no one can hide the truth of our failings or dismantle our better selves. The lessons gathered here are meant to be neither cynical nor idealistic, but resilient and useful.

While some moments of community were long-standing and multi-generational, others may have lasted a week or an hour. I seek to learn how they work. To uncover the pathways that bring us together. To discern the human dynamics akin to how a flock of geese migrates without losing a single goose. To understand that our exchange of love is akin to how photosynthesis enlivens a field of ferns. To understand how an orchestra works together to bring Mozart alive and what happens to the community of listeners as they awaken. To be inspired by the gathering and perseverance of great effort the way thousands accompanied Gandhi on his long march to the sea. Why tend to all this? Because somewhere another child is being born who will ask us things we don't yet know, and we must have some sense of how to account for our time on Earth. As the forgiveness researcher Robert Enright has said, "We need to prepare the hearts of the children for the conflicts they will inherit."

The quarrels that define us are captured in the moment of Israeli prime minister Yitzhak Rabin's death. On Saturday night, November 4, 1995, Rabin was assassinated at the end of a rally in support of the Oslo Accords. He was shot at the Kings of Israel Square in Tel Aviv. Found in his breast pocket was a copy of *Shir L'Shalom (A Song for Peace)* with a bullet hole through it. These words were blood soaked:

Every day the sun will rise and shine upon our land, urging us to . . . walk hand in hand . . . Only when . . . hand in hand can sanity be near . . .

We are always near and far from peace and the sanity of walking hand in hand. In every era. In every situation. Always a pain or sigh away from bloodying the song or singing the song. So much depends on whether we're awakened by compassion to reach out to each other or lulled into watching snapshots of life stream by in images cast off from satellites. Once desensitized, the bombardment of suffering and tragedy sent out hourly around the world becomes a dark narcotic. As Samuel Beckett asks in his play *Waiting for Godot,* "Was I sleeping, while the [world] suffered? Am I sleeping now?"

More than a point of blame, this question is a place to begin, again and again. For when we can listen deeply and give freely, there is a natural evolution from the exploration of an inner self to the practice of care between self and other. My hope is that this book will reveal the power of community and how the life of connection can add more meaning to our lives—that the stories here will detail how we can draw strength from community. And that the conversation of the book will help you develop your own care-based communities.

For the work of community is the practice of care stitching the world together. Ours is a complicated era, and so we need every resource and example of heart and resilience we can find. It is both comforting and challenging to realize that no one person can wrestle from the Earth the song of how we can survive together, and no one voice can sing that chorus. We need each other more than ever.

We Are They

I was waiting in front of my hotel to be shuttled to the airport, when the early sun revealed a block-long line of homeless souls waiting for food. The light illuminated our closeness, our interchangeable fate, and our kinship. Just then, the Ethiopian bellman, who insisted on loading my bags, began telling me about his three-year-old son who was imitating everything he saw his parents do. The early light spilled on our faces as this elegant man, in his adopted culture's uniform, said, "We're careful now what we say and do. He watches and copies everything."

I looked to the weary waiting in line and realized that we all must be careful of what we say and do. For the gifts and cruelty of one culture are watched and copied into the next, one kindness and harshness at a time. The human experiment depends on what we model and what we imitate from generation to generation. So how do we model care? How do we imitate integrity? How do we acknowledge our kinship? How do we learn to animate our gifts so we can feed each other? Every society begins anew while extending the lineage of community throughout the ages.

A recent issue of *Time* magazine reported that

> if all the uprooted individuals ... around the world were to form their own country, they would make up the world's 29th most populous nation, as big as South Korea.

What keeps us from caring for each other? What keeps us from pretending that the world's twenty-ninth-largest population doesn't exist? Is it our fear that we could so easily be them? Is it our fear that if we give to them, we'll drown in their despair? Is it our fear that if we give to those in need, we won't have enough for ourselves and our families? These questions have stirred and thwarted communities and civilizations throughout history. And each generation, each nation, each neighborhood and family, gets to wrestle with these questions freshly. Including us.

This book on community has taken a fifth of my life to research and write. As I was finishing it, a deep divide surfaced in the United States with the 2016 presidential election, a divide that is also being felt in the United Kingdom, in France, and throughout the world.

It seems the need to reanimate a true sense of community is more important than ever. Under all our differences, our capacity to behold, hold, and repair what we have in common is part of a lineage that goes back to prehistoric clans that survived the elements by caring for each other. We need to recover and extend that lineage of care. I hope this book is a contribution to the reawakening of our common humanity and our common capacity.

I was born in Brooklyn, New York, six years after World War II, after the defeat of Hitler and fascism, six years after the Holocaust, in which some of my family perished. As a child, I was frightened by images of the atomic bomb's obliteration of Hiroshima. In grade school, we practiced hiding under our desks, as if that would keep us from being incinerated. I came of age in the sixties, part of a hopeful generation who questioned the war in Vietnam. I later saw the Berlin Wall come down, and, in time, witnessed the first African-American president sworn in on the steps of a White House built by slaves. During my lifetime, there has been a slow, steady awakening of community that has upheld America as the land of the free. Through all this, I have grown to understand that, different as we are in what we believe, there is no they. We are they.

And so, I try to stay true to what I know while listening to the opposite views of others. Listening this way, I've come to see that the underpinnings of our current divisions as a nation fall below politics, below Democrat or Republican. More and more citizens are losing themselves in a world built on fear and hate, where tolerance for difference is tissue paper thin, and their understanding of security is based on striking out against others.

As I witness the racism, sexism, xenophobia, and unprocessed anger that is being unleashed, I fear that our isolation and self-interest, as a government and a people, have poked and stirred the darker angels of our nature. Now, we are forced to take our turn in facing the ever-present challenge: to give in to fear or to empower each other to be brave enough to love, brave enough to discover and accept that we are each other.

For no matter where we come from, no matter how we got here, we all yearn to be seen, heard, and respected. I believe that, under all our fear and brutal trespass, we are innately kind and of the same humanity. Under what divides us, we all long to belong and to be understood. We are they, despite the terrible violence that surfaces between us. And all our gifts are needed to stitch and weave the tapestry of freedom.

From the history of our interactions, we can try to understand what we've learned as a human family. Often, we only look to confirm what we already know, but when we can acknowledge what is true or broken, we can engage others, soul to soul. We can put down our arrogance and admit that we're on the same journey. Then our questions about life create connections. No matter what anyone tells you, we don't ask questions for answers, but for the relationships they open between us. And when we can admit to all that we don't know, we begin the weave of community, by keeping what matters visible a little while longer.

But today, I am afraid that the noise of hate is drowning out the resilience of love. I fear that we are tripping into a dark age. And like the medieval monks who kept literacy alive during the Dark Ages in Europe, we are challenged to commit to a life of care and to keep the literacy of the heart alive.

Now, all the things we have in common, all the endeavors of respect that we treasure, all the ways that we find strength in our kindness—all our efforts of heart—matter now more than ever. We are at a basic crossroads between deepening the decency that comes from caring for each other and spreading the contagion of making anyone who is different into an enemy. And, as history has shown through crusades, genocides, and world wars, if we don't recognize ourselves in each other, we will consume each other.

We must remain open and steadfast in the face of fear and violence. We must never make a principle of the pains and losses that darken our hearts. And we must keep voicing the truth of human decency, no matter the brutalities that try to quiet us. Without this commitment to truth and to caring for others, we will become heartless and lost. Most of all, we must pick each other up when we are heavy with despair. For the sun doesn't stop shining because some of us are blind. Nor will the grace of democracy vanish because some of us are afraid to be in the world and react violently out of that fear.

Still, we are they. And the timeless choice between love and fear, as individuals and as a nation, is not a choice of policy. It is the choice of decency that keeps us human. In the face of the disturbances stirred up by fear, I implore you to be kind and truthful, to be a lantern in the dark, and to call out prejudice wherever you see it. In addition to whatever ways each of us is called to gather, participate, legislate, or protest, I implore you to never stop watering the seeds of human decency.

I implore you to stay devoted to the proposition that, when filled with love, we can work as angels here on Earth, using our caring hands as wings.

FROM I TO WE

We must conceive of ourselves as part of one community. We must support that one humanity through our own spiritually-based community, and not put our own community ahead of that one humanity. If we want a better world for our grandchildren, we must act now. We can't continue to just "regret, regret, regret." Change will come from education, not meditation. A sense of wholeness is a necessity. We must move from "I" to "We."

—THE DALAI LAMA

As pollen gathers and disperses, as inlets form and wash away, instances of meaningful community cannot last. Eventually, they will disperse, not because there is something wrong with them, but because all forms are impermanent and run their cycle. Whether they form for a day or three hundred years, they surface from the reservoir of life-force and eventually join other confluences further downstream. However long, short, wide, or deep a true community might be, its impact is timeless. So the goal is not to make moments of true community last forever, but to inhabit them as fully as possible for as long as possible, and to carry their legacy.

We carry a living wisdom about community within us everywhere we go. As Diogenes said in 220 A.D., "I am a citizen of the world." But somehow, an act of community is needed to understand community. As the philosopher Rudolf Steiner said, "The healthy social life is found when in the mirror of each human soul the whole community finds its reflection . . ." We rely on each other to incubate this wisdom that lives in each of us. Perhaps the old Scottish saying is true: "Loving thy neighbor is the only way out of the dungeon of our self."

Life Around the Fire

What if the healing of the world utterly depends on the ten
thousand invisible kindnesses we offer simply and quietly
throughout the pilgrimage of each human life?

—WAYNE MULLER

Stories make sure that the head and heart meet. Stories make sure
that what is and what is possible travel together. Let me share three,
which describe the why, the how, and the what of community. The
first asks how far we'll go to care for each other, *the why of community*.
The second speaks of learning every day from what transpires between people, *the how of community*. And the third is a creation story
that speaks to the never-ending challenge of living in the world, *the
what of community*.

WAVING THROUGH THE TREES

My neighbor and I wave to each other through the trees, though we
don't even know each other's name. After a snowstorm, we worm our
way out. I admit it's comforting to see another in the open, leaning
on his shovel, his breath clouding as he looks again to the sky. There's
something primal in knowing that we each have a fire we huddle
around. I love clearing the path to our door and leaving the light on.

But if my fire should go out, would he let me in? And for how
long? This is a uniquely human dilemma. We struggle with it every
time we look away from the homeless. Different cultures have different ways of holding the question. The Balinese leave food on their
steps for the kind stranger they've yet to meet. The Connecticut
Yankee trains his daughter in etiquette and the social register. This is

still different from the Holocaust survivor who leaves the door open for an angel he's never seen while guarding against every noise. I lean on my shovel in the snow and my neighbor waves back. For which I am glad. And today, I don't feel the need to know his name or story. Yet isn't it in the steps between our friendly wave and our life around the fire that the work of real community waits?

On the raw side of this question is the moment Elie Wiesel recalls of the Holocaust death march he and thousands were forced to make in the ice and snow of the eastern European night, forced to run barefoot for hours toward Buchenwald. In anticipation of the Allied forces, the SS butted and pistol-whipped the emaciated prisoners on and on. Anyone who slowed or stopped was trampled. Those who fell were shot. In the midst of this hell, a poor soul near Wiesel stumbled to the hard ground. Others nearby fell on top of him. But why? Because they knew he would be killed? Because without thinking they hoped that the SS wouldn't know which of them to shoot? Because some in their exhaustion were ready to surrender their broken lives to keep the bullet from ending his life? There was too much chaos in the air. The guards just beat them all till they got to their feet.

Of all the harrowing, awful, and poignant events Wiesel witnessed as a fifteen-year-old, this small anonymous moment of community is what has stayed with me. I imagine it at the oddest times, while driving home in the rain, while walking our dog in the light snow. It won't let go of me. I think it is a painful koan that holds the essence of community. As kind and brave as it is brutal, this moment is a testament to the lengths we'll go to care for each other, if led or pushed to our true nature. In such pain, in such desperate circumstances, in a frame of mind beaten and starved into numbness, what made these men throw their lives into a pile of compassion? We need to understand. For doesn't the strength of true community wait in the space between us and the fallen?

From waving through the trees to sharing food around our fire to throwing our lives down to protect the fallen, the human experiment of living together continues.

USE DETERMINES MEANING

On November 12, 1857, a huge crowd assembled in the London Library for a meeting of the Philological Society at which Richard Chenevix Trench, the dean of Westminster, spoke. Trench explained why a comprehensive dictionary of the English language was needed and how it might be undertaken in a new way. This was the beginning of an immense community effort that eventually created the *Oxford English Dictionary*, engaging more than eight hundred enthusiastic volunteer readers and researchers, led by four editors over a seventy-year span. That night, Trench spoke in favor of *describing* how people actually *use* words rather than *prescribing* how people *should* use words. It was here that the basic principle of the *OED* was born: that use determines meaning.

This long moment of community devoted to advancing the availability of language to all people would be a stunning accomplishment that, alone, might have reflected an enlightened culture. But in the same year, only seven months earlier, the same British nation, with ignorance and malice, had provoked the Indian Rebellion of 1857, in another case where use determines meaning.

The rebellion took place in Meerut, India, against the British East India Company. The insurgence arose because of what seemed a small thing to the British, whose engineers of war had devised a new breech-loading rifle, the Pattern 1853 Enfield. But the rifle had a fatal defect—not a mechanical fault, but a spiritual flaw. For the Enfield was designed to load a greased cartridge whose tip had to be bitten off before loading. And the British, indifferent to what they viewed as subordinate cultures, greased the cartridges with animal fat, including beef and pork. In shipping boxes upon boxes of rifles and cartridges to India, it never occurred to them that many of the native Hindu and Muslim soldiers (Sepoys) enlisted at Meerut would refuse to put fat from a sacred animal to their lips.

So it was, on April 24, 1857, that eighty-five of ninety Sepoys in the Third Bengal Light Cavalry refused to touch the cartridges. After being court-martialed, they were sentenced to ten years' imprisonment. By placing those Sepoys in irons, the ruling British triggered thousands of Hindus and Muslims to revolt. And though the British quelled that revolt, the sleeping giant of India had been awakened.

The 250 assembled in the London Library seven months later may not have thought much about the rebellion at Meerut or the brutality of the British soldiers, who hanged thousands for sympathizing with the revolt. And if made aware, no doubt, many would have questioned what the *OED* and the Indian Rebellion had to do with each other. But we can question the covenants of a society in which so many were passionate about words but indifferent to the millions of Hindus and Muslims living then under British rule. For at the same time that Trench was speaking in London, the British Empire was flexing its muscle to maintain its harsh domination of India, which would drag on for another hundred years.

Despite all this, we can learn from the beginnings of the *OED* because our inquiry here depends on a similar long-term commitment, not to the life of words, but to the meaning that arises from what happens between people when living their lives together. And I can't help but wonder: What if the reverence Trench invoked around the meaning of words had been invoked around the meaning of our lives?

History proves that we oppress each other when we *prescribe* how people on Earth *should* live together and how communities *should* work; and we give each other tools when we *describe*, with respect and reverence, how people on Earth *actually* live together and how communities *actually* work. And so, this book attempts to gather threads of wisdom from how people have actually woven the fabric of community, to detail, if possible, the working knowledge—both inspired and flawed—of what transpires between people every day. This is how we learn as a human family.

Yet how are we to hold these two moments in London and Meerut in the same year in the same society? What are we to learn from them? If use determines meaning, how do we define honorable use? And when we find these divisions in our own communities, we need to remember how to value people over things.

THE STORY OF RAVEN

While visiting the Museum of Anthropology at the University of British Columbia, Vancouver, I entered a rotunda whose seats are scalloped like ripples in a deep lake. At the center of the ripples, where the stone would have dropped, is an enormous wood sculpture of a large bird on a half-open shell in which humans are waking. Some of the waking figures are eager to come out, while others are hesitant. The larger-than-life carving is on a stone pedestal, settled in a mass of fine pebbles, which are patterned in ripples as well.

The sculpture was carved out of yellow cedar by Haida artist Bill Reid. With the help of other First Nations carvers, it took him ten years to create this remarkable statue. He chose this large project because Parkinson's disease had taken away the steadiness he needed to work small.

The statue portrays the creation story of the Haida people of British Columbia, which centers on the image of Raven. A powerful, wise spirit and trickster, Raven is often depicted atop a clamshell washed ashore in which the first humans are coming alive. Raven is pecking at the shell, coaxing the first humans to come out into the world, for our human destiny requires that we come out of our shell to complete the world. Raven's coaxing is both wise and deceptive, because, once in the world, our journey is not easy and the struggle is ongoing, and knowing as much we might not want to be born. For each generation, the challenge is the same: How to leave our shell and how to help each other live once out of our shell?

I circled Raven several times and felt the presence of Spirit in my own small life, urging me to step out of my shell. I thought of my tribe and realized that the call of every community is to facilitate birth in every way possible and then to help each other on our way once we're here.

The struggle between coming together and breaking apart is epitomized by the fact that before the museum was built, a World War II fort stood in this very spot, and below Bill Reid's carving is a worn-out gun turret. In fact, the architect planned to sit Raven over the turret as a symbol of how we can come together and repair what is broken. Directly above Raven is a circular window in the ceiling, letting in the sky.

This huge yellow-cedar statue, carved by a trembling man and placed between the remnants of war and the open sky, is a true totem: a living image to remind us that though we are born alone, we must live together. I invoke the totem of Raven: of Spirit coaxing us to crawl out of our shells, to stand on the Earth, and to find our way together. History is a tribute to the many ways the human tribe has tried. Why gather and open all these stories, some triumphant, some failed? Because, can't you feel the sea calling? Can't you feel the land waiting? Can't you feel the press of our shell? Can't you feel the wise trickster Raven coaxing us to do more than watch? It is our turn.

For each generation, the challenge is the same: How to leave our shell and how to help each other live once out of our shell?

The Unfinished Painting

Dreams and art are the smoke signals connecting people over time. Stories and myths do the same. Often, we are so greatly taxed by circumstance that we lose the larger view of time and how we are all related, not only to those around us but to those who came before us and those who will come after us. Often when jarred away from the press of my own complications, I feel a sense of this larger tribe that I can't quite name or place. When tossed into great loss or wonder, I feel compelled to understand this unnameable community.

Like last night, when Susan and I went with dear friends to an old small theatre in Three Rivers, Michigan, to see Werner Herzog's luminous documentary *Cave of Forgotten Dreams*, which explores the oldest known cave paintings, discovered in 1994 in the Chauvet Cave of southern France. The 32,000-year-old cave is carefully preserved and the general public is not allowed to enter. Herzog received special permission from the French minister of culture to film these artifacts.

The paintings, the modern efforts to understand and preserve how they came to be, and Herzog's commitment to bring the cave paintings alive—all speak to a sense of community over time. We often suppress or dismiss this sense, because it takes effort and empathy to understand and participate in the enormous arc of life that informs each of us. Yet this is how we discover meaning across time, by putting ourselves in another's place.

What is most remarkable about these cave paintings is their immediacy, their freshness. There is a softness to the horses and bison drawn on rock that conveys their moment of aliveness long ago. Clearly, these early, anonymous artists felt an energy that moves through all life. Their intelligence and feeling transcend space and time.

Carbon dating has determined that markings from different times

11

cover previous markings on certain walls. There are bear scratches overlaid by later human drawings, followed some 5000 years later by more human drawings. These suggest that though each of us thinks we are creating by ourselves, for ourselves, within our own lifetime, life is an unfinished painting that joins us over time. Aware of it or not, we keep adding to another's expression, scratching the same wall of experience, creating an ever-evolving mandala of what it means to be alive.

Given this unfolding, how are we to understand literature across the eons? Or philosophy? Or art? Or translation? Is each work a cave painting, complete unto itself? At the same time, is each effort another layer of strokes, adding to the unfinished painting that keeps emerging, generation after generation? And if this is possible, how do we learn the art of deciphering the pictures that grow from our collective experience, the sum of all our strokes? What wisdom waits there?

In another film, an archaeologist accompanies an Aboriginal man into art-filled caves in Australia. When they come upon an old cave painting that is severely worn, the Aborigine begins to touch it up. The archaeologist is stunned. His companion explains that it is not he alone who is painting, but "that which moves through us all." His people believe it is their job to keep the paintings alive, to keep completing them, and, by so doing, to complete themselves. What sense of community does this way of thinking bring to life? How does this form of responsibility deepen our understanding of what it means to be a global citizen? What does this say about our living, emerging heritage?

A scientist interviewed in Herzog's film notes that we've named our species *Homo sapiens*, which is Latin for *wise man* or *knowing man*. In this way, we have given ourselves primacy and dominion over other life, declaring that we are the only species to have a highly developed brain, capable of reasoning, language, introspection, and problem solving, setting ourselves apart as superior.

The problem is that there's a difference between knowledge and knowing. We can generate and catalogue ever-increasing bits of information, like grains of sand along the shore, without ever experiencing the sea. Given how buried we are in our dunes of knowledge and how little we truly know beyond ourselves, the scientist suggests that we might do better to name ourselves *Homo spiritus*, Latin for *spirit* or *breath*. Then, as we go about our quest for true knowing, we can acknowledge that we are spirited beings aware of this common life-force that moves through everything. Then, knowing becomes how we *engage* this common life-force, not how we *describe* it. Then, community becomes the art and science of understanding and engaging the life-force that moves through everything.

Of all the paintings shown in the Chauvet Cave, I was most touched by the one of four horses neck to neck, part of a larger scene with bison and rhinoceros. I wonder what made that prehistoric artist journey to the depths of this cave and paint this moment on the cold stone? What did he or she see in how the four horses were running in an open plain that the artist couldn't let go of? Was it the light on their necks or the thunder of their hooves or those big glassy eyes taking in everything? Was it the cave person's longing to run as free? The freshness of the connection between the four horses and their seeming awareness of each other echoes the breath of being that moves through everything.

On the way home we talked, at first quickly, enlivened by the paintings of the Chauvet Cave. Then, as the sky streaked its evening blue, hundreds of fireflies mirrored the stars in the highway grasses. We went silent. I was glad to be with my loved ones, glad we saw the energy of those horses captured on the cave wall, glad for the evening sky and the fields of fireflies flaring their small lights, like us. Glad we are forever drawn to this breath of being, to feel it, to know it, to sing it, to paint it, to dig it up once it is buried, and thankful it remains unfinished in us. Who would want the wind to finish or the sea to lose its waves or the sun to stop emitting its light?

The next day I tried to draw the four horses myself—not to replicate them, but to see if I could feel their freshness by joining in, by touching something that was begun so long ago. As I made strokes with the charcoal, I became certain that the things that matter are unfinished paintings that everyone creates and no one owns. More deeply, we are created each time we touch the breath of being, and each time we add a stroke, we are connected to everyone who ever lived. And sometimes, we are briefly aware that we are living parts of the most elemental community of all, the community of life-force that moves through everything.

And what of the unfinished painting we call relationship? Is mis-understanding an unfinished painting that our trust sketches and re-sketches on our oldest wall? Is feeding the hungry an unfinished painting that we must tend to every chance we get? In truth, healing the ill is an unfinished painting that we must touch up and repair whenever we see others breaking down. And stopping the violence and making peace is an unfinished painting of the life-force that moves through everything. Ultimately, caring for each other is the one tribe we all belong to.

All things are connected. The art of community is discovering how.

Community becomes the art and science of understanding and engaging the life-force that moves through everything.

The Aspen Grove

An old friend drove me into the Santa Fe National Forest so we could walk the aspen grove. We stopped along the way to smell some Ponderosa pine. I stuck my nose into the crease of its bark and cupped my hands around it. The tree smelled like vanilla.

We continued up the mountain. At an altitude of 10,000 feet, the temperature dropped thirty degrees. The air was clear. Walking into the grove, which covers almost two hundred square miles, we could see Santa Fe and Los Alamos. We could even see Arizona and Colorado. The path was lined with small red feathery clusters known as Indian paintbrush. Soon the tall, thin aspens were everywhere, their smooth bark stretching like skin to the sky. The continuous rustle of their leaves was like an ocean of small voices arriving through the centuries. If we could just make out their cry, their song, and understand their brilliance.

Walking among them, touching them, listening to their creak and sway, I could feel their connectedness. Aboveground, aspen grow as individual trees, but belowground they're enlivened by one interconnected set of roots. They are the most expansive growth of trees to share a common root system. This means they are one living organism and one living community—at the same time! This is a powerful metaphor for how inextricably knit the life of the individual is with the life of community. What happens to one tree happens to all aspens in the grove. How do they live as one and many at the same time? How do they communicate with each other? How do they sustain each other?

As one living root system, the aspen grove treats each of its trees as a shoot or limb called a ramet. When an individual tree dies, it's as if the grove loses a branch. The grove then rushes nutrients to the damaged area the way immune cells rush to the site of an infection.

The huge root system allows the ramets that are close to water to absorb and send that nourishment to the other connected trees. When we can accept that all humans share the same invisible root system, we, too, can rush nutrients to others who are damaged or suffering.

Quaking aspen, a particular species that grows where avalanches, mudslides, and fires have occurred, is nature's example of relational resilience. The grove roots and regenerates most strongly after disasters. In Yellowstone National Park, a quaking aspen grove grew out of the 1988 wildfires. This is one of nature's gritty forms of resurrection. Likewise, when we can focus on the clearing made between us rather than on the disaster that caused it, we can resurrect and flourish like the quaking aspen.

In the Fishlake National Forest in Utah, there is an aspen grove named Pando, Latin for "I spread." Considered one of the largest aspen groves in the world, it contains about 47,000 individual trees and is estimated to be about 80,000 years old. Shared roots live longer, a lesson for us all.

This is the aspen wisdom we need. We need aspen sensitivity, aspen memory, and aspen compassion. We need to learn how to enliven that depth of connectedness whereby we can feel all of humanity while living our very small, individual lives. In moments of great suffering and love, I believe we do this. But how to understand this capacity and keep it alive when the days are ordinary and we seem so far away from each other?

About a mile into the Santa Fe grove, my friend and I sat on a ledge and waited. Once we were quiet, we could feel the entire grove sway as one timeless aspen *and* as a thousand individual trees on a mountainside in New Mexico. We could almost hear them breathe in unison. I felt certain that in the paradox of the aspen trees waits the secret to our interdependence: being who we are *and* staying connected to everyone.

As we walked back to the car, the path was alight with tiny butterflies circling our feet. Each seemed to hold a question about how to live this way. After a while, my old friend said, "There's a community already existing underground that's growing us into being."

We looked once more and it seemed clear that if all the aspens were to burn to the ground, the community would still be there, ready to begin again. Like the scarred human groves that sprout throughout history.

Shared roots live longer.

Notions of Community

We cannot live for ourselves alone. Our lives are connected
by a thousand invisible threads, and along these sympathetic fibers, our actions run as causes and return to us
as results.

—HERMAN MELVILLE

The sympathetic fibers that Melville refers to can become visible—
but only to those who open their hearts. We are often called to serve
or bear witness to the suffering of strangers in order to discover the
strength and wisdom in connection. These notions of connection
and community are not new, but rooted in many traditions.

The Diné (Navajo) say that seeking wholeness is personal, an
individual journey, while seeking harmony is transpersonal, a communal journey. The Diné word *Ahyo-oh'-oh-ni* means *to bring one into
harmony with everything.* A key purpose of Native American education, this aim for harmony is based on the indigenous notion of *all my
relations* that views all of reality and life as related and interconnected.
Every aspect of life is seen as part of one intrinsic family of existence.

The African view of *ubuntu,* which is often translated as *I am because you are, you are because I am,* implies that we find our humanity
in each other. Archbishop Desmond Tutu says that "Ubuntu is the
essence of being human: that my humanity is caught up in your
humanity." Dirk J. Louw, from the University of the North in South
Africa, tells us that "Ubuntu (a Zulu word) serves as the spiritual
foundation of African societies. It is a unifying vision or world view
[embedded] in the Zulu maxim *umuntu ngumuntu ngabantu,* [which
literally means] 'a person is a person through other persons.' "

Through many paths, we are led to a discernment of relationship
that takes us through our self and beyond our self into the interdepen-

dent mystery, where we find ourselves in each and every living thing, where, as the Hindus say, *Thou Art That.*

The oldest notions of community invoke an underlying network of living connection that is always present whether we honor it or not. Most traditions offer a kindred name for the tribe of humanity through which one person can sense and feel all persons. This timeless connection speaks to the innate sense of responsibility we are each born with to do our best to hold each other up, reflecting in our hearts the hearts of others.

In Sanskrit, the word *Akasha* refers to a collective presence and memory among human beings. In the West, we tend to ignore this, insisting we are separate and unattached. Yet there is molecular and biological evidence of our Oneness and how our very presence influences each other, how being influences being. Consider that two living heart cells, taken from different people and placed in a petri dish, will, over time, find a third common beat. We can draw vitality and strength from these glimpses into the fabric of life, which affirm that we have an innate call to find each other and join. We could say this is the genetic basis for our impulse toward community.

In the summer of 2004, I was in Barcelona attending the Parliament of the World's Religions. One morning, I was sitting with a crowd listening to Dr. Ervin László, a scientist and philosopher who was speaking through translators about the Akasha Field.

Dr. László described experiments in which different atoms were also placed in close proximity. Once atoms A and B would vibrate in harmony, atom A was placed near a third atom, P. Amazingly, the vibration of A and B was imparted to atom P. The reverse appeared to be true as well. Atom A was left with atom P until they vibrated in harmony. Then atom A was again placed closely to atom B. The vibration and harmony of atoms A and P were then imparted to atom B.

When people meditate together, their brain waves quickly harmonize. And when a newcomer joins the group, the newcomer's brain waves harmonize with that of the group. *This suggests that intimacy is a catalyst for the experience of Oneness.* All of this implies that there is a unified field of presence, very near to each of us, that ranges from atoms to cells to souls. The crucial question, then, is: How do we relate to this field of presence? How do we tap into its energy and resources?

As Dr. László spoke, his words were being translated into four languages at once. I realized that what he was suggesting was happening there in Barcelona. I was part of a short-term community of 8000 people from all over the world who had come together because of a common belief in something larger than ourselves. Something was shimmering there between us, like the vibration and harmony generated by those atoms put in close proximity with each other.

Hasn't this always been the power of communities—to somehow break through the trance of their times? Isn't this descriptive of the throngs surrounding Buddha under the Bodhi tree? Or the hundreds gathered to hear Jesus give the Sermon on the Mount? Or the thousands following Gandhi's march of salt to the Indian Ocean? Or the million crowding the mall in Washington to hear Martin Luther King, Jr. give his landmark speech? Isn't this the mystery of self-organizing moments of collective presence?

These instances confirm that there is a subtle, if mysterious, Oneness that cradles us all. We can access the collective presence and memory among human beings and enliven it. Actually, it doesn't take much, once we are opened, to feel the pull of things coming together, whether it be atoms vibrating, strangers meditating, or hundreds gathering around an elder's presence.

As we watch a river from its bank, the current seems impossibly fast. But from the center of the current, the flow of life surrounds us and carries us. Watching from our isolation, the prospect of community seems impossible until we dare to step down and enter. Once in the current of human connection, we are carried along.

Every story of community, large and small, bears witness to how strangers and loved ones alike discover the common human beat and the kinship of presence.

Intimacy is a catalyst for the experience of Oneness.

Bonds That Last

The essence of oneself and the essence
of the world—these two are one.
—Joseph Campbell

When atoms join, they form molecules. When molecules join, they form organisms. When organisms join, they form tissue. When tissues join, a body is formed. Unless interrupted, this is the unfolding of life. Similarly, when hearts are opened, they form bonds. When bonds are deepened, they form relationships. When relationships are inclusive, they expand our sense of kinship. When kinships are strengthened, a community is created. Unless interrupted, this is the unfolding of the social self, which is the atom of community.

These unions are more than a metaphor. Our impulse to join is at first biochemical. So, it helps to examine how atoms join to form molecules. One way is through covalent bonding. A covalent bond is a chemical bond that exists when two atoms share one or more pair of electrons.

As building blocks of life, atoms have a proclivity to join, to combine with other atoms to form molecules. By forming molecules, they grow into something greater than each atom is by itself. This is how a hydrogen atom joins with two oxygen atoms to form water, which is necessary for life to sustain itself. In this way, atoms find each other and join to create the stuff of life, such as protein and DNA. When atoms actualize the chemical bond that joining initiates, they become more together than alone and life unfolds.

Those of us compelled to join become the building blocks of community. When we combine with others, we grow into something greater than our individual selves. People with a common need bond around food, shelter, civil rights, equal pay, or a belief in sobriety.

In this way, we're drawn to work together to solve the great human problems, and create community by becoming more together than alone.

Our capacity to join and complete each other is literally in our DNA. This capacity is at the heart of the social self, which makes community possible. Like water, the bond of community is necessary for life to sustain itself.

We often take for granted the miracle of joining and how it makes life possible. But without our capacity to join, the web of life falls apart. Without our capacity to bond, we are just a collection of mismatching parts. When able to join with other life, the social self awakens and we enliven the miracle of community. The social self is the connective tissue that lets us find what we need in each other in order to grow.

The notions of *Ahimsa, Ren,* and *the Beloved Community* are forms of connection that awaken the social self. These Hindu, Chinese, and African-American traditions are virtues that make community possible.

In Sanskrit *himsa* means "doing harm" or "causing injury." With the *A* before it, the word means "to cause no harm or injury." In its original context, *Ahimsa* doesn't only mean the interruption of harm or injury, but also the commitment to live a non-harmful and giving life. The term Ahimsa can be traced back in Hindu teachings to the Chandogya Upanishad (8th–6th century B.C.), where it's listed as one of the five ethical virtues. The Jain religion (9th–7th century B.C.) holds Ahimsa as the first vow among the living.

Since all life-forms are deeply connected, what we do to others, we do to ourselves. This is an extension of the golden rule. The way of Ahimsa acknowledges that harm begets harm and that the fire of harm can't be controlled. And so, who sets the fire is also set on fire. In the third century B.C., southern India's Tamil poet, the weaver saint Tiruvalluvar, stated this truth as a spiritual law, "All suffering recoils on the wrongdoer himself. Therefore, those who desire not to suffer refrain from causing others pain."

Whether you believe in Karma or not, the ever-present awareness of another's experience helps us stay sensitive to life other than our own. It helps frame our daily actions within the context of more than one generation, the way Native American elders consider seven generations in making tribal decisions. We could benefit greatly from restoring this larger, more heart-centered perspective in all we face and do.

In his struggle for Indian freedom, Gandhi believed that no society can survive without the presence of truth and a commitment to nonviolence. In 1926, Gandhi proclaimed:

> I am not pleading for India to practice non-violence because she is weak. I want her to practice non-violence, being conscious of her strength and power . . . My life is dedicated to the service of India through the religion of non-violence, which I believe to be the root of Hinduism.

We always have the choice to stop harm and to further live a non-harmful life. When harmful, we remain blind to how we're connected and our isolation only makes us more guarded and more harmful. When we can enter the sense of Ahimsa, we get closer to life and all kinds of bonds are possible. In this, the Hindu way is a deeply human way.

The Chinese philosopher Confucius (551–479 B.C.) put forth the notion of a social self—a self inextricably linked to the life of others. Each person is not morally autonomous, but a social being whose identity derives from his interaction and conduct within the broader human community. Central to a healthy and enlivened social self is the core virtue known as Ren, which means "benevolence," "human kindness," or "what ties one to another." Ren is what holds community together. In his Analects, Confucius tells us that Ren depends on "trying to see things from other people's perspectives, and then to do one's best for them with that in mind." Confucius believed that every person has the capacity of Ren within them, which manifests when a virtuous person treats others with humaneness.

Two hundred years later, Mencius (371–289 B.C.) writes that Ren means "to be human" or "to be a person," and that "Ren grows out of compassion, without which we would not be human." Mencius gives this example: A person sees a child playing near the edge of a well and sees that the child might fall in. Ren is the spontaneous appearance of compassion that has us act to save the child. It is our benevolence to others. Ren signifies that we are nothing apart from our social relations, and our interdependency extends into the immediate world and beyond.

As an ideogram, Ren literally means "two-people–ness" or "cohumanity." Our moral life falls apart without Ren. Without a social, relational self, our virtues are scattered and we become a mix of jarring fragments. For example, we might be brave in battle but unkind at home, or ruthless in business but generous in church.

How, then, do we cultivate Ahimsa, a life without harm, and Ren, a life of benevolence, in ourselves and each other? When we can inhabit these qualities, even briefly, we awaken our social self, and are that much closer to what Martin Luther King, Jr. referred to as *the Beloved Community*.

It was the American theologian Josiah Royce (1855–1916), founder of the Fellowship of Reconciliation, who first offered the term "the Beloved Community." Through this Fellowship, King first encountered the concept that he would deepen and bring into our global consciousness.

In his 1957 speech, "The Birth of a New Nation," the young visionary said:

> The aftermath of nonviolence is the creation of the Beloved
> Community . . . The aftermath of nonviolence is reconciliation.
> The aftermath of violence is emptiness and bitterness.

For King, the solidarity of the human family makes the Beloved Community possible. He believed that more lasting than any ideology or sense of politics is the common humanity we discover through our love and suffering. In his last book, King affirmed that "our loyalties must transcend our race, our tribe, our class, and our nation . . ."

He witnessed our common humanity repeatedly during his struggles. In the spring of 1966, several thousand marchers were delayed at the airport after the March to Montgomery, Alabama. King was deeply moved by the sudden unity of the diverse crowd waiting to go home:

> As I stood with them and saw white and Negro, nuns and priests, ministers and rabbis, labor organizers, lawyers, doctors, housemaids and shop workers brimming with vitality and enjoying a rare comradeship, I knew I was seeing a microcosm of the mankind of the future in this moment of luminous and genuine brotherhood.

Where two or more are joined by truth and benevolence, without doing harm, a lasting bond is created that is the atom of all community.

Like water, the bond of community is necessary for life to sustain itself.

Little Raft, Big Raft

Do we go it alone or make our way together? These are our two choices in making the hard journey through existence. These choices are represented by the two prominent Buddhist traditions: Hīnayāna Buddhism, which seeks personal enlightenment (*Hīnayāna* means little raft), and Mahāyāna Buddhism, which seeks a mutual enlightenment with others (*Mahāyāna* means big raft).

Psychologist James Hillman reminds us that these distinctions are also evident in the philosophies of Sigmund Freud and Carl Jung:

> Freud argued that the self is truly non-communal, fundamentally individual. Jung said that we are each make-weights in the scales—that what you do in your psychological life tips the balance of the world one way or another.

When hurt and confused, we can pull in and believe that we can only rely on ourselves. When thrust rawly into suffering, we are quickly opened to a larger definition of self in which we're interdependent with others and the Whole of Life. So we're always choosing between the little raft and the big raft, between going it alone or making our way together. Each has its gifts and each has its burdens.

Our sense of community depends on our foundational understanding of life. If you believe in a world that is not connected or interdependent, but is chiefly competitive, there's a limit to the degree of trust you can find in life, and a limit to the degree of compassion you can wholeheartedly release.

If, however, you believe in a world that is infinitely and irrevocably knit together, in which one spiritual power animates and connects all living things, then there's no limit to the trust that you can invoke beyond your single life. Through that trust, there is no limit to the degree of compassion you can summon toward other living things, and no limit to the kinship you can discover with all aspects of life.

Every day we're faced with a fundamental choice-point that determines whether we can live together or not. We're asked to value life and people over things or to subordinate life to the property and fortifications that surround us. Any religious or social system can join us or tear us apart, depending on which of these paths it supports.

When going it alone and guarding against the harshness of life, we tend to define things negatively, by what they are not, and so miss the strength in defining things by what they are. But defining things negatively only gives us half the story. We in the West often define Ahimsa as "non-violence," which tells us what it's not. But to truly understand the importance of Ahimsa, we have to delve into what it is, a life of engaged understanding and compassion. Stopping violence alone will not cultivate understanding and compassion. This is why, as time went on, Gandhi further defined Ahimsa as "intercommunity harmony."

Similarly, Martin Luther King, Jr. firmly believed that desegregation was not the same thing as integration. He felt that stopping segregation by itself, though necessary, would only produce

a society where men are physically desegregated and spiritually segregated, where elbows are together and hearts are apart. It gives us social togetherness and spiritual apartness. It leaves us with a stagnant equality of sameness rather than a constructive equality of oneness.

If we are to grow, if we are to move from the little raft to the big raft, we have to do more than stop violence and prejudice. We have to commit to understanding their opposites in our hearts, and accept each other as part of a global family. Any true sense of community resides in staying committed to exploring and upholding what we are, as opposed to railing only against what we are not.

The intent of a liberal education has always been to welcome and mix as many viewpoints as possible, because a whole understanding of life requires more than one view of knowledge. Our capacity to learn allows us to mix our ideas and feelings and grow stronger from it. When we let in other knowledge and experience, we only get healthier. Letting in other views helps us live together.

Though we have fragmented our universities and schools with over-specialization and a fundamentalist style of inquiry, the original intent of learning is still sacred and available. In the traditional tea ceremony in Japan, the tea houses are kept small in order to invoke humility by forcing us to leave everything extraneous outside. The contract of true learning is like a small tea house. It only lets us enter with our mind and our heart, leaving our weapons and assumptions outside so we can learn deeply.

Some say the big raft is impossible, that the Beloved Community is a fantasy, that the way of Ahimsa is unrealistic. Yet, though we many never attain them, everything that matters depends on our commitment to keep reaching.

It was Sir Thomas More (1478–1535) who first used the word *utopia* in his 1516 book by the same name. In it, an explorer visits the island of Utopia, which means "Nowhere Land," a land that can't exist and yet is a land worth looking for. In More's Utopia, all things are owned in common, there is universal education for men and women, and religious differences are celebrated. While this has always seemed impossible, it's worth the effort to try to live together in this way. The commitment to aim for our common good is a covenant of humanity.

If the creation of a Beloved Community seems daunting, what matters is the kindness we live out in trying to find it. What matters is the commitment to aim for our common good. The Beloved Community as we imagine it may not exist, but it's a land worth looking for. Perhaps the heart of the Beloved Community is realized by how we live together along the way.

In 1955, after the devastation of World War II, the Japanese government authorized its Agency for Cultural Affairs to honor individuals or groups each year as Preservers of Important Intangible Cultural Properties (*Jūyō Mukei Bunkazai Hojisha*). Out of unthinkable harm a way has arisen to name artists and craftsmen who keep traditions of community alive. These preservers of the intangible are popularly known as Living National Treasures (*ningen kokuhō*). Being designated as a Living National Treasure is a recognition of excellence in an artistic or social field. In essence, the award establishes the recipient as a cultural ambassador, responsible for the dissemination, perpetuation, and future development of their artful form of community.

In our tense and polarized times, we especially need Living Human Treasures to preserve the important intangibles that keep us connected and benevolent, that awaken us to the inevitable fact that the world is the biggest raft of all.

If we are to move from the little raft to the big raft, we have to do more than stop violence and prejudice. We have to commit to understanding their opposites in our hearts.

Keeping Each Other Company

> We must delight in each other, make others' conditions
> our own, rejoice together, mourn together, labor and suffer
> together—always having before our eyes . . . our commu-
> nity as members of the same body.
>
> —FROM A SERMON DELIVERED BY JOHN
> WINTHROP IN SALEM HARBOR, 1630

Many make light of spiritual retreats and the spread of support groups everywhere. Yet these are signs of the human family growing tired of its modern isolation. Increasingly, ordinary people are thirsting for a chance to be together authentically. That an entire subculture has formed outside of religious and educational institutions is a sign that our human needs are not being met by the cult of expertise we have refined. This is not new. Throughout history, small groups have formed when institutions have become dry and ungiving.

We simply need to keep each other company during life's surprising journey. We need moments of real community. Like white blood cells rushing to the site of an injury, people in the modern world are gathering around different injuries to help each other heal. Whether or not these small circles are working, the need for true community is swelling.

In studying people as well as animals, scientists have found that intimacy promotes health while isolation fosters stress, disease, and early death. Led by University of Michigan sociologist James S. House, researchers concluded that social isolation is statistically just as dangerous as smoking, high blood pressure, high cholesterol, obesity, or lack of exercise.

Stress can also come from the press of society, but not necessarily from crowdedness alone. In 1971, Hong Kong and Holland were among the most crowded areas in the world, yet their populations enjoyed strong physical and mental health because they had developed over centuries patterns of human relationship that minimize social conflict and allow people to retain their identity and a large measure of individual freedom.

A strong, respectful social network fosters a healthy sense of belonging. A community with a close-knit web of connections has a lower rate of heart disease. This is called the Roseto effect, named for a town in Pennsylvania that had an unusually low rate of heart disease. At the time, Roseto was an Italian community with strong family ties and a long immigrant history. From 1954 to 1961, the men of Roseto had nearly no heart attacks. All other factors being the same in nearby communities, Roseto's good health was attributed to an active caring community.

Carl Jung believed that the inner work of individuation informs healthy community building. When individuated and transformed, we're more capable of true relationship. The more congruent we are individually, the healthier our connections with others. When we are not individuated and whole, we think we have to push off from others in order to preserve our inner freedom. Or we think we have to push off from the turmoil of our unexplored psyche with strategies of survival for a hostile world. But once we experience inner and outer health, we can be who we are in the presence of others and support each other.

Modern research affirms the ancient truth that connection is essential. Finding a companion—any companion, from pets to a partner—can alleviate stress. Stanford psychiatrist David Spiegel found that by spending ninety minutes a week with a support group, women with metastatic breast cancer doubled their average survival time, from nineteen months to thirty-seven months. In the same vein, pet owners enjoy better health than people without pets. The very act of stroking a dog can lower heart rate and blood pressure, both the person's and the dog's.

When at our healthiest, we are informed by who we are, not by what we do. In the great Native American nations that flourished around 1000 A.D., members of the Anasazi and Cahokia tribes rotated their service in the community, changing roles to help the whole—building, planting, and making tools. Career as we know it didn't exist. There was no individual route to wealth or distinction. The life of the community was their career. Not only did this strengthen the social fabric of the tribe, but it also provided variety in the life of the individual. Most importantly, it gave individuals the chance to define their identities by other than what they did. Who they were was defined by their relation to the human whole and the natural whole, of which they were a part. These Native American citizens didn't see themselves as builders or planters or toolmakers, but as individual spirits with many skills. Their identities were fueled by a sense of being that was greater than themselves or their roles.

Some people fear that being adaptable to a life of community will rob them of their individuality. They identify with their accomplishments and ambition. When asked who we are, we often respond that we are what we do: I'm a doctor, I'm a teacher, I'm a salesman. Or we say that we are what we aim for: I want to be a pro athlete, I want to be president, I want to be a rock star. There's nothing wrong with accomplishments, it's how we view them that can be problematic. We need a larger identity that gives worth to the intangible and essential elements that make up who we truly are, alone and together.

In a driven society, we lose touch with a greater perspective. In their traditional society, Native Americans had an encompassing view of life, community, family, and themselves. The recurring question for each generation is how to restore that wider, deeper perspective that lets us know ourselves as part of a larger, living, interdependent whole.

Physicist Arthur Zajonc reminds us that Albert Einstein established that no one thing or place has a privileged point of view; that is, no one point of view holds the entire truth. Therefore, the primacy of any one point of view is not only invalid but damaging and disrespectful to the inherent unity of life, which can only be understood and experienced through relationship and the accumulation of all viewpoints.

Through the language of physics, Einstein's declaration of relativity affirms what the core of all spiritual traditions begins with—the fact that we are more together than alone, a central truth we often forget. How we live this truth when we know it, and how we recover it when we forget, creates community.

Environmentalist Paul Wapner suggests that the most corrosive point of view, which infects most fields of knowledge and education, is anthropocentrism. In other words, we see life and the world as human-centered and that all resources and life-forms are here to serve, feed, clothe, and comfort us. Paul and other environmentalists have demonstrated that the primacy of this human-centered view has fueled the depletion of the planet and the trampling of other species and life-forms. Anthropocentrism has become a social form of cancer by which the human cell has become aberrant and ravenous in how *we*—and it is *we*—are surviving by eating the whole.

The threat of self-centered living is grave. The physical world and our ability to inhabit it depend on how we recover from these impoverishments in order to restore the natural web we are born into.

These timeless, relational skills help us keep each other company: the effort to make other conditions our own, the effort to find authentic connection and intimacy, the effort to retain our identity and individual freedom, the effort to create a healthy social sense of belonging, the effort to face who we are and be who we are in the presence of others, the effort to have our relationships (and not what we do) define who we are, the effort to undo our human-centered, privileged view, and the effort to restore an encompassing perspective of life.

All this reminds me of a tribe in the Amazon that has preserved the skill to see stars during the day. I don't remember the tribe's name or location, but I can't stop wondering: What have they retained? And what have we lost? In so many ways, we are lights for each other, irrepressible lights of spirit born to constellate. Yet, in the press of our days, we lose sight of each other. Just how do we rediscover the ability to see each other during the day? How can we track the human constellations by which we navigate the dark? This is a calling that no generation can escape: enlivening our hard-earned efforts to keep each other company.

Like white blood cells rushing to the site of an injury, people in the modern world are gathering around different injuries to help each other heal.

An Exercise in Faithfulness

Despite all our differences, the unity of
mankind will assert itself irresistibly.
—CARL JUNG

In my thirties, I almost died from a rare form of lymphoma. During that time, I encountered a strange and potent inversion of how we claim to care for each other in America. While it's widely known in the province of law that we are innocent till proven guilty, once ill, we find ourselves in the province of medicine where we are sick till proven well. Even when healthy, the language presumes borrowed time: we're not considered well, but in remission. This makes those who survive an anomaly rather than a resource.

This inverted way of holding the future impedes our attempts at community. This dark forbidding sense fuels the plague of worldwide cynicism in which everything is assumed guilty till proven innocent and sick till proven well. Dr. Stephen Toope, president of the University of British Columbia, has pointed out that one of our more urgent challenges is to *engage* the cynicism of our age, not to condemn it or minimize it.

It's helpful to remember, as the American poet Philip Levine has said, that the opposite of innocence is not guilt, but experience. Essentially, we need to relearn how to walk together without seeing everything we encounter and touch as bereft before we meet it.

Such cynicism is a cultural form of smog, dimming what is possible and clouding the best of our history. It just might be that learned helplessness carried in the heart is the burden of depression, and learned helplessness carried in the mind is the burden of cynicism.

No matter how intelligent its argument, cynicism is more a symptom of despair than a philosophical stance or a resolve to be pragmatic. Just as damaging is ungrounded idealism, which jumps over the hard work it takes to be here together. Like an alcoholic who is one drink from his demon or one drink refused from his higher power, we're all one gesture from being the cruelty we have suffered or one kindness from helping each other heal in the open. What we do when our arm is raised, about to strike or soothe, will determine the next hundred years.

Yet without denying the violence that scars the face of history, we can believe in the possibility of community. Since we're never far from violence or peace, we need a sense of faithfulness that will stir the better versions of our selves. Rudolf Steiner speaks of such faithfulness as the commitment to keep the true being of each other in view, no matter how briefly seen, especially when another acts in confused and hurtful ways:

You will experience moments—fleeting moments—with other persons. These human beings will appear to you then as if filled, irradiated, with the archetype of their Spirit.

And then there may be—indeed, will be—other moments. Long periods of time, when human beings are darkened. But you will learn to say to yourself at such times, "I remember [their] archetype. I saw it once. No illusion, no deception shall rob me of it."

Always struggle for the image that you saw. This struggle is faithfulness. Striving for faithfulness in this way, we shall be close to one another, as if endowed with the protective power of angels.

In the quote from Howard Zinn which I cite as the epigraph to this book, the historian urges us to keep the true being of community in view, no matter how briefly seen, despite the long, dark periods we encounter.

This quandary—between our struggle and possibility, between violence and peace—is not new. It is simply our turn in the endless odyssey of human beings striving to be ethical and loving to each other. In Jacob Needleman's book *Why Can't We Be Good?*, he recounts Rabbi Hillel's call to a brutalized Jerusalem in 30 B.C. "to 'remember itself'—that is, to reestablish a relation to the inner, transcendent source of its ethical rules and principles." This is a timeless call, painfully relevant today.

Other cultures voice the same call. Consider the African concept of *Sankofa*, which is an Akan word from Ghana that means, *We must go back and reclaim our past so we can move forward, so we can understand why and how we came to be who we are.*

We must also be careful not to mythologize or idealize the past, but to draw strength from what lives in the bones of the human family. In this spirit, the Jewish tradition offers the ethic *Tikkun Olam,* which is Hebrew for *You are here to repair the world.* This instruction is at the heart of the Talmud. Since we are the world, we are here to repair ourselves, the way a cloth is made whole when its threads are repaired.

We gather and disperse like cells in the bloodstream, depending on each other and our community. For without a healthy bloodstream, there is no home for cells, and there is no bloodstream without healthy individual cells. For human beings, this interdependence translates to being an individual in a community. For there can be no self without a home, and there can be no community without healthy individuals. Life-giving cooperation is crucial: between cell and bloodstream, individual and community, self and home.

Just where can we look for such balance? While history has launched models for community—philosophies, manifestoes, utopias, and dystopias—I am compelled to look for and bear witness to the actual moments of community that have somehow worked along the way. Let the organic nature of the human journey be our teacher. Let us face the stubbornness and fear that triggers us to be cynical and violent, while never losing sight of our better selves.

We're all one gesture from being the cruelty we have suffered or one kindness from helping each other heal in the open.

Cooperation or Resistance

The humane sense of community envisioned by Confucius beholds society as a structure of human relationships that can be maintained and renewed through daily rituals. Believing that a healthy society is based on a healthy individual, Confucius said, "To put the world in order, we must first put the nation in order; to put the nation in order, we must first put the family in order; to put the family in order; we must first cultivate our personal life; we must first set our hearts right." Toward this end, Confucius emphasized veneration and obedience to family, elders, and rulers; in general, aligning our individual needs with the greater needs of the community.

For thousands of years the Confucian model served, at its best, as a noble basis for living together caringly on Earth. But for thousands of years, Confucian thought has also been misused by autocrats and dictators to solidify their power and to oppress those under their rule.

Gandhi on the other hand gave us a way to organize community around basic human rights in order to resist oppressive social systems. In his early pamphlet, *Hind Swaraj (Indian Home Rule)*, published in 1909, Gandhi addressed British rulers by declaring:

> We cease to play the part of the ruled. You may, if you like, cut us to pieces. You may shatter us at the cannon's mouth. If you act contrary to our will, we shall not help you; and without our help, we know that you cannot move one step forward.

Given the world Gandhi was born into, his efforts to affect a more humane sense of community hinged on "[our own] ability to preserve order without the assistance of the ruler . . . to non-cooperate with the system by withdrawing all the voluntary assistance possible and refusing all its so-called benefits."

It's an ongoing challenge to discern what best serves the common good: cooperation with the social order or resistance to the social order. When to cooperate and when to resist? Perhaps this can only be answered by asking in any given situation if the people at risk are being treated as a means to an end or if their well-being is the goal.

Confucius might ask Gandhi, "Under what circumstances would you cooperate?" And Gandhi might ask Confucius, "Under what circumstances would you resist?" Before answering, I can imagine each deferring to their counterparts in future generations. Though both, no doubt, would bow to the mysterious power that appears when people tend to each other beyond any sense of self-advantage.

Perhaps no one soul can answer these questions. Perhaps we need to ask each other what matters before giving ground or standing firm. Perhaps we live into the answers when we dare to lend our voice to what feels true. Perhaps there's a Confucius and Gandhi in each of us who sparks the X and Y chromosomes of community. Perhaps every time we step toward each other, we take a turn toward our communal well-being. And no matter how often we fail, we still can rely on our untapped nature. As Martin Luther King, Jr. said, "I believe what the self-centered have torn down, the other-centered will build up."

> A mysterious power appears when people tend to
> each other beyond any sense of self-advantage.

Just Take a Pebble

Don't ask the mountain
To move, just take a pebble
Each time you visit.

—JOHN PAUL LEDERACH

The work of change takes time and commitment, one pebble at a time. Earlier, I mentioned the Hebrew phrase *Tikkun Olam*, which means, *You are here to repair the world*. Accepting that we're in need of repair minimizes our temptation to be seen as special or elite. This keeps us closer to all that matters. The Jewish understanding is that we repair the world by making the fragmentation of creation whole again.

The work of repairing the world is endless and beautiful. It's harder when we're not fully who we are. When we don't develop and express our own values, the social currents of the day fill us the way water fills a hole. Not because the norms of every society are pernicious but because, like gravity, collective values have their own social gravity. If we're not grounded and fully engaged, our gifts will be muffled and our good intentions will be neutralized. The life of our gifts depends on not hiding.

So how do we show our gifts, put things back together, and resist feeling special by separating ourselves from those we help? Over time, I've learned that there are six efforts of balance that can repair us.

- *The First Balance:* To remember that we're not separate from those we try to help or outside of whatever we try to repair. We are changed by all that we encounter, and we have a responsibility to reveal the physics of this process.

- *The Second Balance:* To enter the smallest task wholeheartedly with an awareness of the Whole of Life, helping others from a sense of connection and not isolation.
- *The Third Balance:* To meet the outer life with our inner life. Aristotle said, "We have a right to censure a work of art that makes us feel terror or pity without an inner necessity to do so." We must commit to the inner necessity of overcoming terror and pity.
- *The Fourth Balance:* To engage the world beyond the dualistic press of history, not letting our heart be governed by left or right, up or down, right or wrong, good or bad, surface or depth, but looking for how all views contribute to a unified whole. To engage all sides of paradox, always remembering that the whole is greater than the sum of its parts.
- *The Fifth Balance:* To commit to participating in life and not just watching. If you're a reporter, at what point do you put down the camera and hold the screaming child?
- *The Sixth Balance:* To have the courage to bear witness to how things come together with the same urgency as we bear witness to how things fall apart.

In 1969, U.S. Air Force lieutenant S. Brian Willson was caught in forces beyond his control. He was shipped as an intelligence officer to Vietnam and, while inspecting a napalmed village, was devastated to see the carnage. He came home questioning the war from both sides, and began a life of protest against war and, as importantly, against the values that lead to war.

Eighteen years later, Willson and fellow veterans David Duncombe and Duncan Murphy were sitting on a railroad track, protesting the shipment of munitions from a naval weapons station in California to Central America. Anticipating a takeover of the train, the conductor was ordered to rush the crossing. While Duncombe and Murphy were able to slip aside, Willson was run over by the train, which severed one leg, mangled the other, and damaged his skull. Through his difficult recovery, Willson has only strengthened his grace as a peacemaker.

In his memoir, *Blood on the Tracks*, he offers this:

I believe human beings come into the world with the archetypal characteristics of empathy, cooperation, and mutual respect. We are wired as social beings. Yet these fundamental characteristics have been buried under an avalanche of narcissistic, egocentric behavior fueled by a modern materialist culture.

Sociologist Margaret Mead speaks to the separation that unconscious materialism can create when she says, "Having two bathrooms ruined [our] capacity to cooperate." What Mead is suggesting is that without a context of care with which to use things, the things begin to use us. This has been the insidious curse of progress, not because progress is evil, but because those of us intoxicated with progress stop giving our attention to the life underneath all the progress.

To begin to effect change, we return to John Paul Lederach's simple but profound invitation: Take a pebble from the mountain each time we visit.

Here is another example, of a grandmother learning from her grandson. Puanani Burgess and her family live in rural Hawaii, in Waianae, a native community on the island of Oahu, forty-five miles from Honolulu. They live on a two-mile rural block. She tells this story of her mother Popo and her two-year-old son Poha.

At seventy-six, Popo would stroll around the rural block with Poha, showing him the cows and horses. But Poha had no reaction. After four such walks, Popo thought, *If he has no interest, I won't bother.* Finally, during one more walk, Popo said, "Look, Poha, look at the cows and bright horses." The little one still had no reaction at all. Then, for some reason, Popo slowly creaked her way down to the ground next to Poha to see what the little one could see. He could only see the tall grass. She laughed and lifted him above her head and then, for the first time, little Poha saw the amazing cows and bright horses. He clapped his small hands and began to laugh and point.

Such a simple but profound lesson: See what others see first. It's an indispensable practice of community and compassion. Forget philosophies and persuasion and negotiation. See what others see first. Then we can lift each other so we can all see the bright horses. This is how our gifts meet the world.

The work of repairing the world is endless and beautiful. And since we are the world, we are here to repair ourselves.

QUESTIONS TO LIVE WITH

I offer these questions as a way to personalize and expand your relationships within your own community. They involve reflection, deep listening, honest conversation, and an encouragement to engage in local action where you live. I invite you to use these questions in the small groups you might convene. And I invite you to use a personal journal as a home for your reflections.

+ The Dalai Lama has called kindness a religion. Bring four or five friends together. In conversation, have each of you describe an ancestor you admire in the lineage of kindness. In the next three weeks, practice the religion of kindness in one small way, individually and as a group.

+ In your journal, describe a moment of community you have witnessed or experienced in which hardship or suffering has led people to work together for the common good. What made this moment possible? Bring this conversation to someone you are currently working with, and plan to work together in a specific way for the common good.

+ Our limited or expanded sense of community depends on whether we believe in a world that is not connected or in a world that is inextricably woven together. Bring four or five friends together. In conversation, have each of you tell a story of a time when you felt disconnected from the rest of life and of a time when you felt knit into the fabric of the Universe. Describe the inner and outer circumstances that lead to feeling disconnected and connected. In the next three weeks, describe one way your immediate community feels disconnected and act on restoring that connection.

+ *Tikkun Olam* is Hebrew for "You are here to repair the world." Since we are the world, we are here to repair ourselves. Bring four or five friends together. In conversation, have each of you describe one way you need to repair yourself in order to change the world. What is the first step in this healing? In the next three weeks, commit to taking that first step.

+ There are two prominent Buddhist traditions: Hīnayāna and Mahāyāna Buddhism. Hīnayāna Buddhism seeks personal enlightenment (*Hīnayāna* means little raft), while Mahāyāna Buddhism seeks a mutual enlightenment with others (*Mahāyāna* means big raft). Bring four or five friends together. In conversation, describe what kind of raft each of you is building and why. In the next three weeks, make plans for where and how you can build the next piece of your community raft together.

+ Bring four or five friends together. In conversation, have each of you describe your personal experience of being ignored by others and your experience of being interdependent with others. As a group, discuss the difference between being ignored and being interdependent. In the next three weeks, identify a practice in your community that is ignoring others and how you might make that practice more interdependent.

+ Bring four or five friends together. In conversation, have each of you describe one way your family and community support you in being who you are and one way they dissuade you from being who you are. Then, describe one way you support those around you in being who they are and one way you dissuade those around you from being who they are. In the next three weeks, identify a practice in your community that dissuades others from being who they are and how you might support those involved in more thoroughly being themselves.

ISLANDS IN TIME

The first peace, which is the most important, is that which comes within the souls of beings when they realize their relationship, their Oneness, with the Universe and all its Powers. This center is really everywhere, it is within each of us. This is the real Peace, and the others are but reflections of this. The second peace is that which is made between individuals, and the third is that which is made between nations. But above all we must understand that there can never be peace between nations until [we first know] that true peace which is within the souls of beings.

—BLACK ELK

We are tied together in the single garment of destiny, caught in an inescapable network of mutuality. And whatever affects one directly affects all indirectly.

—MARTIN LUTHER KING, JR.

As one drop of honey can let us know the nature of sweetness, one moment of giving can let us taste the sweetness of living together on Earth. As one moment of loss can open our heart to the pain of others, one moment of breakdown can let community rush in, the way water rushes the break in a wall.

And while it's impossible to portray the entire history or impact of community, I can bear witness to the inspiring and demanding moments of giving, building, and heart. My hope is to lift these emblematic moments and stories up to the light as you would a prism, in an attempt to disclose the many colors at work when we try to live together.

The word *holm* (pronounced *home*) means a small island in the middle of a river or stream. These moments of giving, building, and heart—these moments of community in the river of time—are moments of home. I offer these islands in time as a way to begin such a conversation and invite you to tell these stories and discuss them, if you are moved, and to add moments and stories of your own.

The Two Tribes

In the beginning, when the first humans came across each other, the more fearful one said, "You're different. Go away." The other said, "You're different. Come, teach me what I don't know." While our reasoning has grown more complicated throughout the centuries, our reactions are essentially the same. "Go away" or "Come, teach me."

Since the beginning, the two tribes have had their philosophies. The "Go away" tribe believes that human beings by nature are self-serving and untrustworthy, in need of control. The "Go away" tribe believes in stringent laws and constraints, both moral and legal, to ensure that people don't run amok. The "Come, teach me" tribe believes that human beings by nature are kind and trustworthy. The "Come, teach me" tribe believes in cultivating laws that empower freedom, to ensure that people actualize their gifts through relationship.

The truth is that we are born into both tribes and can move from one to the other, depending on the level of our fear. The times of genocide throughout history mark the extreme, malignant manifestation of the "Go away" tribe. Distorted by fear, it's not enough to say, "Go away." For strident, unbridled fear turns to anger, which normalized turns into prejudice and hate. Such deep, embedded fear tries to exclude those who are different, to make them invisible, to exile them, jail them, hurt them, and—in extremely ugly cases—persecute and kill them.

Times of enlightenment throughout history mark the extreme manifestation of the "Come, teach me" tribe, which fosters wonder, learning, compassion, and cooperation. Empowered by trust, curiosity turns into interdependence and a belief that we need each other and our diversity of gifts to make life whole. This ethic is what gave rise to democracy in the first place. This is why America has grown so strong from welcoming immigrants for over two hundred years.

We as a nation have moved between periods of isolationism and inclusion as people shift between the two tribes. Today, our nation has coagulated into these primary camps and we seem to be heading into another period of isolationism and fear of those who are different. I pray for our return to each other.

I believe it's imperative that we educate our children to live according to the fundamental dynamic that all the spiritual traditions teach: that we are all parts of one indivisible whole, which love and suffering reveal. And while we come apart from time to time, and push each other away in our fear, the natural resting position of life on Earth is to join in order to release the life-force inherent in the biological, societal, and mystical fact that the whole is greater than the sum of its parts.

Trust, courage, and the ability to listen are the agencies of heart that allow us to rejoin. These are the qualities that each soul has waiting within it like golden seeds to be watered by the strength of our kindness. This is the purpose of community: to water these seeds and to join and rejoin.

We need each other and our diversity of gifts to make life whole.

Hospitality

SHELTER

My grandfather was a gentle soul who became a letterpress printer in New York City, only to lose his job during the Great Depression. With little to eat, he'd bring strangers home for dinner. When Grandma would pull him aside with "We don't have enough," he'd kiss her cheek and say, "Break whatever we have in half. It will be enough." He taught me that basic shelter is the first form of hospitality: a place to sleep, something to eat, something warm to wear.

In Ancient Greece, *Xenia* was the ethic and custom of showing kindness to a stranger. The word means *guest-friendship*. This was a form of hospitality shown to those far from home who happened by your door. Behind this basic form of kindness is a deep trust in human nature, that without provocation we mean each other no harm.

In India, hospitality is based on the principle *Atithi Devo Bhava*, meaning "the guest is God." The assumption here is that the stranger bears a gift that no one may know about which loved into the open will complete us all. The same belief is found in the Jewish principle of *Hachnasat Orchim*, which means "welcoming guests."

Practicing shelter-hospitality, Panera Bread Company now has four non-profit community cafés in St. Louis, Dearborn, Portland, and Boston. Each community café is based on shared responsibility, aiming to ensure that everyone who needs a meal gets a meal. People are encouraged to take what they need and donate their fair share. There are no prices or cash registers, only suggested donation levels and donation bins.

At the heart of all welcome is the humble recognition that though we open our door today, we may well be in need of an open door ourselves tomorrow. The kind spiritual teacher Henri Nouwen confirmed this, when he said:

53

We live in a desert with many lonely travelers who are looking
for a moment of peace, for a fresh drink and for a sign of encouragement so that they can continue their mysterious search
for freedom . . . Hospitality is the ability to pay attention to the
guest.

AFFIRMATION

Affirmation of our true nature, which is just as important, can be
understood as inner shelter. We each need to have the authority of
our own being and our place in the larger Universe confirmed. Out
of this affirmation, the social self is enlivened and community is
possible. Mythologist and storyteller Michael Meade puts it this way,
"Everyone needs some help learning who they already are. That's the
root of genuine education and the task of real culture."

Bread for the Journey, a leader in neighborhood community-
based giving for over twenty years, has helped individuals give back
to their communities. In acts of affirmation-hospitality, local Bread
for the Journey chapters across the country have donated more than
$4.5 million to diverse community-based projects, all through mod-
est, well-placed grants of no more than $3000. These grants have
helped teach teenagers to build computers, two at a time, from spare,
used parts, keeping one and giving one away. The seed money has
supported elders in solving homelessness in their community, and
taught young people to make bicycles in order to give them to low-
income residents who can't afford cars. There are hundreds of stories
like these. Every effort that enables those in need to give affirms their
own worth and the worth of those they give to.

OUR LARGER HOME

Hospitality helps us remember our larger home, the web of relationship and connection, and the Oneness in which we live. We tend to
forget these essential connections, and when we do, we can wander

for a long time, desolate and inconsolable. Mother Teresa witnessed this disconnection her whole life and concluded that "if we have no peace, it is because we have forgotten that we belong to each other."

Even in our solitude, we need to stay connected. The philosopher Hannah Arendt, who survived World War II, declared:

> No human life, not even the life of a hermit in nature's wilderness, is possible without a world which directly or indirectly testifies to the presence of other human beings.

This is why every tribe, tradition, and spiritual path has rituals and symbols: to help us remember who we are and the web of relationship we are a part of. A great example of a symbol ritualized to help us remember our larger home is the use of sacred *wampum* in the Native American tradition.

Originating with the Algonquin tribe of the Northeast, the average wampum belt was about six feet long, containing more than six thousand beads made from white or purple shells gathered from the sea. Wampum was considered an aid in preserving the oral tradition of the tribe. Each bead contained a tribal memory. The more beads, the more sacred the wampum belt. In essence, it was a story belt which preserved the collective memory of the tribe.

The string of sacred wampum was often held by a speaker to verify that he was speaking the truth. This tradition of speaking the truth involves certain rules of engagement when listening to each other. To begin with, each must accept the other as they are, putting aside assumptions and expectations; each must accept the other as equal; and each must be honest, clear, and forthright. What a sound way to face each other.

When the Europeans arrived, they mistook wampum as simple currency and never inquired into its sacred nature. And without knowledge of our stories, the sanctity is lost and the sacred is reduced to mere currency. This happens every time I objectify you without taking the time to inquire into the personal history and meaning of what passes through our hands.

We might do well in our own lives to form a bead or gather a shell for every important passage we live through. Creating our own wampum belt will give us the strength to accept each other as we are, and to speak truth to each other.

SPIRITUAL HOSPITALITY

Sociologist Ivan Illich defined *spiritual hospitality* as *helping another cross a threshold*. This is a beautiful way to describe the work of love: to help another cross a threshold. Illich doesn't say that we define what that threshold is for another, but that we wholeheartedly help another cross the threshold that is of importance to their own growth, as they define it. This means we don't impose our values on those we try to help. Spiritual hospitality demands that we do not guide, steer, or keep others from the threshold that is theirs to cross.

The modern hospice movement is a compelling example of spiritual hospitality, helping others cross the threshold of their life into death. Hospice workers will tell you that the difficult privilege of helping others transition to their death affirms the workers' own true nature and helps them remember our larger home.

Physician Elisabeth Kübler-Ross brought dying into the open. Though the first known hospice appeared in Europe in the eleventh century, Kübler-Ross's groundbreaking book *On Death and Dying* initiated the modern world in a more humane and dignified approach to death. Her devotion to facing the inevitability of death exemplified the healing power of choosing love over fear. Her love helped to seed the modern hospice movement, which has helped so many.

When asked what stirred her to work with the dying, she recalled hitchhiking through the ruins of post-war Europe. In Poland, she visited the liberated concentration camp of Maidanek. The degradation that she saw there transformed her. She said, "I would never have gone into the work on death and dying without Maidanek."

Being so deeply touched by the Holocaust shaped her life's inquiry. Later, at the University of Chicago, she held interviews with terminal patients onstage, exploring the process of dying in public. What gave her the courage to bring death into the light? What made her invite ordinary people out into the open? What made her turn to the wisdom of the tribe?

The words *hospice* and *hospital* trace back to the Latin *hospitium*, meaning *hospitality*, and to the Latin *hospes*, meaning both *guest* and *host*. What else can love provide but hospitality? And what keeps us from offering our love and hospitality? Somehow, this physician had the courage to step through fear with love and talk to death. In her courage, she reaffirmed the truth that we are all brief guests on this Earth and only through our love can we be humble hosts to each other in this amazing passage.

The dying tell us—when we love enough to listen—that the deepest hospitality erases the distinction between guest and host. When moving through fear and pain and death together, we can no longer tell who is welcoming and who is welcomed, or who is caring and who is cared for. This is the bedrock of a Beloved Community.

When we participate wholeheartedly in these forms of welcome, we are at home in the world. When we hold back and cut people off, we suffer and are lost.

The writer Caroline Kettlewell points to the difference between feeling at home in the world and feeling lost when she says:

If a heart could fail in its pumping, a lung in its breathing, then why not a brain in its thinking, rendering the world forever askew, like a television with bad reception?

One enduring purpose of hospitality is to pump the heart that fails, to fill the lung that collapses, and to re-establish a clear reception in the mind. For without hospitality and welcome, our world fragments and shrinks. As the historian Robert Bellah says:

If we don't understand a larger coherence of life, wisdom remains a private experience.

Community organizer Pilar Gonzales speaks of the Apache custom of *returning the order*. She says, "I can't cross a threshold or enter a home or relationship without giving in some measure what was given to me. I am compelled for the sake of the world to leave a gift for a gift; whether that means doing the dishes or listening to the suffering of my host."

This is a good way to practice hospitality, by returning in some measure what is given to us.

To speak and hear the truth, each must accept the other as they are, putting aside assumptions and expectations; each must accept the other as equal; and each must be honest, clear, and forthright.

Of Two Minds

Socialism never took root in America because the poor see
themselves not as an exploited proletariat but as temporar-
ily embarrassed millionaires.

—John Steinbeck

Westerners have always been of two minds about what we want
from community, whether to help each other or to give each other
space to make our own fortune. By contrast, for centuries, the First
Peoples of North America practiced a sacred gift-giving ceremony
known as *potlatch*, which, hard as it is to imagine, was criminalized
by both the Canadian and U.S. governments for about seventy
years.

Potlatch means *to give away*. Often held in winter, the potlatch
ceremony was a communal way of distributing wealth and resources
among those in need within the tribe. It was also a means for resolv-
ing grievances and maintaining and expanding social relationships.
The ceremony's givers gave away as many personal belongings as
they could afford. And potlatch recipients were obligated to give
away more than they received, when they could. While there was
great variation in how potlatch was practiced, it was woven into the
fabric of the First Peoples of the Pacific Northwest in Canada and the
United States, including the Heiltsuk, Haida, Nuxalk, Tlingit, Makah,
Tsimshian, Nuu-chah-nulth, and Kwakwaka'wakw tribes.

Held on the occasion of births, deaths, adoptions, and weddings,
a potlatch was hosted by a house within the tribe. A house might
consist of a hundred members. During a potlatch, titles would be
transferred to others in the tribe and gifts were made of oolichan
(candlefish), dried food, oil, canoes, Chilkat and Hudson's Bay blankets, animal skins, and ornamental coppers. It was the distribution of

large numbers of Hudson's Bay blankets that first drew government attention to the potlatch.

The ceremony was also marked by the competitive exchange of gifts, in order for elders to maintain their power and authority within a tribe. Still, the gift-giving at the heart of potlatches remained incomprehensible to Europeans and Americans, perhaps because such generosity seemed to threaten the pragmatic model of accumulation and self-interest that was taking hold of the white world racing toward modernity. Once the potlatch was made illegal, Native American "regalia was seized and, in some cases, burned in front of families to whom they belonged. Some potlatch participants were tried and sent to prison."

The potlatch was also considered by the Western governments to be a major obstacle to Native American assimilation. In 1875, the missionary William Duncan wrote that the potlatch was "by far the most formidable of all obstacles in the way of Indians becoming Christians, or even civilized."

If the missionaries had not been blinded by their sanctimonious propriety, they would have apprenticed with the First Peoples to learn how to better love their neighbor. Essentially, the potlatch ceremony has a kinship with the lineage of kindness by which Jesus fed the multitudes when he took five small barley loaves and two small fish supplied by a boy and turned them into enough to feed five thousand.

The Abenaki elder Joseph Bruchac reminds us that America and its free-market system, which grew out of Calvinism, is based on the values of personal acquisition. People were taught that they would be rewarded in Heaven for what they amass while on Earth. In direct opposition to this worldview, the potlatch ceremony sanctifies the values of generosity, and measures a person not by how much he owns, but by how much he gives away.

So, at a time when dreams of greed and prosperity were being ennobled as a birthright of white settlers and their governments, potlatching was made illegal in Canada in 1884 and in the United States in the late nineteenth century, largely at the urging of missionaries and government agents who considered such giving to be wasteful, unproductive, and contrary to their values. The worship of economic progress and self-interest had made the notion of giving uncivilized. As a society, we are still recovering. For the insistence on making everyone the same undermines both nature and society.

In 1888, Chief O'waxalagalis of the Kwagu'ł made his now-famous remarks to the anthropologist Franz Boas:

> We will dance when our laws command us to dance, we will feast when our hearts desire to feast. Do we ask the white man, "Do as the Indian does?" No, we do not. Why, then, will you ask us, "Do as the white man does?" It is a strict law that bids us to dance. It is a strict law that bids us to distribute our property among our friends and neighbors. It is a good law. Let the white man observe his law; we shall observe ours. And if you [have] come to forbid us to dance, begone; if not, you will be welcome to us.

It took another generation to repeal these laws that made gift-giving illegal. In 1934 and 1951, the U.S. and Canada, respectively, lifted their bans on the potlatch ceremony.

Just what are we to learn from this long moment of cultures clashing over the nature and purpose of community? Perhaps there is a clue in the notes of Franz Boas after his time with Chief O'waxalagalis:

> The so-called *potlatch* of all these tribes hinders the single families from accumulating wealth . . . [yet] every present received at a *potlatch* has to be returned at another *potlatch*, and a man who would not give his feast in due time would be considered as not paying his debts.

This points to a troubling assumption that has plagued communities throughout history: that self-interest is more crucial to survival than serving the common good. While in certain instances self-interest is unavoidable, caring for the self in an integral way strengthens the common good, the way healthy cells strengthen the immune system in any given body.

The sanctity and wisdom of the potlatch ceremony invoked over centuries is that caring for each other is a form of paying our debt to the community for helping the individual grow, the way we might care for the soil in gratitude for the immense harvest it continually yields. Potlatching evinces a covenant of care that is at the heart of all social programs in all cultures, whether for the elderly, the ill, the orphaned, the broken returning from war, the mentally ill, or the displaced. Underneath the sacred vow of the First Peoples to give to each other is the acceptance that everyone will be in need at some time or another. And secondly, the vow to give to each other is based on the living faith that, though there will be times of scarcity, there is always enough for everyone. Yet even today, these twin covenants seem to threaten the Western mind intent on accumulating wealth, because those who serve the economic god refuse to believe, even in times of abundance, that there is enough for everyone.

I am not making an argument against capitalism or for socialism. I am speaking to the more elemental question of kinship that all living species have struggled with throughout time: whether to cooperate for the common good or go it alone. The criminalization of giving starkly renders the difference between life organized around self-interest and life organized around a covenant of care. Which system governs our time on Earth together: the power created by self-interest or the power inherent in our inborn connection? There is an endless history for each. Yet none of it matters if we can't discern what makes us lose and regain our social trust, if we can't recover the resilient belief that we are more together than alone.

Social critic Noam Chomsky says, "Power systems do not give gifts willingly." But people do. And natural systems give gifts willingly. The sun never holds back its light and warmth, the sea never holds back its water, and the wind never holds back its invisible power. Left to our own nature, the human community never holds back its light and warmth or its care and innate impulse to build and repair.

Are we only here to accumulate wealth at the expense of each other or to offer our feast of giving in due time to pay our debt to all that lets us live? Aren't we struggling with these two minds today? Aren't we, in our fear of being powerless, accumulating power for its own sake? Haven't we lost the power of connection and kinship generated by the embodied act of giving?

The struggle between self-interest and care lives in each heart. We are asked to work these choices every day, and the life of relationship, family, and community depend on what we choose. When driven by hardship, our care is often diverted by our fears, and the truth of our situation and of those around us is often obscured by our race toward a prosperity defined by others. All the while, we are challenged, as every generation before us, to enliven the honorable work of creating enough for everyone.

The struggle between self-interest and care lives in each heart. We are asked to work these choices every day, and the life of relationship, family, and community depend on what we choose.

Fairness

If you do not change direction, you may
end up where you are heading.

—Lao Tzu

In Eindhoven, in the Netherlands, there is a five-way junction of roads where over the years the accident rate had increased. To try to prevent collisions, city officials added different types of signage: large bright warning signs and then yellow arrows painted on the road. Then they lowered speed zones in and out of the juncture; then they installed more traffic lights. But the accident rate wouldn't abate.

Finally, a young civil engineer suggested that they remove all signage completely and restore the intersection to how it was before modern government tried to improve it. Since nothing else had worked, the city officials agreed. Within a year, the accident rate almost vanished.

With no instructions or directives, individuals began to assume their personal responsibility in making their way. Without signage to follow, they began to resume eye contact with fellow travelers and everyone began, quite naturally, to negotiate the complex flow of human traffic. Given the chance, ordinary people will re-establish lines of communication in a way that honors their own needs and the needs of the whole.

This tells us that we innately know how to live together. Laws and rules are helpful, for sure, and necessary to regulate some human behavior. But excessive direction precludes our firsthand experience and the necessary chance to assume personal responsibility for how we interact.

Personal responsibility broadens our view. While it may be dangerous to remove a pedestrian *Walk–Don't Walk* light at a busy intersection, relying solely on the light is equally dangerous if the light becomes a substitute for our own seeing. At best, a sign will remind us of the situation so we can look up and see the road for ourselves. Too much signage—spiritually, psychologically, ethically, or pragmatically—robs us of the chance to develop our own spirit, psychology, ethics, and usefulness in the world.

Signage and rules, on the road and in our lives, are most useful in removing impediments to our innate sense of care and fairness. Primatologist Frans de Waal has seen that bonobos and chimpanzees have an inborn sense of fairness. If two chimps are given equal rewards for a task, they will perform that task without question. But should one be given a grape, which is valued more than a cucumber, the one given the cucumber will become enraged.

Chimps demonstrate a sense of fairness about how they are treated, but bonobos demonstrate a sense of fairness regarding others, which chimps seem incapable of. A bonobo given the more valued grape will not continue a task until the other bonobo is given the same. Bonobos are imprinted with this awareness of the plight of others, perhaps with the primal DNA of social justice. The disturbing question is: What happens to humans that interferes with our awareness of the plight of others? What allows us to continue when we know that those beside us are not being treated fairly?

Dr. De Waal concludes that the origin of this sense of fairness in primates comes from their experience of cooperative relationships. Perhaps our human obsession with self-reliance has blinded us to the work and gift of cooperative relationships. Perhaps we've become so isolated in our use of technology that we've stopped empathizing with others and have lost touch with our inborn sense of fairness. If so, what form of social remediation do we need to regain our sense of equity for others?

Given the chance, ordinary people will re-establish lines of communication in a way that honors their own needs and the needs of the whole.

Living in Fear and Scarcity

Death is not the biggest fear we have; our
biggest fear is taking the risk to be alive.
—DON MIGUEL RUIZ

I once heard someone say that the game musical chairs is a training ground for the fear of scarcity. There is always one less chair than there are people, and so, even as children, we're prompted to practice racing each other to have enough. Rather than learning how to share what we have.

Today, reality shows, which have little to do with reality, serve as a collective tranquilizer. Under the guise of being participatory, they seduce viewers into thinking that they have actually taken an action in a community by voting for contestants. In fact, viewers are still isolated and longing for connection, while the shows reinforce self-interest motivated by scarcity and fear. Viewers fantasize about being on the shows and winning, rather than face the lives that are truly theirs to live.

Shows like *Survivor*, *The Apprentice*, and *Fear Factor*, to name a few, define success as the ability to outwit, outperform, out-stomach, and out-bully others in order to secure money and celebrity. In *The Apprentice*, success is determined by appeasing a patriarchal authority at all costs. *Survivor* is a romanticized training ground for the winner-take-all mentality that informs the most ruthless kind of leadership. There, the voting among rivals for who stays on the show is a test of duplicity and betrayal. *Fear Factor* titillates viewers with a vicarious glimpse of people mustering the nerve to perform terrifying acts, all for the sake of winning. These contrived situations replace the miracle of finding the extraordinary in the ordinary with the need to devise more and more jarring acts so that the perverse defines what is extraordinary. This, in turn, is the source of shock—not the source of wonder.

These situations are all innovative forms of gambling, which is really about risk-taking and not necessarily about wagering money. In his novel *Siddhartha*, Hermann Hesse comments on this when the main character Siddhartha loses his way in a life of gambling. After tumbling down that road for several years, he realizes that gambling provides the thrill of chance, which serves as a distraction and poor substitute for the experience of genuine risk. I think these shows do the same thing. They deter us from the genuine risks that await us all: to face things truthfully, to love each other honestly, and to risk living a genuine life, alone and in community.

One crucial difference between chance and risk is that genuine risk is lived through and not watched. And it is *the living through* that is most satisfying and rewarding. It is *the living through* that leads us to a deeper experience of life. The thrill of chance, on the other hand, arises when we imitate risk. Then, we need chance to escalate in order to stay thrilling, as our imitation of genuine risk is seldom satisfying or rewarding. This is why the wager has to increase each time we gamble. Likewise, the emotional ante of these reality shows continues to escalate in order to have viewers keep wagering their attention and affections.

Paradoxically, the reality show ethos—where we gather and watch for something to happen—has inverted the gifts needed to participate in actual reality. One of the greatest stories of seeking God and truth is nested in the novel I mention above. In *Siddhartha*, the young seeker goes out into the world in earnest conversation with life itself, with unscripted experience. He seeks out certain mentors but discovers unexpected teachers along the way.

Siddhartha's timeless journey unfolds from an open mind and an open heart, from giving and not getting attention. And what awaited Siddhartha awaits each of us. For we are all seekers who trip out of our self-designed plan to lean further into the world, until the journey shapes us. So, staging an experience and filming what happens defeats the whole purpose of exploration.

What matters in life most often shows itself when no one is looking. It occurs in unplanned moments of revelation, not in a filmed episode with the world watching and the meter running. All my experience tells me that Spirit doesn't show itself this way, though it could happen, since Spirit is everywhere. Several of these reality projects have good intentions to inspire people in their own search for God and truth. In some instances, they might inspire the participants, but I fear the generic reality show is voyeuristic, giving us a vicarious taste of the journey without taking the risk to enter our own life and embark on our own journey.

These shows tell young people that through self-interest and cut-throat behavior they can stay on the show, and by doing anything to anyone or even to themselves, they can please their peers and the authority they work for in order to gain money and celebrity. Subtly, these shows are teaching our youth to watch the thrill of chance and to avoid the more life-fulfilling work of genuine risk.

Now, there are those who ask me to calm down: it's only entertainment. But I remember watching channel five wrestling when I was a kid with my grandfather. He enjoyed it so, though he seemed to always know it was staged. Today there are many who don't know or care that these versions of life are staged. All this has taken us further into a culture that has lost the distinction between what is real and what is acted. This loss of reality began when an actor became president. Then, a wrestler, and a weight lifter known as the Terminator, became governors of two states, and in 2016 a former reality TV figure became president. Even politicians get training in acting. All to stay on the show.

It reminds me of the Roman Colosseum, where Christians were thrown to lions for sport and gladiators fought to the death to entertain the multitudes, dissipating their thirst for rebellion. Through the use of television and technology, the web of reality shows has inadvertently become our virtual Colosseum. And if hell is the cost of false living, then we have cultivated a hellish culture that can no longer tell what is real.

But if we are interested in finding each other and living the one life we are given to the fullest, we need to navigate through a house of mirrors that will stun us into a trance that will keep us from things that matter. It will keep us from the real world. And so, our ability to find truth and meaning becomes even more crucial. For once we lose the distinction between what is real and what is false, it is twice as hard to find our way. It is difficult to fly from the birdcage if you see the bars as branches in which to nest.

Genuine risk is lived through and not watched.

The Migration of Care

In America, our sense of self-reliance is so embedded in our "Live free or die" ethic that, when we mean to honor what we've been through as a society, we often re-enact the conflict and the suffering rather than the freedom we won through the conflict. For example, there are annual re-enactments of the Civil War battle at Gettysburg (July 1–3, 1863) rather than annual healing conversations about race. And there are annual re-enactments of the Revolutionary War battles at Saratoga (September 19 and October 7, 1777) rather than public forums on the deeper meanings of freedom.

Perhaps we distort what matters because, as *National Geographic* photographer Dewitt Jones points out, we as a culture are obsessed with "being the best *in* the world" rather than "being the best *for* the world." It seems that whenever we compare and count, we lose access to the depth of our kinship. This doesn't mean we never have to compare or count, just that we have to be wary of making these mind-sets codes to live by.

Other cultures have done a better job of caring for each other. In his classic, *The Practice of the Wild*, Gary Snyder tells us of a practice of common care that's still part of Swedish law, which

> allows anyone to enter private farmland to pick berries or mush-rooms, to cross on foot, and to camp out of sight of the house.

This custom turned law makes room for the stranger passing through.

In Africa, *Osusu* is a community practice of pooling savings and sharing those monies with those of the group who are in need. Members will give what they can, as little as one dollar or as much as a hundred dollars a month. The communal pot is then given to one member of the group. The next month, the communal pot will be given to the next member of the group. This will continue till everyone in the group receives the pot. Then the cycle will begin again.

Osusu has been practiced for generations in Nigeria and has long been part of the Yoruba tradition. Osusu groups depend on trust and cooperation. Such communal sharing rises out of a belief that each person's survival is tied to everyone else.

So what do we model and what do we imitate? Again, we're brought back to the core question: Are we in this together or are we fighting to make it alone? What do we place value on and what do we pass on to our children: that sharing or hoarding is the way to survive? It's a strange truth that those with less tend to share more. Perhaps because once we've suffered, we understand and feel each other's fate more easily.

In our modern Western culture, fear isolates us from each other so much that it's difficult to discern when it's safe to reach out to others. Yet we so desperately need the balm and care of community. How do we undo these tangles? How do we recover our common sense of living? What skills are necessary to find each other and to feed each other? What can we do in our day-to-day lives to reconnect and share some of what we have?

To surmount our isolation and fear, we could learn from the monarch butterfly who migrates over four generations across an entire continent. Amazingly, the next butterfly, born where the last one died, knows innately where to go and picks up the path of migration where the last left off. If one butterfly dies in a meadow and the next is born there a month later, the newborn still knows where to go and how to continue the path of its ancestor.

How does this happen? No one really knows. With a delicate persistence, the first three generations of butterflies live from two to six weeks, and the fourth butterfly completes the migration to warmer climates such as Mexico and California, living six to eight months until the whole process begins again. Often, these butterflies land in the same trees, year after year, the way humans learn the same lessons time and time again.

The summer breeding ground for monarchs can span more than

a million acres. And every fall, the monarch makes its way south, traveling up to 3000 miles to refind its winter roost, the way seekers make pilgrimage to ancient holy sites.

The question remains: How can we resolve our differences, from one generation to the next, passing on our Collective Wisdom, while inhabiting our very individual lives? Perhaps lineage is the migration of human nature across generations. If so, how can we participate more fully in this journey?

Once the noise of our pain and discord is settled, there is something in each of us that knows where to go as soon as we're born and where to keep going when feeling lost. Some call this migration of heart—resilience. Others call this dynamic participation in the life that moves through us—the reseeding of Spirit from one awakened being to the next. Together, the migration of wisdom and care from one generation to the next—until the child assumes what the parent has learned—is what the best of tradition tries to evoke.

The small things we can share and model will make a difference.

Perhaps lineage is the migration of human nature across generations. If so, how can we participate more fully in this journey?

Whole-Mind Thinking

What you see and hear depends a good
deal on where you are standing...

—C. S. LEWIS

When our worldview becomes fragmented, we no longer feel the connection of all life in our heart and no longer see the cause and effect of all actions in our mind. The resulting turmoil and isolation can be unbearable.

One purpose of imagination is to reveal and restore the web of connection we participate in. But living in fragmented ways—never seeing or accepting the consequence of what we do—erodes our capacity for imagination and connection. Inevitably, we slip into the near-sightedness of literalism whereby we can only comprehend what is before us. Literalism erodes our ability to connect the dots. We return to a flooded house unable to fathom that leaving the water running had something to do with it. We wake in a society filled with random acts of violence unable to fathom that how we treat each other and educate each other has played a part in creating the conditions for that violence to erupt. Literalism blinds us to the consequences of our actions and so, creates conditions for violence, thwarting the compassion of community.

If the chemicals on my lawn leach into your water supply, making it undrinkable, there is cause and effect. And if we never see or hear certain people in our communities, they will eventually resort to drastic measures to be seen and heard. There is always cause and effect. One part affects the other. One part keeps the other alive. The practice and failure of our awareness of each other has gone on forever.

Being a citizen of the world—a wakeful member of the largest living community known as humanity—requires us to keep the ways we are connected in view and to base our actions toward each other on the larger effects our actions will have on those connections.

The American naturalist Henry David Thoreau (1817–1862) refused to pay a poll tax in July 1846, because he believed that the funds would be used to support the Mexican-American war. This armed conflict was waged between the United States and Mexico from 1846 to 1848 in the wake of the 1845 U.S. annexation of Texas, which Mexico considered a province of its nation. At the time, Thoreau was living in the woods surrounding the New England village of Concord, Massachusetts.

Thoreau saw how the tax funded the war, and didn't want to contribute to this violence. The municipal officials of Concord did not see what the tax and the war had to do with each other. They simply saw a vagabond being disobedient to the basic obligations required to be a member of their smaller community. They didn't see the obligations required to be a member of the larger human community. So they arrested and jailed Thoreau. Ralph Waldo Emerson, who also lived in Concord, visited Thoreau in jail and asked, "Henry, what are you doing in here?" Thoreau replied, "Waldo, the question is what are you doing out there?"

When my wife, Susan, and I first moved from upstate New York to southwest Michigan, we owned a van. In New York State, annual car inspections required every vehicle to have a functioning emissions control device, which we supported in concept but complained about whenever the expensive contraption under our car wouldn't work and needed to be repaired.

In the thousand details of moving, I realized once in Michigan that our van's inspection had lapsed. I quickly found an auto shop and was surprised to learn that there are no required car inspections in Michigan. Since the emissions control device on our van wasn't working again, I asked about that and was told that there were no emission regulations in Michigan. The mechanic glibly said, "No worry on that. The winds blow north. It just all goes into Canada." Just what are we doing in here and out there?

When a break in whole-mind thinking—the effort to keep our

worldview as large as possible—fragments our lives, it creates a form of social insanity whereby we become our own unconscious enemies, undoing the good efforts we make.

For instance, two random shootings, in Las Vegas (January 4, 2010) and Washington, D.C. (March 4, 2010), were perpetrated with guns sold to the shooters by the Memphis Police Department. As a source of revenue, police departments across the country resell guns confiscated during arrests; then they turn around and head back out into the streets to track down criminals who seem to have an endless supply of guns. Here our inability to see cause and effect is starkly dangerous.

Even more incredible is the fact that, in Tennessee, the practice of reselling guns is now required, and that this was signed into law by Governor Phil Bredesen on the very same day (March 4, 2010) that the mentally disturbed man, armed with a gun purchased from the Memphis Police Department, walked up to an entrance of the Pentagon, approached two police officers, and calmly opened fire, wounding the officers before they shot him. This sequence of events is social insanity, tantamount to fire departments selling gasoline and matches in order to raise money.

The wholeness or brokenness with which we see and feel each other in a daily way has real consequences. We are challenged at every turn to recover and honor the obligations required to be a member of the larger human community. Perhaps the greatest gift we've lost is the largeness of view by which we feel the web of life and all its connections.

Healthy communities depend on their ability to understand and foresee both connection and cause and effect, because everything is connected and interdependent. We're challenged to remember that, just as bodies are made of organs which are made of tissue, communities are made of neighborhoods which are made of families which are made of individuals. Each part informs the whole.

As human beings living in an increasingly complex human hive, the social insanity we are falling into is a collective disease of disconnection, which only the re-awakening of our compassion can heal. Otherwise, like James Thurber, we will find ourselves sipping coffee by a window, watching bulldozers cut down elm trees to clear a site for an institution for people driven insane by the cutting down of elm trees.

Being a citizen of the world requires us to keep
the ways we are connected in view.

Learning Together

Like a dormant seed, humanity has taken a long time to flower. Almost six million years ago, we first began to walk upright. More than three million years ago, we invented stone tools in Kenya. A million years ago, we discovered fire. That means we walked about in the dark for five million years before having access to warmth and light that we could somewhat control. It wasn't till 3000 B.C. that we invented papyrus in Egypt and began to write on paper. Assyrians created the first aqueduct in the ninth century B.C. In 431 B.C., the first hospital was opened in Sri Lanka. In 859, the first degree-awarding university was opened in Morocco. At the same time, gunpowder was invented in China, and education and self-destruction began their endless conflict.

Our creativity and ingenuity expanded rapidly. In 1285, the first eyeglasses were created in Italy. In 1514, Copernicus asserted that the Earth revolves around the sun, declaring that we are not the center of everything. Two hundred years later, in 1740, the first symphony was written. In 1826, the first photograph was taken in France. In 1835, the first revolver was put together and violence became intensely personal.

We continued to devise tools of communication and protection. In 1871, Antonio Meucci invented the telephone. Eight years later, in 1879, Thomas Edison filed a patent for the lightbulb. Six years later, in 1885, the first gas-powered car was on the street. In 1903, the Wright brothers made their first airplane flight. In 1925, the first television was created. Two years later, in 1927, the first talking picture was filmed. In 1952, Jonas Salk discovered a vaccine for polio. In 1967, the first heart transplant was performed. Two years later, in 1969, humans walked on the moon. In 1975, the first personal computer was turned on. In 1982 the Internet was created. And in

2014, Google unveiled a driverless car, eliminating our need to steer on the road.

Yet, we were developing inwardly and relationally even before we discovered fire, evolving our sense of interdependence and community along the way. I want to focus on three ancient islands in time when communities flourished, when learning was expansive and diverse, and when our understanding of what is possible between us was strengthened. These progressive communities were the Gandhara Empire, which existed in what is now Pakistan (2nd millennium B.C.–7th century A.D.), the middle Chan school of Buddhism in China (755–907), and the reign of the Buddhist ruler in Tibet, the monk-king Yeshe-Ö (c. 959–1040). Each advanced the power of learning.

The Gandhara Empire was established by Kushan nomads from northwest China, who were open to Buddhist ways from Asia, Greek ways from the Mediterranean, and Hindu ways from India. From the outset, Gandhara was multicultural and inter-religious. During this era, the first images of Buddha in human form appeared, and statues of Buddha and Apollo were at times interchangeable.

Gandhara gave rise to one of the first great learning centers in history, Taxila University, where more than 10,000 students attended from all over the world. At its height, Taxila offered more than sixty-four fields of study, including the Vedas, philosophy, Ayurveda, agriculture, surgery, politics, archery, astronomy, commerce, futurology, music, dance, the art of discovering hidden treasure, and the craft of deciphering encrypted messages. Taxila, which in Sanskrit means "city of cut stone," had a law school, a medical school, and a school of military science. Students were enrolled at the age of sixteen after completing their basic education, and generally lived near their teacher, as many as five hundred per instructor.

Knowledge was considered too sacred to be exchanged for money, so there were no fees at Taxila University. Education was paid for by the society at large, especially by rich merchants and wealthy parents, and no qualified student was turned away. Most students did manual labor for their keep. Examinations were not required, but a student had to master one area of knowledge in order to move on. No degrees were awarded, as the mastery of knowledge was considered a reward unto itself, and using knowledge for self-interest was considered sacrilegious.

The Gandhara Empire reached its height under the reign of Kanishka the Great from 128 to 151. Under his rule, Taxila University thrived, the trade route known as the Silk Road was developed, important monasteries were built, and the inclusive Mahāyāna form of Buddhism, which seeks a mutual enlightenment with others, became a social ethic of the time. This was a kind era of multiculturalism and social compassion.

Our next island in time, the middle Chan school of Buddhism in China (755–907), spanned 152 years and was a creative period akin to the Italian Renaissance. The middle Chan period began in 755, when a rebellion against the Tang emperor divided China into autonomous regions. It became a time of harsh persecution for Buddhists. As a result, essential, informal schools formed around a nexus of dynamic teachers who dissuaded any single-minded followers. During this era, dozens of gifted masters lived in an area equivalent to the northeastern United States. Over time, a web of inquiry and practice evolved into a network of teachers available to all. Students would travel and study from master to master in a fertile cross-pollination that formed the foundation of a spiritual lineage that would flourish for centuries, shaping Mahāyāna Buddhism and Japanese Zen as we know them today.

In the more typical formation of community, alignment and allegiance to a shared set of values is required. What's instructive and exciting about this self-organized, open network of living masters is that this community wasn't based on sameness, but on the commitment to integrate the whole of many, diverse ways of thinking. The organic network of Chan masters demonstrates that true learning depends on an animated sense of belonging to an understanding of life greater than any single set of values or following any one revered leader. It supports the notion that our direct connection to life is the building block of our direct connection to each other.

In the sacred pursuit of cross-cultural knowledge that took place at Taxila University in northern India and the informal cross-pollination of knowledge in southern China, the honest search for meaning while listening to others gave rise to vital communities.

A third island in time occurred in Tibet, during the reign of Yeshe-Ö (c. 959–1040), the first noble lama-king. In thirty years of rule, he revitalized the teaching of Buddhism and built the Tholing Monastery to ensure the legacy of Buddhism throughout Tibet.

Yeshe-Ö assumed the throne when his uncle, King Tashi-gon, died without an heir. One of his first acts was to sponsor twenty-one novitiates to be trained as monks under leading gurus in Kashmir and other parts of India. Their charge was to translate Buddhist scriptures from Sanskrit to Tibetan. The extreme conditions of northern India proved fatal to all but two of the young men, Lekpai Sherap and Rinchen Zangpo. Yet it was Rinchen's translations that seeded Buddhism in Tibet for centuries.

In 1024, Yeshe-Ö brought a master, Atisha, from Bengal to Tibet to write *A Lamp for the Path to Enlightenment*, which became a classic for the Tibetan people. In it, he reformed how monks are trained so that their spiritual education would center on the mentor-student relationship. This set the tone for valuing apprenticeship in all fields of knowledge, and can be seen as the ancestor of the craft guilds in the Middle Ages in Europe, the British tutorial as it appeared at Oxford and Cambridge, and the modern concept of internship.

In our long journey to living well together, these ancient yet progressive communities cultivated these timeless ethics: that meaningful knowledge is free and learning is its own reward; that lasting knowledge is independent of its teacher and found by integrating the whole of many, diverse ways of thinking; and that the mentor-student relationship is a building block of community.

We owe much to these early endeavors. The following questions, which come from their efforts, are good barometers of our willingness to learn and good indicators of the health and openness of our relationships, whether in friendship, in a family, in an organization, or in a community: Do you believe that what matters and holds us together is more lasting than our self-interest? Do you believe that learning is its own reward? Do the people you live with and work with believe that knowledge that lasts is independent of any teacher? Do those who love you and support you encourage you to follow what is alive and to keep integrating what feels true? Are you currently a student learning from a mentor? At the same time, are you willing to be a mentor to a willing student?

When faced with discord and division, when thinking we're so different, we can reclaim this timeless truth: that no one owns the wisdom that restores us. We can knit our divisions by entering our ongoing apprenticeship with kindness, accepting that everyone in need is a teacher. These lessons are waiting just beneath the anger and self-interest of our day.

We are all apprentices, walking about in the dark for long periods of time before stumbling into the timeless reservoir of warmth and light. It's the power of learning that brings us there.

Through the power of learning together, we are reminded that what matters is free, that learning is its own reward, and that lasting knowledge is independent of its teacher.

From One to Another

What is a bee without its hive?
—PUANANI BURGESS

Being alive is being part of the community of life. Remembering that we belong is an act of community. Acting out of this knowing is an act of compassion. We are all tied together in invisible places, the tearing of which diminishes us.

Martin Niemöller (1892–1984), a Lutheran pastor born in Germany, held anti-Semitic views before World War II, but he opposed the Nazification of German churches and for this was imprisoned in several concentration camps until 1945. After being released, he expressed his deep regret for not having done enough to help the victims of the Nazis. He is known for this poem:

> They came first for the Communists,
> and I didn't speak up because I wasn't a Communist.
> Then they came for the Jews,
> and I didn't speak up because I wasn't a Jew.
> Then they came for the trade unionists,
> and I didn't speak up because I wasn't a trade unionist.
> Then they came for the Catholics,
> and I didn't speak up because I was a Protestant.
> Then they came for me,
> and by that time no one was left to speak up.

We are constantly challenged by what it means to be in community. In his essay *What is Art?* Leo Tolstoy said, "Art is the passing of feelings from one human heart to another." In his Nobel Prize speech, William Faulkner said, "It is [the writer's] privilege to help man endure by lifting his heart . . ." In their novels both bear witness to the difficulty of the human journey by invoking a compassionate realism. Their insights and approach help to define the art of community, which keeps evolving. So we need to keep asking: What skillful means of being and doing does community require of us?

An anonymous social worker from Sacramento, California, extended herself further than Martin Niemöller but wonders if she opened herself enough:

> I work at a private park that provides daytime services for the homeless. When it rains, our shoe-exchange rack fills with wet shoes as the dry ones are claimed. The hot coffee quickly disappears, and people sit in gazebos to get the rest they didn't get during the night, their wet clothes steaming under the propane heaters. Men and women who are destitute themselves often ask me to do something for "that old man over there who shouldn't be out here" or "the young kid on the bench in the corner." Sometimes I can offer little more than a friendly smile and perhaps a pair of dry socks I found in a corner after I was certain we had run out.
>
> I go home on days like this physically and emotionally exhausted, happy to strip off my rain gear and warm up. Sometimes when I ride my bike past the city's rapidly growing tent community, I wonder: What exactly is it that keeps me from inviting them inside with me?

Whether we watch and do nothing or do something and feel it's not enough, we always reach an edge of limitation in caring for others that humbles us. Keeping that edge authentic demands a commitment to self-honesty.

In this anonymous worker's moment of community, we see how love can break down the boundary we keep building between self and other. From this one caring moment, we can lift up some traits that indicate when a community values all of its people:

- when public space is available to all
- when in times of basic need, those with enough provide food, clothing, and shelter for the common good
- when the wisdom of those suffering helps us to understand and heal the suffering
- when those who find something to give when there seems to be nothing left are turned to as leaders
- when those who help the community survive are turned to as social engineers
- when those who keep asking what keeps us from doing more are turned to as teachers.

Perhaps this is the secret to a compassionate society: to give to strangers until they no longer seem strange, and to let in others until the risk to care mysteriously adds to our life. The fact that the park in this story is private and not public tells us that we still have a long way to go. Ultimately, in the health of one resides the health of all.

This reaching back for others is a timeless sign of the good-hearted among us whose very strength of kindness makes community possible. This innate concern for the journey of others is the story of the Buddhist Bodhisattva, who seeks to use his or her kindness and wisdom to help others wake. An ancient teaching story describes the nature of a Bodhisattva:

Three people are walking through a desert. Parched and thirsty, they spy a high wall ahead. They approach and circumnavigate it, but it has no entrance or doorway. One climbs upon the shoulders of the others, looks inside, yells "Eureka" and jumps inside. The second then climbs up and repeats the actions of the first. The third laboriously climbs the wall without assistance and sees a lush garden inside the wall. It has cooling water, trees, fruit, and the like. But, instead of jumping into the garden, the third person jumps back out into the desert and seeks out desert wanderers to tell them about the garden and how to find it. The third person is the Bodhisattva.

Every time we pause to help someone climb a wall or cross a street or face an illness, we are a Bodhisattva. Every time we check on the neighbor who has no one and listen to her stories of a time long gone, we are a Bodhisattva. Every time we hold those in pain or offer a mirror to someone who has forgotten who they are, we are a Bodhisattva. When others do this for us, they are Bodhisattvas.

Remembering who we are is the first step to remembering that we are all the same and that our well-being depends on each other. The challenges remain: to receive truth from each other along the way and to help each other endure by lifting one another's heart. While we can neither save the world nor ignore it, we can better the world by reaching back for each other when we stumble.

> We are all tied together in invisible places,
> the tearing of which diminishes us.

Entrainments of Heart

> There is one soul and many tongues, one spirit and various
> sounds; every country has its own speech, but the subjects
> of speech are common to all.
>
> —TERTULLIAN, C. 217

In creating any kind of community, it's important to recognize that we at heart are the same and connected under all our differences. This fundamental view of life as interconnected and interdependent affects how we educate and govern. In every age, seeking truth and meeting trouble bring us together and make our underlying connections visible. In 1838, James Fenimore Cooper argued that a free community is based on "the necessity of speaking truth, when speaking at all; [and] a contempt for all designing evasions of our real opinions."

Yet there's a difference between telling the truth and experiencing the truth. When we open our heart to concerns beyond our own, we start to experience the truth we're all a part of. This opening to concerns other than our own is the stitchwork of community. I saw this quote from Martin Luther King, Jr. painted on a newspaper vending machine:

> An individual has not started living until [they] can rise above
> the narrow confines of [their] individualistic concerns to the
> broader concerns of all humanity.

Under all the ways we can study and learn, it's an open, truthful heart that lets us live in rhythm with others. This impulse to share the journey is a fundamental force of nature. In physics, *rhythm entrainment* is a phenomenon where if two objects vibrate in a similar way long enough, they entrain each other to a third, common amplified wave, which, in turn, is louder, stronger, deeper, and more far-reaching than their singular rhythms. Strange as it seems, this is how TV remotes work.

In a social sense, the vibration of the heart makes the fabric of community visible, through its capacity to entrain with the rhythms of others. Tending to the life around us can invoke an *entrainment of hearts*. Such ways of tending to life include caring, truth-telling, listening, entering silence, being vulnerable, and telling stories. Embodying these aspects of being invoke the common rhythm between living things, which we then feel as a bond of relationship—louder, stronger, deeper, and more far-reaching than our singular feelings.

The Maori, the indigenous people of New Zealand, have a custom of sharing their breath. They touch noses and take in each other's breathing and, in this nonverbal way, affirm that their lives are connected. They do this every time they meet and leave each other. In sharing their breath, the Maori entrain their hearts and find their common rhythm.

Our heartfelt attention to life as a whole yields a knowing that gathers throughout time, which can be understood as *Collective Wisdom*. Jung termed this storehouse of knowing across generations as the *Collective Unconscious*. This web of knowing across all time may be the largest community of all, a community of souls.

The latest thinking in neurobiology affirms our common web of knowing. This micro-science is exploring the kinetic energy that exists between cells and how the information passed there enables each cell to do its part in a concerted way that none could do alone. It's compelling to view the energy fields that exist between cells as a collective neuro-conversation that enables life to happen at its most elemental level. In this way, the common rhythms of neurology can be seen as a biological form of collective wisdom. In essence, each person is a dynamic biological community.

In our everyday encounters, we stumble into the question: How do we understand and access the magic of what we know together which no one can know alone? Because of the subtlety of this knowledge across time, every tradition has its mystical way of inquiring about our place in the community of life. Many traditions offer mystical schools of inquiry devoted to embodying our direct connection with life as a whole.

Within the Jewish tradition, listening for the indwelling presence of God helps us know the truth of life. The story of Rabbi Zusya of Hanipol speaks to this. The rabbi taught in the 1700s in the town of Tarnów in southeastern Poland. A Hasidic leader, he spent long hours studying the Talmud. One day, he left his students to read a certain passage. A day later, his students found him still dwelling on the first page. They assumed he had encountered a difficult notion and was trying to solve it. But when a number of days passed and he was still immersed in the first page, they were troubled. Finally, one of them gathered courage and asked the master why he didn't move to the next page. And Rabbi Zusya answered: "I feel so good here, why should I go elsewhere?"

This story points to the reason for all learning. Under all our struggles, what we learn as a human family is that all paths and choices are vehicles for love to do its work wherever we are. When we can devote ourselves to what we find in each other, we welcome life wherever it may show itself—in a stranger or a bird or an old familiar lighthouse. Or in the animated conversations that flit from park bench to park bench in the city where we live. Each moment, if entered, can connect us to the whole of life.

Within the Buddhist tradition, *Vajrayana* holds the spiritual aim of embodying ultimate truth with the vow to help others in their path to liberation. *Vedanta*, which literally means "the end of knowledge," is a mystical path within the Hindu tradition that seeks to uncover the relationship between the unknown and unseeable aspects of life and the knowable and seeable aspects of existence.

Within the Islamic tradition, Sufism aims to release the experience of joy that comes from overcoming our lesser self, while trying to experience the Divine in everything. Mystics within the Sikh tradition believe that the Oneness of God is manifest in the practical life of truthfulness and service.

Within the tradition of Jainism, *Moksha* is a mystical path that works toward our unification with all life, in the belief that this unification will liberate us from our rebirth into the cycle of suffering.

Within Judaism, the *Kabbalah* is a course of study meant to sur-face the relationship between the unchanging, eternal mystery of life and the finite experience of human beings.

At the same time, Christian mysticism explores experiences of the soul that have no physical or earthly cause, trying to know and honor the unseeable Divinity that holds everything together.

And the mystical qualities of Taoism hold that we are born to live in accord with the larger, intangible current of life, the way a fish finds and swims with the current of the sea.

Each of these traditions offers an entrainment of heart by which we can experience the common rhythm of life, as it beats now and throughout the community across time we call Eternity. These are not abstract paths. Some people use the mystical path as a way to retreat from living in the world, but the true value of entraining our heart to the rhythms of life is that it enables us to live *more fully* in the world, with greater resolve and compassion.

Regardless of where you're drawn to look, the practice of staying connected to life reveals the larger frame of all that joins us. If we can't stay open to all that is larger than us, we will live from a self-centered frame of reference that will narrow our range of experience. The larger our frame of reference, the richer our understanding of how we can live together.

Imagine you're driving alone along a road. If you limit your view of life to the one road you're on, everything that comes along can seem an intrusion. But if you view life as a network of infinite roads, of which your road is one, the influx of other life seems inevitable, even desired.

When we can view the road we're on as one path within a geo-graphy of paths, then the rich, all-encompassing community of life seems ever-present and healing. Our path then includes the migra-tion of antelope, flamingos, and salmon, and the currents that clouds follow as they blanket the globe, as well as the migration of stories between generations, and the evolution of insight passed among the wisdom traditions throughout the centuries.

Being part of such a diverse geography of possibility informs our choices, even if we never stray from our personal road. The larger our perspective, the more rhythms of life we encounter. The more rhythms of life we encounter, the deeper and broader our experience. The deeper our experience, the more fellow travelers we admit. And the more fellow travelers we admit, the deeper our compassion and strength of heart. This is how community grows.

The abalone farmers in the East China Sea were compelled by the vast forces of life to find their common rhythms and work together. In generations past, lone fishermen would bob and drag their nets for abalone in the open sea, drifting near each other, but keeping their distance. Until a typhoon made it impossible to survive alone. And so, the lone fishermen tied up together in order to outlast the swell and pound of the storm. Once the storm passed, they discovered it was easier and more efficient to fish together.

Today, floating villages exist in the China Sea with platforms tied together for miles, to protect each other from typhoons and to share resources and tools. A similar interdependence is found in the floating fishing villages that string across Tonle Sap, a lake in Cambodia that swells to more than five times its normal size in the rainy season when the Mekong River floods the nearby forests and plains.

These are not just instances of survival, but times when life shows us that, if we can follow the common rhythms that bind us, we can come alive in the web of connections that holds the world together.

So when the waves you can't see get choppy and hard to withstand—in love, in suffering, in our search for life's meaning—tie up with whoever is near, so you can withstand the storm together. And once you're comfortable with the bonds between you, let others tie up when necessary. It will only make you stronger. Whether we realize it or not, or like it or not, we're all part of a floating village, trying to bring up enough from the deep to make it to tomorrow.

The web of knowing across all time may be the
largest community of all, a community of souls.

Our Struggle and Possibility

The world changes in direct proportion to the number
of people willing to be honest about their lives.

—ARMISTEAD MAUPIN

I was heartbroken to learn of those innocent children slain in Newtown, Connecticut, on December 14, 2012. Such heartbreak sweeps away the differences we stand behind, at least for a while. It's always been the work of community to keep the kinship revealed by heartbreak out in the open once the shock subsides. I still think of those little ones.

I still think of their parents and siblings. I can barely imagine their loss. At the time, I thought we might tremble enough to make no weapon automatic. I thought we might be shaken enough to no longer ignore those with mental illness. I thought we might look up and recognize each other, in our pain, as more fragile and connected than anyone imagined. But most of us have become inured to the senseless killing, as if it were uncontrollable, like tornadoes or lightning strikes.

How we're ripped open by the natural and unjust forces of life, how we discover how close we really are in that ripping, and how we settle in the numbness of life going on—this cycle from tragedy to compassion to acquiescence has gone on forever. But keeping the heart open, no matter what opens it, is how we move from our struggle to our possibility, as individuals and as a community. And holding those who suffer is where healing takes place.

After we're broken by tragedy, we're very close to being ethical and loving. The moral conscience of a society is measured by how well it threads its justice with its compassion. Yet, while we've constantly aspired to bring who we are and what we do together, it's eluded us

91

forever. When the going gets rough, we've always struggled with how to live together and how to care for each other.

We often think self-interest will protect us from the hardships of life, when all it does is consume us until we become part of the hardships wearing on others, unwilling to own the harm we inflict. Leo Tolstoy spoke of this when he said:

> I sit on a man's back, choking him and making him carry me, and yet assure myself and others that I am very sorry for him and wish to ease his lot by all possible means—except by getting off his back.

And told that America was making progress with regard to civil rights by those still perpetuating racism, Malcolm X replied, "If you stick a knife in my back nine inches and pull it out six inches, there's no progress. If you pull it all the way out that's not progress. Progress is healing the wound that the blow made."

Having the courage to put ourselves in another's shoes is the fulcrum by which a society becomes humane. This edge between kindness and cruelty separates the haves and have-nots of any community. Eldar Shafir, a professor at Princeton, has explored the psychology of poverty and offered compelling evidence that the pressure of not having what is basic to survival (food, clothing, shelter) dominates how we think and behave.

Shafir uses the metaphor of a suitcase: When we have a large enough suitcase, we don't need to worry whether or not everything will fit. We gather what we need—and more importantly, what we'd *like* to take with us—close the suitcase, and off we go. But when we have too small a suitcase, our mental energy must always deal with an added layer of concern and make choices about what will fit. Now we have to prioritize and value one thing over another, because we can't take everything with us.

It's easy to see that the psychology of scarcity taxes the thinking and energy of people living in poverty. Having to constantly make these added decisions is fatiguing. Such harsh living drains children of their focus and attention, making it difficult to learn. And when living without basic necessities, every mistake matters. Making a math error of a few dollars in your checkbook when you only have sixty will mean less food that week. Professor Shafir suggests that the long-term damage of the psychology of poverty is that "the source of scarcity begins to capture you." What you lack and need begins to shape how you see the world, how you think, and all you do.

This is powerfully true of any sense of scarcity we live with, including our inner impoverishments. A poverty of love, community, or respect can imprison our heart. The psychology of poverty divides and drives nations as it does individuals. It's easy and misguided for those with more than enough to blame the poor for their own plight, to say that they just need to work harder, make better choices, and pick themselves up.

It's just as easy and misguided for those secure in love, community, and self-worth to blame the lonely and insecure for their emotional poverty. This kind of thinking only impedes the growth of a compassionate and mature society. Until we fall, we don't understand why it takes so long to get up. Until we lose our way, we have no patience for indecision. Eventually, we land so close to the shallow breathing of another that it doesn't matter where we're from or where we're going, if we're living like a waterfall or asleep with our eyes open. The only thing that matters is the hand we offer and the assurance that everything will be all right, though we really don't know.

When we've suffered through our own experience, we can empathize more with others who suffer. Civilizations throughout history, like the Roman Empire, have weakened and devolved because their social contracts lacked true empathy. These societies were torn by classism and a deep-seated fear that made those who had more protect themselves from those who had little. Other civilizations, like the Iberian Peninsula in Spain in the tenth century, had social contracts based on true empathy and the notion that we share a common destiny. It's interesting that France, the Allied country left most in ruins from World War II, had periods after the war that leaned emphatically toward socialism, which, whether it works or not, tries to care for all the people.

Humanist and activist Elesa Commerse reminds us that "community by itself isn't an antidote to all our ills. Community needs to be diverse to be healthy. A strident, homogeneous community can lead to fascism and genocide. Consider Hitler's Germany and the Ku Klux Klan in the United States." When we can try on another's life—see for a moment what they see, and feel for a moment what they feel—then we begin to trust and embrace our differences. Then, the totality of life's diversity keeps strengthening the common force of life we share.

So, how are we to understand the senseless killings that plague the American landscape these days? It's easy to label the broken and lonely who are shooting up movie theatres and elementary schools as crazy psychopaths. Indeed, they are. It's easy to throw our hands up in disgust and say they have nothing to do with us. But while these broken, aberrant souls are responsible and accountable for the harm they perpetrate, it's not that simple. Just as an aneurysm occurs in the body because a weakened artery wall can't withstand the force of a pressurized and stressed system, these weakened souls are social aneurysms, waiting to explode in response to the pressures of a society that can't calm itself.

While these individuals are responsible for their actions, we are responsible for creating a stressed and pressurized society that is relentless on the weakened members among us. A mature society commits to relieving the stress points in its community while holding those who snap responsible for the harm they do. What can we do to calm and stabilize our larger community? Where are we relentlessly stressed? Are we mature enough to tend to the broken parts as well as the pressurized whole?

In our modern world, we focus more on diagnosis than on comprehensive awareness, more on isolating and eliminating what seems problematic (smart-bombing the problem) than on healing troubled parts by enjoining them to the whole. This way of isolating and eliminating problems may fix things in the short term, but it seldom repairs the fundamental issue. As Linda Bowen, the executive director of the Institute for Community Peace in Washington, D.C., says, "The prevention of something (violence, fear, prejudice) doesn't ensure the presence of anything (peace, love, openness)."

In one of his speeches, Martin Luther King, Jr. cited the last verse of "America the Beautiful" as an injunction for true community:

May our country, on the brink of war, take to heart the final refrain of "America the Beautiful:" "America! America! God mend thine ev'ry flaw, Confirm thy soul in self-control, Thy liberty in law."

May our country, on the brink of social chaos, stitch and heal our every flaw. May our society, on the verge of coming together or breaking further apart, confirm our kinship of soul in the deeper reflection that quiets our fear and aggression. May our community, on the edge of breaking through into a collective form of open care, grow our liberty in the creation of more humane laws. Facing what's wrong, divided, or missing only clears the way. Holding the broken as well as holding them accountable is the challenge of our times.

> The moral conscience of a society is measured by how well it threads its justice with its compassion.

QUESTIONS TO LIVE WITH

+ Bring three friends together and invite two new people into your group. In conversation, have each of you discuss an island in time you have experienced in which two or more people have worked well together, a time when two or more people have brought into being an accomplishment or quality that neither could have brought about alone. As a group, discuss the lesson in these stories and how they can apply to the community you live and work in.

+ Four sustaining forms of hospitality are shelter, affirmation, remembering our larger home, and spiritual hospitality (helping another cross a threshold). Bring three friends together and invite two new people into your group. In conversation, have each of you discuss a time when you were given one form of shelter. Then explore your readiness to offer some form of shelter to someone in your community.

+ The thrill of chance serves as a poor substitute for the experience of genuine risk. Chasing thrills rather than facing genuine risk affects how hidden or open a community can be. Bring three friends together and invite two new people into your group. In conversation, have each of you tell the story of a time when you pursued the thrill of chance rather than facing the genuine risk before you. Then describe a genuine risk you are each facing right now and how you might meet it.

+ Bring three friends together and invite two new people into your group. In conversation, have each of you describe what learning together means to you. How do you practice learning in a daily way? How do you learn from others? And how can you support the power and practice of learning in your family and community?

✦ Bring three friends together and invite two new people into your group. In conversation, have each of you describe a time when you discovered that you were more together than alone. Then discuss if your community is working well together. Finally, identify a need in your community that you can address in a way that will bring people together.

✦ Bring three friends together and invite two new people into your group. In conversation, have each of you describe your own struggle with scarcity and abundance. Tell the story of a time when you lived in fear that there wouldn't be enough, and tell the story of a time when you felt certain that there would be enough. As a group, discuss if your community operates out of a sense of scarcity or abundance, or a mix of both. Then, identify what you can give to an area of scarcity in your community.

✦ Bring three friends together and invite two new people into your group. In conversation, have each of you describe one gift you inherently have to offer the world. Then, as a group, explore how you might extend and combine your gifts to make a difference.

CENTERS OF LIGHT

Truth is an eternal conversation about things that matter, conducted with passion and discipline. Truth cannot possibly lie in the conclusions of that conversation, because the conclusions keep changing. So if we want to live "in the truth," we must learn to live in the conversation rather than in its conclusions of the moment. Truth—which comes from the same word that gives us "troth"—is found in staying faithful to the fact that we belong to each other in community.

—PARKER PALMER

The struggle between self-interest and cooperation is an ongoing conflict that has shaped civilizations and their philosophies throughout history. This conflict has been the difference between warring nations and peaceful nations, between the countries the less fortunate flee from and the countries they flee to.

Whole societies have based their social contracts on whether they believe there's enough to share and whether there's enough trust among their people to share what they have. People who have lived out that trust have created centers of light.

Is it really as simple as sharing what we have? The living out of real trust is always complicated. But in the heart of it, to trust in each other and believe that whatever we have is enough has been the foundation of the most compassionate and enlightened societies on Earth.

Spiritual traditions have always held that it's the trust between self and other that empowers compassion and peace. Inevitably, the wisest and kindest among us have always discovered that helping each other is helping ourselves.

Voices of the World

I was at the Parliament of the World's Religions in Barcelona, where Spanish and Catalan are the native tongues. I can't speak either, but listening to everyone without knowing what they were saying was like moving through a field of birds startled into flight, each singing at the light and looking for each other.

On the second day, I attended a workshop with a group of Spaniards. Forty of us stared at each other for a long time, because the hired translator didn't show. But we had to begin. Only our care and want to help and understand came through. Not having access to each other's words meant that we couldn't hide behind them or mistrust what was said or suspect a subtext. That day, moments began to spill open and we had to gesture and reach for something in between. Though I didn't understand a word that was said, we understood each other completely.

After a while, a young man came by and offered to help. He was so adept at translating that he listened to each story in its entirety before putting it into English. Before he would translate, I found myself listening beneath the noise of our words: to the tilt of a head, the wince of a heart, the sudden laughter at self-recognition, the lifting of hands, the dropping of hands, and the silent stare when someone would fall off what they meant to say.

As the conversation wound down, the father of our young translator came into the room to pick him up, and he was surprised to find his son so involved. After a while, the father spoke. It was clear he was sharing something very personal. Slowly, his son translated, "My father says he has a mental illness and it has prevented him from loving his family well. He takes pills now, but doubts if he'll ever be cured. He suffers greatly and feels ashamed."

The son stared off into what seemed like a long familiar silence and the Spanish father began to search his troubled mind, as we waited to see what he would unearth. Finally, as if under a heavy load, he uttered something, which his gentle son translated as "My father says, 'Sometimes, my suffering is greater than my shame and I must speak.'"

Someone blurted out a stream of Spanish. The son translated, "There are two ways to free the heart: the breaking in of suffering or the flying out of love." The words floated then sank between us like stones thrown into the sea.

That evening, we were drawn to tell stories of our own fathers, and I fell into the tale of my mother's father from Romania, one of six sons scattered across the globe. That night, he came to me in a dream. I rushed into his arms, as I did when a boy, shouting, "Poppi! Poppi!" He hugged me, then stroked my cheek and said, "Stop with these big, big stories. I was just a man."

In that unadorned room, that day in Barcelona, we fell into an unexpected moment of community. Faced with no common way to speak, we somehow stayed present to each other until our common humanity surfaced. No one knew what to do, but no one left. And no one pretended to understand what was happening or being said. That created an authenticity among us that drew the young translator to join us and offer his gift.

Staying present and not pretending allows a space of truth to open that others can join.

Such honest company lets the wisdom we all carry surface. Such honest meeting makes it safe enough for a father to admit in public before his son that "sometimes, my suffering is greater than my shame and I must speak." Such depth of admission, heart to heart, makes it safe for a stranger to cough up wisdom such as "There are two ways to free the heart: the breaking in of suffering or the flying out of love."

Whether two or two hundred, whether temporary or lasting, isn't community the oasis of heart we kneel before and drink from after withstanding the rough weather of life? Though we so easily forget the worth of such company, we need to commune in this way— which means *to share one's intimate thoughts and feelings, commune* (a cognate of the word *community*) from the old French meaning *to share what is common.*

We need to look for what we have in common. And finding it, not leave or pretend, but dare to be who we are in public, before family and strangers, until our ancestors come in dreams to remind us that we are all just pilgrims who need each other, travelers who carry bits of truth and wisdom we don't understand until brought to life between us. We need to commune in this way, so we can endure these things and grow.

> Staying present and not pretending allows a space of truth to open that others can join.

The Seeds of Our Nature

Nalanda University was an ancient center of learning for six centuries (5th century–1193 A.D.) in Bihar, India. One of five monasteries, Nalanda was part of an extraordinary network of learning centers between which great scholars would move easily from position to position.

Nalanda was one of the world's first residential universities, and scholars and students attended from as far away as Tibet, China, Greece, and Persia. Considered an architectural masterpiece, the university accommodated more than 10,000 students and 2000 teachers in eight compounds and ten temples. Its several meditation halls and classrooms were placed among lakes and parks.

In his diary, the Chinese pilgrim Xuanzang described the towers of the university and how its forest of pavilions and temples seemed to "soar above the mists in the sky." He noted that monks from their cells "might witness the birth of the winds and clouds."

The Chinese monk Yijing wrote that matters of curriculum and administration required discussion and consensus by all those living and working at Nalanda. If a single monk objected to a matter, it would not pass. Yijing confirmed that

> if a monk did something without consent of all the residents, he would be forced to leave the monastery.

Over the centuries, the university assembled one of the most extensive libraries in history, accumulating hundreds of thousands of volumes housed in a nine-story building where ancient texts were carefully copied and preserved. Known as Dharma Gunj (the Mountain of Truth), the library of Nalanda held the most diverse, complete, and renowned collection of Hindu and Buddhist knowledge in the world at the time.

Tragically, in 1193, Nalanda University was brutally sacked by the fanatic Turk general, Bakhtiyar Khilji. Thousands of monks were beheaded and burned alive. The library was vandalized and burned, and the smoke of all those books lingered over the hills for six months.

How do we hold such noble effort and such travesty? Imagine all that wisdom gathered, page by page through the centuries, one monk at a time: preparing the ink, scribing the sutras, pressing them dry, stacking them on the shelves. Imagine the various texts rolled and unrolled, generation after generation, by teachers eager to discuss the quandaries of living carried in all those stories. Imagine the lineage of teachers and students gathering knowledge from the books like studious bees harvesting pollen and spreading wisdom in the world.

Now imagine the raging Turks fevered to stop this invisible power that they couldn't find or slay. Imagine the first handful of agitated warriors trampling through the library, their horses stumbling over books as they set them aflame, and the cries of those gentle monks helpless to stop them. In the horrible wake of the slaughter, picture the stories in those books smoldering for days, distilling to their essence, dispersing and hanging in the air. Imagine the smoke of all that wisdom rising for months from the mounds of ash, to be inhaled by the land and those farming the land. Day after day, the resin of what took centuries to record swirled into a fine dust that settled on the skin of those just born. Imagine the essence of all that learning filling their pores and lungs, informing in time, without anyone knowing, the kindness of one person stopping to free the stuck wheel of another's cart. Perhaps the lasting purpose of all wisdom is to slip its container so it might imbue the living with a generous mind and a strong heart.

This magnificent harvest of wisdom over six hundred years, and its brutal destruction and release through the vile burning of it all in one day, reveals another paradox: that the inexhaustible essence survives beyond all inexcusable violence. As a soul leaves the body that has carried it when the body dies, to rejoin the reservoir of all Spirit, wisdom leaves the book that has carried it when the book is destroyed, to rejoin the reservoir of all wisdom.

These examples of the best and worst acts of humanity challenge us to work with the reality that cruelty and injustice occur. But while the things that crack us open are often cruel and unjust, what they open within us matters more.

The French Expressionist Georges Rouault (1871–1958) wrote, "The just, like sandalwood, perfume the axe that strikes them." In other words, kindness, torn open, spills on everyone. Wisdom burned is never lost, just absorbed. And illumined truth is still true, even when obscured by the clouds of our tangled humanity.

In heartache, we can darken our understanding of reality and bow only to the *grim effects* of our nature: the violence, the cruelty, and the relentless self-interest. All the while, we're asked to cultivate *the seeds* of our nature by tending to the fact that we're capable of all things: the equanimity *and* the violence, the kindness *and* the cruelty, the awareness of others *and* the self-interest. We are both the wise old monk copying the ancient text and putting it on a shelf *and* the seething Turk cutting his head off. Only by understanding that the potent seed in us is capable of both can we cultivate our better selves.

The enlightened community of Nalanda University and its barbaric slaughter prove that we're always lighting the truth and burning the truth. The history of learning, whether formal or informal, whether in great universities and monasteries or in small cafés, is the lineage of lighting the truth. Every time we give of ourselves to listen and reflect, to feel and so deepen our compassion, we counter the burning of truth.

And however we gather—in a circle like Native American elders, or in rigorous dialogue like a minyan of rabbis, or in the silence of a Quaker meeting, or in a cancer support group in the basement of a hospital—we do so to participate in the lighting of the truth, to better understand the seeds of our own nature, and to understand how we're capable of all things. We gather to quiet our rage and cynicism and to stir our responsibility. We gather to engage all aspects of our nature. We gather to inhabit the gift of our humanity through which we might witness the birth of the winds and clouds,

through which we can come alive together, in the lighted pocket of
the time we have.

> Only by accepting the fact that we're capable of all things—the
> equanimity and the violence, the kindness and the cruelty, the
> awareness of others and the self-interest—can we cultivate our
> better selves.

The Chamber of Time

On a breezy morning in May in New York City, I caught the four train up to Eighty-sixth and Lexington, walked to Fifth, and waited in a line that wrapped around the Neue Galerie, a museum for German and Austrian art. We were there to stand before Gustav Klimt's luminous portrait of Adele Bloch-Bauer, *The Woman in Gold* (1907), one of five paintings seized by the Nazis during World War II from the Bloch-Bauer family in Vienna, and recovered after years of effort by their heirs.

For all of Klimt's innovative rendering and use of gold leaf, it's Adele's eyes that shine the most. More than a hundred strangers gathered and leaned in to see her, then backed away to let the next person get closer. Some like me waited for a second look. I was struck that we live in a time and place where such treasures are preserved and made available.

This hasn't always been the case. For much of human history, the wonders of art were the private treasures of emperors and kings, bequeathed to the next monarch, stolen by generals and bishops, or destroyed by those so enraged by their oppressors that they were blind to the medicine carried in art. Some destroyed beauty in a rabid imposition of their own primacy, unable to tolerate anything that is not them. Like the Turks in the 1100s who burned the great Nalanda library. Or the stern clerics of the Spanish Inquisition in 1478 who destroyed anything secular. Or the Nazis in World War II who burned books and stole more than half of Europe's art, and who when defeat was certain tried to burn centuries of cultural treasures. More recently, the Taliban dynamited the ancient stone Buddhas in Afghanistan, and Islamic fundamentalists smashed antiquities in Iraq, Syria, and Mali.

Yet somehow, the more fundamental covenant—that no one

owns art or literature or music—has prevailed. Today, anyone can find their way into a museum, in America and other countries, to drink from a sense of all that is larger than us, and all that has come before.

Leaving *The Woman in Gold*, I wandered down Fifth Avenue to the Metropolitan Museum of Art, one of the largest museums in the world. Opened in 1872 by railroad executive John Taylor Johnston, the Met originally offered Johnston's personal art collection. Thankfully, it wasn't satisfying for him to keep all that art to himself. The founding superintendent of the Met, George Palmer Putnam, was also the publisher of early American authors such as Washington Irving, William Cullen Bryant, James Fenimore Cooper, and Edgar Allan Poe. The artist Eastman Johnson was a co-founder.

Here I was, 150 years later, returning to this public crossroads of the ages, as I have done perhaps twenty times in my life. I return to the Met as I return periodically to the Pacific Ocean, to stare into its vastness, for its sense of Eternity. At the shore of the Met, no one is denied access; a donation is only suggested. The museum itself is a tribute to our impulse to share. The fact that museums exist around the world is an affirmation that time is a reservoir that no one owns.

I climbed the steps and wandered in to meet some old friends. In the sunlit hall of sculpture on the first floor, I paused before Rodin's *Age of Bronze* (1876), a life-size statue of a young man on the edge of maturity, his soul about to leap from his mouth. A few hundred feet away is Rodin's larger-than-life *Burghers of Calais* (1889), the moment the town leaders agreed to give their lives so their village would be spared by its conquerors. The anguish of their resistance and acceptance reflects our own when life demands more than we think we can give.

I sat to take in the burghers again. I watched others as they were stopped by the living bronze, startled by their own internal gasps. I moved on and, an hour later, found Van Gogh's paintings, *Olive Trees* (1889) and *Wheat Field with Cypresses* (1889). In these paintings, he dismantles the appearance of outer forms. In these oils, he invites us to look beneath what we normally see, like a physicist or biologist asking us to look through his microscope. Though it's only thick strokes of paint on canvas, the sky is aflame, the ground is an ocean, and the trees are rushes of wind. When I first saw these paintings twenty years ago, I understood that, like the common energy enlivening all the natural elements, all the emotional states we're given are at heart the same. Our aliveness simply hardens into lightness or darkness, into trouble or peace.

On another floor, in another century, I stood before Hokusai's incomparable woodblock print, *The Great Wave off Kanagawa* (1830–1832). It points so compellingly to the magnitude of nature and our small insistence to work together in the face of all odds.

Finally, I wound up where I knew I would, in the Asian wing, in a dimly lit room where soft lights encircle ancient statues of Buddha, making each rise from the past. In all my visits over the years, these thousand-year-old carvings seem to breathe, if I sit before them long enough. It's the eyeless and handless Buddha I return to. He's my attendant spirit. He reminds me that when we can put down our habits of seeing and stop grabbing and taking, then we can truly behold each other.

Where else can you go and be touched by what others have touched a thousand years ago? Museums open us to the lineage of human effort. These gathering places are living moments of community. And the individual pieces of art show us how to live and stay connected. Though we try so hard to hide what we feel, every sculpture, whether prehistoric or modern, captures the moment that life pokes us in the heart. They mirror what we carry within us.

When I left that day, I sat on the museum steps overlooking Fifth Avenue, on the edge between the lessons and encouragements of the past and the challenges of our day.

Art shows us how to live and stay connected.

Seat of the Muses

History is necessarily personal: the annals of the centuries
are nothing more than individual days sewn together, and
those who keep the records use their own needle and thread.

—LILY ROTHMAN

The impulse to share what we gather is at the heart of all community. For sharing what we know and what we hold sacred knits the torn fabric of the tribe. From the earliest times, museums and libraries have been repositories of knowledge and testaments to the history of human relationship. They serve as wellsprings for every generation from which we can renew our understanding of how to relate and persevere. Without their reminders, we're doomed to haul and swing the blunt tools of self-interest forever.

The word *museum*, from Greek *Mouseion*, means "seat of the Muses." One of the oldest museums in the world, located in southeastern Iraq, dates back to 530 B.C. Its collection of antiquities was curated by Princess Ennigaldi in honor of her father, Nabonidus, the last king of the Babylonian Empire, who was an early archaeologist. One of the first efforts to preserve art was spawned by the love of a daughter for her father. Princess Ennigaldi had the museum built within her palace grounds near her living quarters, so she could visit it daily. Most of the artifacts had been excavated by her father and dated back to the twentieth century B.C. The museum included some items that belonged to Nebuchadnezzar II.

Early museums were only accessible at the whim of the monarchs who created them. Often, kings and queens and generals didn't want to inspire yearnings for a better life in their oppressed peoples and so limited access to the long view of human ingenuity, creativity, and resilience.

113

It wasn't until the Renaissance that museums began to be conceived as public spaces. In 1471, at the beginning of his papacy, Pope Sixtus IV donated a group of ancient sculptures to the people of Rome, which eventually developed into the Capitoline Museums. What made him suddenly want to give these treasures to his people? In 1506, Pope Julius II, a lover of classical art, purchased a remarkable statue, *Laocoön and His Sons*, one of the great Greek representations of human form. Discovered in a vineyard on the outskirts of Rome, the statue was still partly buried and tangled in the roots of the vineyard when Julius sent Michelangelo to examine it. Seeing this masterpiece unearthed before his eyes shaped Michelangelo's vision as a sculptor. Pope Julius put the statue on public display in the new Belvedere Courtyard one month after its discovery. *Laocoön and His Sons* was the original piece of art in what would become the Vatican Museums.

In 1662, Georg Eberhard Rumphius, a botanist working for the Dutch East India Company in Indonesia, built the first public botanical museum in Ambon, the capital of Maluku Province. Almost a hundred years later, the British Museum was opened to the public in 1759, largely formed around the collections of physician Sir Hans Sloane after his death. Sloane, who wanted to share his fascination with objects of the past, bequeathed his collection to the nation, and an act of Parliament established the "universal museum." In 1769, the great Uffizi Gallery in Florence was established for the people of Tuscany by the House of Medici. A few years earlier, in 1764, Catherine the Great of Russia began an art collection of master works. Over the next twenty-seven years, she would commission the building of galleries to house her ever-growing collection, which would eventually become the Hermitage. A New Hermitage, commissioned by Nicholas I, was open to the public in 1852. The Prado Museum in Madrid was created by Charles III in 1785 to house the royal collections and was open to the public in 1819.

With the advent of the Age of Enlightenment in Europe and later, the Industrial Revolution, the power of monarchies waned. The chaos and vitality of fledgling democracies began to shape the global consciousness of community, affirming, often without knowing, the indigenous sense of shared history that native peoples have embodied since prehistoric times.

A turning point that gave the public access to museums occurred with the creation of the Louvre in Paris. During the French Revolution, the Louvre, originally built as a twelfth-century fortress, was transformed from the private royal collection of art and antiquities established by Louis XIV into a public museum. In May 1791, the National Assembly, the guiding body of the revolution, declared that the Louvre would be "a place to preserve the national memory ... a place for bringing together monuments of all the sciences and arts." On August 13, 1792, Louis XVI was imprisoned and later executed and the royal collection in the Louvre became national property.

In 1836, the enormous bequest of the English chemist James Smithson was accepted by Congress to fund the United States National Museum, now the Smithsonian Institution in Washington, D.C.

By their sheer existence, public museums are a testament to the inherent if mysterious human gift through which we create lasting conduits of beauty out of ideas, imagination, spirit, and raw materials, generation after generation. Yet the artifacts lie so still that it's hard to remember that each was held and shaped by a pair of living hands building, carving, painting, or repairing.

Museums preserve the best of what we as humans create, reminding us of the enduring beauty we're capable of. They may also reveal the sacred as it resides in the moment before us.

Recently, in a museum in Indonesia, an early statue of Kuan Yin, the Buddhist goddess of compassion, was put on display. Within weeks, there were exceptionally long lines of local people waiting to bow and pray to Kuan Yin.

At first, the museum administrators were pleasantly surprised. The museum never had so many visitors. The staff made a concerted effort to maintain the decorum of the museum, and to keep the crowd orderly. They tried to have the locals stay in line within the velvet ropes and move along in a timely fashion, so everyone could see Kuan Yin. But week after week, the lines kept growing until they stopped being lines and swelled into crowds who ignored the ropes as they chanted and left flowers, beads, and candles at the foot of Kuan Yin. Many sat on the floor of the museum in meditation before her. To the local people, this statue wasn't an exhibit but a holy shrine, the reappearance of a lost deity.

Unexpectedly, a veil had lifted. As the museum tried to preserve an artifact that had been held sacred in the past, it revealed a sculpture that is still sacred in the present. In essence, the museum stopped being a museum. It was as if a picture of a rare flower had come alive and now the preservers had to decide whether to keep sunlight from fading the picture or to water the living flower. The curators had been challenged to become gardeners.

This is the ultimate fulfillment of every act of preservation: to bring the sacred alive again. The hope of every museum is to seed moments of living community *between* generations.

Museums and libraries serve as wellsprings for every generation from which we can renew our understanding of how to relate and persevere.

Clearings for Renewal

After visiting the Metropolitan Museum of Art, I felt like a citizen of a historical community that has no nationality and is not restricted to any one era or continent. I wandered into Central Park and meandered along its carefully appointed paths whose trees and large outcroppings frame tableaux of the city. The park itself seemed a place to preserve our natural and collective memory. I couldn't help but think of the thousands who had walked these paths before me, and who would do so after me.

Like museums, public parks are living tributes to our deep yearning to be in each other's company, and to be alone together in nature.

When I lived in Albany, New York, I fell in love with Washington Park, an 81-acre park built in 1870 using a design by John Bogart, who worked and studied with Frederick Law Olmsted, who designed Central Park. Both parks have paths that intersect in common meeting grounds in order to weave the rhythm between solitude and community. They lead us into ourselves and into nature, and then into the soft and sudden company of others.

This feature of Olmsted parks—the creation of common meeting grounds—is a foundational covenant of healthy communities, which allows for and nurtures both the integrity drawn from solitude and the compassion that evolves from being with others. A healthy community provides for both.

Frederick Law Olmsted (1822–1903) was the Rembrandt of park design. He and his sons were involved in the design and creation of more than 6000 parks and university campuses throughout North America and Canada, including Central Park and Prospect Park in New York City, the University of California at Berkeley, Stanford University, Mount Royal Park in Montreal, the parkway system in Buffalo, the Emerald Necklace parks in Boston, the landscape surrounding the

U.S. Capitol in Washington, D.C., and the scenic park surrounding Niagara Falls. His contemporaries marveled at Olmsted and one wrote, "An artist, he paints with lakes and wooded slopes; with lawns and banks and forest-covered hills; with mountain sides and ocean views."

The first to use the phrase *landscape architect*, Olmsted is considered the father of landscape architecture. A constant learner, he traveled to England in 1850 and visited Birkenhead Park and Derby Arboretum, which impressed him greatly and stirred his imagination. In 1858, Olmsted began his partnership with the architect Calvert Vaux. Together, they won a design competition to create Central Park. Their design was known as the Greensward Plan. Construction began the same year, continued during the American Civil War, and was completed in 1873. The park would occupy 843 acres and include a latticework of thirty-six bridges accenting the tapestry of paths and common meeting grounds. Sheep grazed freely in the meadow in the park, until New Yorkers during the Great Depression poached the livestock.

Including public parks within towns, campuses, and cities was to a great degree birthed and developed by Frederick Law Olmsted. He saw public parks as an enactment of democracy where, through the creation of common meeting grounds and shared clearings for renewal in nature, individuals can be alone together. And the reflection and joy of being alone and together can add to the health of the whole community. Like notes running together into chords and chords merging to form a symphony, the music of one becomes the music of the many.

Olmsted was also committed to creating and maintaining open space, so that citizens could renew themselves by connecting to everything larger than themselves. He foresaw that the greatest threat to his public parks would be the urge to fill these spaces as the cities grew. This principle of maintaining open space is crucial to the health of democracy. And it holds true that the greatest threat to our kinship is our urge to fill our inner spaces as we grow. So maintaining open space in our minds and hearts is just as crucial to the health of community.

During the same century, the wilderness began to be seen as a public resource for our ongoing dialogue with nature, and the notion of free and public national parks came into being. There is no finer account of this social miracle than the 2009 documentary by Ken Burns, *The National Parks: America's Best Idea*.

Though Presidents Lincoln and Grant rejected the entitlement and fervor of our expansion as a nation, America pushed relentlessly in what it called its Manifest Destiny to settle and develop the North American continent coast to coast. At the same time, nature artist George Catlin (1796–1872) was the first to question the trampled path such expansion would leave behind. When Catlin traveled the northern Great Plains, he grew concerned about the destruction of Native American culture, wildlife, and the wilderness. It was Catlin who first imagined the idea of a national park.

Over the next thirty years, as railroads crossed the country, the economy burgeoned and Native American populations were sub-jugated and decimated. Over the same thirty years, writers James Fenimore Cooper and Henry David Thoreau and painters Thomas Cole and Frederic Edwin Church offered compelling portraits of the wilderness as a timeless inner resource to be protected and treated with respect, a natural and secular form of church. But while this non–human-centric appreciation of nature seemed new to an indus-trialized white culture, Native American nations had lived within this reverence for thousands of years.

On June 30, 1864, in the throes of the Civil War and in the midst of this tension between expansion and preservation, Lincoln granted the state of California the properties known as Yosemite Valley and the Mariposa Grove on condition that they would "be held for public use, resort, and recreation; [and] shall be inalienable for all time ..." Giving public rights to land was unprecedented.

Forty years later, in 1903, naturalist John Muir took a camping trip with President Theodore Roosevelt. Experiencing the majesty of Yosemite firsthand convinced Roosevelt that access to the vast stretches of untouched wilderness in America is essential to the renewal of the American character. On June 8, 1906, Roosevelt signed the Antiquities Act, which gave the president authority to turn public lands into national monuments. Three months later, on September 24, 1906, President Roosevelt proclaimed Devils Tower in Wyoming as the first national monument.

In 1933, Franklin Roosevelt consolidated all national parks and national monuments into a single national park system. He also created a National Park Service, which today employs more than twenty thousand Americans, maintains more than four hundred national wilderness sites, and welcomes more than 275 million visitors a year.

It took the Park Service thirty-one years to name and include such natural landmarks as the Everglades in Florida, Joshua Tree in California, Jackson Hole and the Grand Tetons in Wyoming, the Petrified Forest in Arizona, and Haleakalā in Hawaii. By the early sixties, national seashores were included, such as Cape Hatteras in North Carolina, Cape Cod in Massachusetts, and Point Reyes in Northern California.

But just as the marvels of freedom must be understood within the horrific context of slavery and its violent oppressions, the marvels of our national parks and wilderness sites must be understood within the context of the horrific destruction of the Native American people, a travesty that sullies the ground on which this immense achievement stands. Still, our network of public parks and natural wilderness sites makes available the largest living museum in history, one that has no walls and which lets us renew ourselves by communing with what is naturally sacred, leaving it untouched. Given how central communing with nature is to the Native American way of life, we would do right to rejoin our wilderness endeavor with the Native American nations' sacred history with the Earth. In this way of community, they are our ancestors.

There is no greater public communion with nature than to tend and preserve the original reaches of the Earth. Together, our urban parks and our natural wilderness sites form the ultimate expression of a common meeting ground which our early Native ancestors knew as their homeland.

Through the creation of common meeting grounds and shared clearings for renewal in nature, individuals can be alone together.

Where We Meet

Community exists only when people
know each other's stories.
—**WENDELL BERRY**

The first definition of *Commons* refers to land that no one owns but which everyone benefits from and cares for. The simplest way to understand this is to imagine that you and I live on opposite sides of a lake. Our homes are personal and private, but the lake, which gives us water to live by, belongs to no one. The lake between us is the Commons. It is in our common interest to protect the lake from pollution.

Stewardship of the Commons is essential to the lifeblood of community. In his seminal book *The Practice of the Wild*, Gary Snyder says:

> Between the extremes of deep wilderness and the private plots
> of the farmstead lies a territory which is not suitable for crops. In
> earlier times it was used jointly by the members of a given tribe
> or village . . . The commons has [therefore] been defined as "the
> undivided land belonging to the members of a local community
> as a whole."

In the grasslands in Mongolia, shepherds maintain their individual homesteads but share and care for the vast grazing pastures, which are too big for any one person to own. Lobster fishermen in Maine maintain their small buoyed fisheries but share and care for the common waters, which no one owns. The air we breathe is yet another crucial Commons, which everyone experiences privately but which no one person can contain, and which we all must care for.

Equally important are the resources that constitute our Community Commons, the covenants of relationship that bind us, which exist between us but which no one person owns. And the Commons of Ideas, the web of foundational truths that bridge us and sustain us. And the Mystical Commons, the Unity of Life that we all depend on, like the water that fish live in.

Each form of Commons invokes our stewardship: of common land, of common resources, of common truth, of the Unity of Life that informs every life. In whatever realm, caring for the Commons is how we practice being more together than alone.

Another form of Commons is the river of dialogue between people over time. A great example of this is the Talmud of the Jewish tradition, an open-ended conversation held over centuries through commentary. The Talmud is described as the Oral Law. In eastern European villages, rabbis would gather hundreds of students for lessons and conversations, caring for the life of questions, which, like the air we breathe, everyone needs but no one owns.

Shlomo Yitzhaki (1040–1105), known as Rashi, was a medieval French rabbi who authored extensive commentaries in the Talmud. According to Abraham Heschel, "Rashi *democratized* Jewish education . . . He made the Talmud a popular book, everyman's book. Learning ceased to be the monopoly of the few." Rashi believed that lasting knowledge is a form of Commons that everyone needs but no one owns.

In ancient Greece, Aristotle convened his students on the grounds of the Lyceum, a public meeting place in Athens situated in a grove of trees. Aristotle would amble through the colonnades and covered walkways with his students as he explored life's questions, opening a path of inquiry that everyone needs but which no one owns. Aristotle's school became known as the Peripatetic school. *Peripatetic* comes from the Greek word which means "given to walking about," a term also used to describe philosophers not affixed to any particular school or tradition.

As the rural Commons is the land between farmsteads, the urban Commons is a public space, a town square or marketplace, maintained between homes and shops, where people can gather and share stories. The European town square is an urban Commons that appeared at the center of major cities from Spain to Sweden during the Middle Ages.

Today, it goes by many names: *agora, forum, piazza, plaza, Platz, platea, piata, náměstí, rynek,* and *trg.* Well-known squares around the world include the Red Square in Moscow, the Palace Square in St. Petersburg, Tiananmen Square in Beijing, the John F. Kennedy Platz in Berlin, Trafalgar Square in London, and Times Square and Bryant Park in New York City.

Above all, the town square serves as a place for story and dialogue. It's the common hive individuals return to after finishing their chores and wanderings. I'm reminded of a story that took place just off the old town square in Santa Fe, New Mexico. One of the oldest bookstores in the city, Collected Works, was moving about three blocks from San Francisco Street to Galisteo. On the day of the move, more than a hundred volunteers showed up and formed a line from the old storefront to the new. And one by one, they passed book by book, all day long, until the move was complete.

This is an image for the Commons across time: people showing up to help move the stories of the tribe from one living home to another, a book at a time, a person at a time, just off the public square, story by story, hand by hand. At our best, we are stewards of knowledge that everyone needs but which no one owns, passing what matters from seeker to seeker, from generation to generation.

Gary Snyder affirms that we need to enliven the "Mind of the Commons," in which we stop trying to develop and own everything but care for the common resources that sustain life:

> There is no choice but to call for the "recovery of the commons"—and this in a modern world which doesn't quite realize what it has lost. Take back . . . that which is shared by all of us, that which is our larger being.

We have to make an art of caring for what everyone needs but which no one owns. We can do this by tending to our relationships minute to minute the way we breathe constantly. We can do this by tending to the common grasslands that grow between us. We can do this by keeping the town squares where we meet free and vital. We can do this by keeping the life of dialogue between us true and vital. We can do this by meeting in the open and passing our stories between us from one home to the next.

> Caring for the Commons is how we practice
> being more together than alone.

The Forest Community

During World War II, the Bielski partisans created a community in the forest of Belarus in resistance to the Nazis who were hunting them down. Their resistance was courageous, and just as inspiring was their insistence on building a life together with what they had.

After the German invasion of the Soviet Union on June 22, 1941, the Nazis occupied western Belarus, killing thousands of Jews in the Nowogrodek District. Once their parents and two brothers were killed, the three surviving Bielski brothers—Tuvia (1906–1987), Asael (1908–1945), and Zus (1910–1995)—formed a small resistance group. They fled to the nearby Zabielovo forest, where the group comprised about thirty family members and friends.

The elder brother, Tuvia, a Polish army veteran, was asked to lead the group, known as the Bielski Otriad. Asael became his deputy, while Zus was placed in charge of reconnaissance. As part of a Jewish farming family in the village of Stankiewicze, the brothers knew the region well. With the help of non-Jewish friends, they were able to acquire guns. Later, they captured German and Soviet weapons, and equipment from Soviet partisans.

The Bielskis encouraged Jews in Lida, Minsk, and other ghettos to escape and join them in the forest. They sent guides into the ghettos to escort people into the woods. In late 1942, a special mission saved more than a hundred Jews from the Iwie ghetto just as the Germans planned to liquidate it. By the end of 1942, the Bielski group had grown to more than three hundred people. While fighting against the Germans, the Bielski brothers provided a safe refuge for Jews, particularly women, children, and the elderly.

Until the summer of 1943, the group moved about in the forest. But in August 1943, the Germans began a massive hunt for Jews on the run. The manhunt involved more than 20,000 military personnel and SS officers. A reward of 100,000 Reichsmarks was offered for Tuvia Bielski's capture. The brothers feared that the local peasants might betray them. And so, in December 1943, the Bielski group created a permanent base in the Naliboki forest, a swampy, barely accessible region on the right bank of the Niemen River.

It was in this primitive setting that the Bielski group formed a community. Despite opposition from within the group, Tuvia never wavered in his determination to accept and protect all Jewish refugees, regardless of age or gender. The Bielskis never turned anyone away. The community began to organize the skilled workers among them into workshops, including cobblers, tailors, carpenters, leather workers, and blacksmiths.

In addition, they established a mill, a bakery, and a laundry. The leadership managed a crude infirmary, a school for the children, a synagogue, and even a courthouse with a jail. Workers supplied the camp with food and cleared the land where possible for the cultivation of wheat and barley.

Tuvia improvised constantly. He divided his people into teams. Building teams would search through the deserted villages to bring back window frames that sometimes still had glass, as well as ovens, boilers, barrels, and kitchen utensils. Another team would plow the fields and dig for potatoes. Another team concentrated on building living quarters. Unless sick or elderly, everyone in the camp was engaged in doing useful work.

Tuvia insisted that, as a community, they had the ability to take care of their own needs and the needs of other partisans. He urged his people to keep working together, saying, "If we should die trying to live, at least we live like human beings."

There was one basic rule in the forest community: all members were expected to exchange all services free of charge, and any member could have something repaired for free—a pair of shoes, a coat, a gun. Services were bartered for food, medication, and arms. When reduced to a common need to survive, the exchange of money became irrelevant.

The Bielski Otriad sustained life in the forest for four years. More than 1200 Jews from the forest community survived the war and have now increased to 20,000 through five generations. After the Soviet occupation of Belarus in 1945, Asael was drafted into the Soviet Red Army and killed six months later in the Battle of Königsberg. Later that year, the war ended and the Otriad dispersed. Tuvia returned to Poland, then emigrated to Israel. In time, Tuvia and Zus settled in New York, where they began a trucking business. When Tuvia died in 1987, he was buried on Long Island. A year later, he was exhumed and given a hero's funeral at Har Hamenuchot, the hillside graveyard in Jerusalem.

Stories like this confirm that, no matter what's taken away, there's always a pebble to stand on that can become a foundation. In the midst of disaster, injustice, and fear, it's as important to commit to building a new life together as it is to flee the injustice and persecution.

If we should die trying to live, at least we live like human beings.

Without Ever Pushing

I'm not so interested in how they
move as in what moves them.
—PINA BAUSCH

Through Wim Wenders's extraordinary documentary *Pina: Dance, Dance, Otherwise We Are Lost* (2011), I became aware of Pina Bausch. My wife, Susan, and I watched in awe, unable to move afterward. We both felt we had discovered a force of being. Yet we realized that Pina had already come and gone, having died in 2009.

A visionary dancer and choreographer, Pina Bausch (1940–2009) directed the dance company Tanztheater Wuppertal, which has been a vibrant creative community since 1973. Focused on rendering the human condition in its full majesty and complexity, Pina was a quiet and compelling master, modeling in both her being and dance the authenticity we all need to find in the midst of life's joys and sorrows.

It's rare that dancers stay in one company for long, yet Pina recruited dancers from around the world who remained with her for years, no doubt because of the constant challenge of her pieces and the process of their creation. Some, like Dominique Mercy, now sixty-one, had been at her side for decades. Pina's dancers are still performing together, even after her death. In fact, she was one of the few choreographers who welcomed aging dancers. She welcomed vitality at any age.

Pina was devoted to love and truth as abiding principles by which people can work and live together. She trusted her own authenticity as a tuning fork by which to reveal the larger forces we all must work with, and she trusted the authenticity of everyone around her. Pina

128

knew that dances could only be discovered if everyone involved brought their love and truth into the dance.

Pina's dances are incredibly raw and beautiful, and their co-creative process is useful in understanding the human condition. No matter the problem a community faces, we can trust in our own experience and in each other. Most often, the things we face require more than one person's insight or talent to fully comprehend and resolve. People like Pina Bausch, who grow the life-force out of those around them, are models of the most useful, gracious leaders we can become.

Dominique Mercy described Pina's co-creative style of unfolding a dance this way:

What is particularly remarkable is her unique way of making you discover what there is within yourself. I've seen that time and again. She has something which makes each dancer go further than they ever thought they could, and yet she achieves this effortlessly, without ever pushing.

Pina would invite each dancer to discover their deepest connections to life. She said to one dancer who was shy, "You need to keep searching," not presuming to tell her for what. To another longtime dance partner, she would say before a performance, "You need to scare me tonight." And to a younger dancer, "I need something touching joy from you."

The themes of Pina's astonishing pieces show her respect for the co-creative process and the interdependence of our aliveness. In them, men and women are constantly leaning on each other, moving things out of the way of each other, losing and finding each other—all in the midst of natural elements, such as water, stone, and soil.

Pina was born in 1940 in Solingen in the German state of North Rhine–Westphalia, the third child of August and Anita Bausch. Her parents owned a café attached to a small hotel, where little Pina would sit quietly under the tables, watching customers. Occasionally, she would break into impromptu dances. She recalled that, as a child, "I loved to dance because I was scared to speak. When I was moving, I could feel."

In 1960, she went to New York City on a scholarship to the Juilliard School, where her teachers included Antony Tudor, José Limón, Alfredo Corvino, and Paul Taylor. She began to choreograph in 1968. Her first piece, *Fragmente*, used music by Béla Bartók. In 1972, she became the artistic director of the Wuppertal Opera Ballet. In 1973, she renamed the dance company Tanztheater Wuppertal and decades of dance innovation and immersion began.

One of Pina's seminal dances, *Café Müller* (1978), portrays the café she often visited as a child. In a simple setting of tables, chairs, and doors, a small woman dressed in white enters the café. Two more women appear, one of whom is blind. They hesitate to step further, as the tables and chairs obstruct their way. Two men appear, committed to removing these barriers. Eventually the blind woman and one of the men stand face-to-face.

Unvarnished and bare, this piece holds the central challenge and gift of being human together. The dance is deeply moving because it reveals the DNA of all relationship: the never-ending tangle between those in need and those who need to help others make their way, and how we take turns. In *Café Müller*, it's profound to see how moving forward when we're blind and getting things out of the way are essential to the human dance. This is also the rhythm of compassion. Both positions are equal and necessary.

For years, the film director Wim Wenders had wanted to work with Pina and the Tanztheater Wuppertal. Finally, as they were collaborating and bringing the documentary into being, Pina suddenly grew ill, was diagnosed with advanced lung cancer, and died within five days. Everyone was devastated and Wenders announced that they would not make the film. But a few weeks after Pina's death, the dancers decided to continue working together as a company and insisted that the film go forward.

The life and work of Pina Bausch is proof that one person's authenticity and loving presence can create a community. Whether we create a dance or build a hospital or irrigate a field, when we empower what lives within each other, we strengthen our humanity. For working together wholeheartedly is one of our greatest natural resources. The heart, when watered like a seed, will produce food for generations.

> Community is the never-ending tangle between those in need and those who need to help others make their way, and how we take turns.

The Web of Knowing

The ebb and flow of knowledge throughout history has been as important as money, food, or shelter. The old maxim "Knowledge is power" is true, but what kind of power has always been the question. While there are always those who insist on power over others, it is relational power that brings us to our full potential. Throughout history, there has been an endless debate about whether protecting our fair share or distributing our fair share is the best way to survive. There is also an ongoing debate about whether guarding knowledge or freely giving knowledge away is the best means for civilization to grow.

In truth, a web of knowing exists across all time that reveals the largest community of all—the human community. This web of knowing, which connects all nations and religions, depends on the efforts of those who preserve and share knowledge. Ultimately, each of us shoulders the responsibility to preserve and share what matters. And those devoted to keeping knowledge free are part of a great and tireless lineage that sustains community resilience.

The most recent landmark in this evolving web of knowing is Wikipedia, a supple and muscular medium that offers "free knowledge for everyone." Jimmy Wales and Larry Sanger launched Wikipedia on January 15, 2001, to be a free, worldwide, self-organizing knowledge center housed on the Internet.

In appropriating *Wiki-Wiki*, which is Hawaiian for *quick*, and merging it with the word *encyclopedia*, Wikipedia was named as a learning tool that offers quick collaboration and access. Democratic, non-profit, and self-correcting, Wikipedia has organically evolved over time from being completely open to being semi-protected. Today, registered users worldwide can create, edit, and modify articles. The content is live and constantly growing and being shaped in a global conversation.

Through the inexhaustible flow of the Internet, the free access of worldwide knowledge is now like air or water. Both the Internet and Wikipedia within it serve as technological commons, spaces that no one owns but which everyone shares.

In the tradition of the Jewish Talmud, which is a dynamic home for a two-thousand-year-long conversation full of stories and commentaries, Wikipedia has, in sixteen years, offered a similar open-ended conversation with endless evolving viewpoints. As a consequence of its open structure, Wikipedia "makes no guarantee of validity" with regard to its content, since no one is ultimately responsible for any of the information appearing in it. However, mild restrictions have been implemented to ensure content accuracy without limiting the democratic, free shaping of the material. An arbitration committee now determines the accuracy of questionable content.

Sustained mostly by individual donors, Wikipedia received $51 million in donations in 2015 in seventy currencies. Across all editions of Wikipedia, there are nearly 35 million articles in 288 languages. Twelve of the language editions have more than one million articles each. As of May 2015, Wikipedia had almost 26 million accounts, with about 100,000 active authors and about 72,000 active editors. Twelve thousand new pages are created every day. A full-time staff of about two hundred people maintains the matrix of relationship that is Wikipedia.

Over the past ten years, I have found the breadth and accuracy of Wikipedia articles to be increasingly reliable. Like the Aspen grove whose massive forest rises from an interconnected root system, Wikipedia is weaving and spreading knowledge in a democratic and enduring way.

From the beginning, wisdom has been distilled from our experience into something precious and life-giving—guarded in every culture by a mythic god who appeared after some arduous trial, as if the one weaver of all knowing has assumed a different face in each phase of history.

In Egyptian mythology, the one weaver came to Earth as the moon god Thoth. As the guardian of wisdom, his first task was to ensure that neither good nor evil won, but that their struggle remained balanced and ongoing, so that human beings would always have the chance to choose. After treacherous battles, Thoth's care and counsel allowed warriors to find the wisdom they needed to recover their sight. Thoth also created writing, which allowed knowledge to be preserved and passed on.

In Babylonian mythology, the one weaver appeared as the god Nabu. In Hindu mythology, the one weaver appeared as Saraswati, the goddess of knowledge, music, and art. Known as the keeper of Celestial Waters, she offered a drink of wisdom to those who were humbled by life.

During the Aztec era, the one weaver appeared as Quetzalcoatl, the god of learning. In one seminal story, the virgin Chimalman conceived Quetzalcoatl by swallowing an emerald, only to be hit by an arrow in her womb, which caused her to birth the jewel of wisdom into the world.

To this day, the weaver of all knowing keeps incarnating in each generation. In our time, the one weaver has dispersed into the many who are ordinary guardians of knowledge. No more gods, just us worker bees of consciousness, who secrete the honey of knowledge one drop at a time, in modern forms such as Wikipedia.

So if you're curious about anything that exists beyond your daily life, drink from the living river of all knowledge and participate in the timeless web of knowing, not just by receiving knowledge, but by doing your part to gather it, preserve it, and pass it on.

> Freely giving knowledge away is the best
> means for civilization to grow.

A Common Song

We're all creating a quality of life.
—MASTER POTTER RICHARD BRESNAHAN

For thirty-five years, Richard Bresnahan has been the visionary force behind the pottery program at Saint John's University in Collegeville, Minnesota. A stunning example of a community living out its values around a shared process of work, the program describes itself as embodying "the Benedictine values of community, hospitality and self-sufficiency as well as the University's commitment to the integration of art and life . . ."

I heard Richard speak at the Kalamazoo Institute of Arts when I accompanied my wife, Susan, who is a potter. She has apprenticed in an ancient form of communal wood-firing, done in an Anagama kiln, a massive open space that looks like a stone whale. The enormous kiln originated in Korea and migrated to Japan. In Japanese, *anagama* means "single-chambered." A working group of potters save the pots they have shaped for months, and in the spring and again in the fall they fire the kiln for five days straight, each shift of potters caring for the fire and raising its temperature roughly fifty degrees an hour. The firing takes weeks of preparation. They all cut, split, and haul six or seven cords of wood in various sizes. Then they take days to load the kiln, packing the shelves tightly, but leaving more space near the floor of the kiln, so the fire will be forced to move around their unfinished wares. The fire is set and the journey of trusting the fire and depending on each other takes over.

Designed by Richard Bresnahan and constructed with the help of apprentices and volunteers, the Anagama kiln at Saint John's can fire up to 12,000 works at a time. It's the largest wood-burning kiln in North America. It takes six weeks to load and is usually fired in the fall. For ten consecutive days, sixty volunteers work in firing shifts around the clock. Once the firing is done, the kiln is sealed and allowed to cool for two weeks.

During his talk, Richard said that "we're all creating a quality of life." He suggests that, regardless of the form, whatever we shape—a pot, a basket, a poem, a dance, a home, a ship, a garden, a song—each is a creation unto itself *and* each is a thread in the communal work of art we call *a quality of life*, which we keep creating and sustaining together.

As whales are born with an instinct for the deep, we're each born with an impulse toward creating a quality of life. No matter the type of work that leads us there, following that impulse is the destiny of each soul. And so, we search to find our medium through which aliveness can express itself. Following our instinct for the deep, we find each other.

In areas of the Atlantic and Pacific Oceans, whales basically sing the same common song. When a new verse is added, they all incorporate it. How do they learn this and share this? As humans, we have a greater capacity to communicate and yet we resist adding to our common song.

Occupying the same geographical areas, which can include large ocean basins, whales tend to sing similar songs with slight variations. But whales from different regions will sing entirely different songs. Though, once together, they will find a common pitch. This common whale song is constantly evolving over time. Old patterns are not repeated. In essence, whales stay current, freshly evolving their communication with each other. A task for us all.

Most whales, especially humpbacks, compose patterns of sound that are strikingly similar to human musical traditions. What helps whales be such good communicators is that the speed of sound is roughly four times greater in water than on land. Profoundly, it's easier to hear in the deep. When in the deep, we have a better chance of staying current and hearing our common song.

When we follow our instinct for the deep, we discover our common song, which brings us alive. Through this unfolding, we make our contribution to the common good. From generation to generation, all that we learn and create adds to this living work of art we call a quality of life.

The following rituals and practices exemplify efforts to restore our quality of life, which we stitch and mend, again and again. We stitch a thread and unravel it. We rip a hole in what binds us and then we mend it.

For hundreds of years, the Mexican people have practiced the ritual of *fiesta*, which is broadly known as a celebration of dance, food, and song. More deeply, a fiesta is not just a celebratory event, but a time of mending social wounds, a time to heal relationships and ask for forgiveness. From a narrow individual perspective, all we see is the party. From a broader social perspective, a fiesta is a pause in the rigors and tangles of life to renew troubled bonds, and the *result* of that healing is a celebration filled with dance and song. The ritual of fiesta can deepen our skills of listening and empathy, and open us beyond our self-interest, which in turn can help us restore our common quality of life.

Another compelling custom is *dream-walking* or *dream-sharing*. Taught for generations by the Iroquois nation, dream-walking is the process by which each person's individual dreams and sufferings are interpreted to find communal meaning. Those meanings, woven together, are then used to blueprint the dream of the community. We need to rediscover how the inner life of the individual can help to blueprint the dream of our community—in fact, we have an urgency to do so.

Iroquois dreamwork was a precursor to Freudian and Jungian dreamwork, and is similar to the dream techniques used by psychologists today. The difference is that while Freudian dream interpretation focuses on what the dream reveals for the life of the dreamer, and Jungian dream interpretation explores how the life of the individual is influenced by the Collective Unconscious, Iroquois dream-walking discerns what the dreams of individuals mean for the life of the community.

In the Iroquois culture, the *Ononharoia*, which means "turning the brain upside down," is an annual dream-walking festival during which the tribe opens itself beyond the ordinary thinking of daily life. The festival begins with *dream-renewal*, a time when those who were cured of illness during the past year offer dances for the health of those who helped heal them. Then there's time for *dream-sharing*, when members of the tribe share dreams that have changed them or which they don't yet understand. Finally, there's the *Ceremony of the Great Riddle*, in which the shamans of the tribe attempt to interpret the dreams shared as visions and instructions for the larger community.

In our modern world, we need to open ourselves beyond the ordinary thinking that meets daily tasks in order to remember our basic kinship. In the rush of survival, we need to pause long enough to turn our brains upside down in order to see each other freshly. In this regard, the relational aspects of dream-walking offer us skills by which we can consciously tend to the social fabric of our community. We would do well to gather regularly in an effort to bring into view the dream of our community. We would do well to consult our elders, dead and alive, and to consult our history, evoking our dreams and goals, as well as our wounds and scars—all for the good of the community and the common quality of life we long for.

Each of these communities—the Anagama potters, the common song of whales, the Mexican fiestas, and the Iroquois dream-walkers—has relational skills to offer us. The concerns they uphold are at the heart of every community throughout time: to create and maintain a quality of life, to find and sing our common song, to mend our wounds and heal our relationships, and to discover the blueprint for the tribe by interpreting our dreams. These are the threads we'll keep weaving and mending till the end of time. We can't control that eternal twine. We can only care for the strands that we weave or unravel during our watch.

From generation to generation, all that we learn and create adds to this living work of art we call a quality of life.

Larger Than Ourselves

Alcoholics Anonymous (AA) is widely known for its worldwide community. While I am not an alcoholic, I have many loved ones who are in recovery or who have been the children of alcoholics. Along with the cancer support groups that helped save my life, it was the raw and committed humanity of the AA rooms that stirred me to create my daybook, *The Book of Awakening*. I saw firsthand how thoroughly used daybooks were: marked up, folded, torn, and carried everywhere. Even more used and worn, though indestructible, are the twelve steps that alcoholics devote themselves to in their recovery, which were first put forth by Bill W. and Dr. Bob.

In December 1933, nine months after the end of Prohibition in the United States, Alcoholics Anonymous was established as a mutual aid fellowship by a New York stockbroker, Bill Wilson, and an Akron, Ohio physician, Dr. Bob Smith. Their primary purpose was to help alcoholics "stay sober and help other alcoholics achieve sobriety." The contract with alcoholics wanting help was straightforward and stated clearly, "[We have] to hang together or die separately. We [have] to unify our Fellowship or pass off the scene."

In 2016, the worldwide membership of AA was estimated at more than two million, with over 100,000 groups meeting in approximately 150 countries. The anonymous covenant of AA helps to focus those involved on the truth of their lives and not on the false masks they've created. Members who sustain sobriety eventually agree to a language of honesty and compassion:

> At its core it remains simple and personal. Each day, somewhere in the world, recovery begins when one alcoholic talks with another alcoholic, sharing experience, strength, and hope. (*The Big Book*)

The underlying notion of fellowship and the core relational skills put forth by the twelve steps are healthy codes to live by, whether we're addicted to anything or not. To invoke the humility that so much is beyond our control widens our compassion. To restore our belief in something larger than ourselves, regardless of what we've been taught, enlarges our acceptance of life. To take a moral inventory of our character and our flaws can only awaken our better angels. To make amends to those we've directly harmed or injured can only strengthen the cords of life. To face ourselves and change our behavior is how we change the world. And the commitment to stay conscious once awakened can only serve to illuminate us and those around us.

The first principle of AA states that "our common welfare should come first; personal recovery depends upon AA unity." This is a perennial wisdom that all relationships stand on: our personal recovery depends on the bedrock of our collective unity. The way that individual blades of grass depend on the sod in which they grow.

> The commitment to stay conscious once awakened can
> only serve to illuminate us and those around us.

Questions to Live With

+ We are capable of great creativity and great cruelty. Each of us can build libraries and each of us can burn books. Bring four or five friends together. In conversation, have each of you describe a time when you built something and a time when you broke something. What led you to be creative and what led you to be destructive? In the next three weeks, bring this conversation about creativity and cruelty to another part of your community.

+ Go on a journey with a friend or loved one to visit a museum. Be open to what you discover there. When moved by a piece in the museum, linger long enough to hear it speak. Then find a quiet space in which to discuss the experience with your friend or loved one. In the next three weeks, make an effort to bring someone else in your community to this museum.

+ Frederick Law Olmsted, the landscape architect who designed and built Central Park in New York City, envisioned common meeting grounds where people would come upon each other after walking in solitude. Set out with a friend or loved one to arrive at a common meeting ground after you each experience a period of solitude. Once there, listen to each other's experience and concerns. Then determine how your experience of solitude affected your experience of community. In the next three weeks, identify a common meeting ground in your community and contribute to it in some way.

+ The notion of "the commons" refers to land which no one owns but which everyone benefits from and cares for. The commons can also refer to common resources, common stories, common truth, or a common tradition or wisdom. Bring four or five friends together. In conversation, have each of you tell the story of a form of "commons" that you benefit from and how you might contribute to its care.

+ Living well together involves moving through our blindnesses while getting things out of each other's way. Bring four or five friends together. In conversation, have each of you describe a blindness you are encountering in yourself or with those you live with or work with. Then, describe one thing you need to get out of each other's way. In the next three weeks, invite the people involved in your stories to describe these elements from their own point of view. Follow up by having a working conversation about how you might remove the things in each other's way.

+ Bring four or five friends together. In the spirit of Iroquois dream-walkers, have each of you share a dream. After discussing how each dream speaks to the dreamer's life, explore the dreams together for how they may speak to the dream and needs of your larger community. In the next three weeks, take a step in your community toward implementing one aspect of what your dreams point to.

+ Bring four or five friends together. In conversation, have each of you tell the story of someone who has been a mentor to you. What did they teach you? Are you passing this learning on? How? In the next three weeks, tell the story of your mentor to someone else in your community and ask them to describe a mentor who helped shape them.

WITH AND AGAINST COMMUNITY

Since the Renaissance, we've been exalting the individual and not the community. That, coupled with modern social mobility, has only entrenched that emphasis. Therefore, in modern times, we are all in a diaspora and all exiles in our own land. Therefore, the need for community and the re-learning of the skills to build community around the world is essential.

—RABBI ZALMAN SCHACHTER-SHALOMI

We are strange creatures; drawn to what we need, only to walk right by it or harm it. What is it in us that can't see what's before us? What makes us seek out what is magnificent only to level it to our size? Not all of us. Not all the time. But we are all capable of this smallness that turns away from the magnificence we seek.

The Grand Canyon is 277 miles long, from four to eighteen miles wide, and over a mile deep (6000 feet). As best we can tell, the Colorado River set its course through the canyon at least 17 million years ago. For all that time, the river and its tributaries cut their channels through layer after layer of rock, exposing the magnificent Colorado Plateau. Early on, the canyon was inhabited by the Pueblo people, who considered the Grand Canyon (Ongtupqa in Hopi) a sacred, living site. Native Americans lived in and around the canyon for more than 4000 years until a severe drought in the late thirteenth century caused them to move.

It wasn't until September 1540 that white men arrived in the canyon when Captain García López de Cárdenas, with the aid of Hopi guides, led Spanish soldiers down the magnificent rim. He was sent to find the fabled Seven Cities of Cibola, rumored to be cities of gold. Not finding what they were looking for, they turned their backs on one of the world's natural wonders and left. They showed no interest in the culture or wisdom of the Hopi nation or the Zuni people who had created the Seven Cities of Cibola. They only had one form of gold in mind.

This smallness of mind is not reserved for white people. It lives in all of us. The condor, the largest flying bird in the western hemisphere, glides through the Andes Mountains and along the Pacific coast of western South America. High up with their wings spread, condors can glide for hours. With their large black frames and ruff of white feathers at the base of their necks, these majestic birds were thought by early peoples to be messengers of the gods. Primarily scavengers, feeding on animals already dead, such as deer or cattle, condors roost at elevations of 9,000 to 16,000 feet, on inaccessible rock ledges. They are one of the world's longest-living birds, with a life span of fifty years.

Even in how we name these majestic creatures, our smallness shows itself. For only the hunter in us would name something that lives without killing a scavenger or vulture. In Andean mythology, the condor is associated with the sun deity and is believed to be the ruler of the upper world. It is considered a symbol of power and health by many. And yet, in Peru, they are commonly shot. Peruvians also have a brutal ceremony known as *arranque del cóndor*, in which a live Andean Condor is suspended from a frame and punched to death by horsemen as they ride by.

How can we see the beauty and life-giving power in such a bird and still want to destroy it? This inner and ancient conflict between our need to find a home within everything larger than us and our dark need to break everything larger than us has kept the human experiment stymied forever. What are we to learn from this as we relive it again and again? How many times is the peaceful one beaten and the magnificence of the earth trampled because there is no gold? What are we to do with this difficult knowledge?

Though I don't understand how it reaches me, I feel a place within me that goes back before my life. From that place, I carry a drop of care and wherever I can offer this drop of care, it preserves the majesty of life. It is this drop of love that can stop us from beating things that fly. If we can bring it out of each other, it is this drop of reverence that can stop us from trampling the wonders we come upon.

Carrying the Water

When overwhelmed by the suffering,
bring water to the first you find.
When you can't grasp, embody.

All life depends on water. As such, access to water has become a universal right in the world, regardless of faith, country, privilege, or poverty. Throughout the world, in a legal and common law way, people, corporations, and countries have access to water, but no one owns the water. What this means is that if a river passes through your land, you can use it, but not divert it, dam it, stop its flow, or damage its purity as it passes through your land to another.

This says a great deal about our responsibility as guardians of what passes through our care. It says that the deepest resources are not ownable, but shared and passed on. As such, we can easily equate water with Spirit, wisdom, and the communal ways of being. We can also call that deeper stream which no one owns, the common good. For all life depends on the common good, which passes like a river through the land of our care. Just like water, we can use each other and honor each other, but not divert one another, dam one another up, stop each other's flow, or pollute the common good as it passes through our hands to another.

In Hindu lore, Saraswati, the Hindu goddess of knowledge and art, was born out of the Saraswati River, the invisible river that carries the waters that sustain all life. Her name means "the one who flows." From the earliest times, the invisible river sustained our natural resources *as well as* our human and spiritual resources, carrying actual water *and* the water we have come to know as truth and love.

Saraswati's ageless counterpart is the serpent-demon, Vritrasura, who is driven to hoard all the water on Earth. And so the endless struggle was set: whether to be one who flows or one who hoards. In the Rigveda, the sacred collection of Sanskrit hymns (c. 1500 B.C.), we are given a profound instruction. With help from her brother Ganesh, the provider and remover of obstacles, and Indra, the god who connects all things, Saraswati killed the demon who would hoard the Earth's water. It is eternally true that working our way through obstacles until we can connect all things helps move us from being one who hoards to being one who flows.

Those who would carry the water and those who would hoard the water keep appearing, again and again, within us and between us, so that we have chance after chance to learn this lesson well. This is why we wake one more time. Unspoken or not, aware of it or not, we take incarnation to earn our way back into the lineage of those who would carry the water, one more time.

In the Haitian tradition, a story called "The Chief of the Well" speaks of a time of drought when the streams are dry and the wells are parched. There's no place to get water. The animals meet to discuss the situation and decide to ask God for help. God creates a well that will have unlimited water, as long as one of the animals serves as caretaker and welcomes all who would come in need. The lizard Mabouya volunteers. But, intoxicated with his newfound power, Mabouya becomes a gatekeeper, not a caretaker, and sends everyone in need away. Eventually, God replaces the lizard with the frog, who croaks to all, "Come! This is God's well! The hole in the ground is yours, but the water belongs to God."

In each generation, we are challenged to be the caretaker of resources that outlive us. In each generation, we are called to discover what is ours and what is God's and to learn anew what turns the caretaker in us into a gatekeeper.

The acequia is a good model for caring communally for resources. An acequia is a sluiceway or gravity chute that flows down a mountainside, providing water for a village. The Spanish word *acequia* (a-sā'kē-e), which means "ditch" or "canal," comes from the Arabic *al saqiya*, which means "water conduit." Late in the eighth century, the Islamic occupation of Spain brought this technique of irrigation to southern Europe.

When Spanish explorers came to the Americas, they found indigenous acequias already in use. In the Andes, northern Mexico, and the American Southwest, acequias exist as the outgrowth of ancient systems that carry snow runoff to villages and distant fields. Many South American villages settled around the mouth of an acequia that begins high and out of sight in the crags of a mountain. There, the source-water collects all winter near the top and with the thaw it streams into the village.

In Peru, entire villages climb their acequia each spring to clear rocks and tree limbs and snake nests, which during the winter block the path of water the village depends on. On the east side of Santa Fe, New Mexico, the Acequia Madre winds itself through the city for seven miles and eventually ends in the village of Agua Fría. The Acequia Madre or mother channel is the third oldest acequia in the United States.

In 2012, more than forty people turned out for the four hundredth annual spring cleaning of the Acequia Madre. Wearing rubber boots and gloves, seven-year-old Sierra Lindsey raked leaves and debris from the ancient ditch. Alongside her was Steve Reed, who has helped clear the acequia for fifteen years. He leases water from the ditch each year for his garden. As he stuffed leaves in a black garbage bag for the city to haul off, he said, "This is a real community effort. You get to know your neighbors. You become friends. It helps maintain community cohesion."

Keeping the acequia clear and flowing is a useful metaphor for interdependence and cooperation. Keeping the acequia clear—both the actual acequia and the acequia of humanity—bears learning how to do well.

When we can let the common good flow freely between us, we can feel the presence of all those who've come before us, as well as those who will follow. Holding ourselves open to the lineage of the common good lets us know our place in the human community over time. Consider those places in the Northwest where underground springs connect networks of inland ponds and small lakes. It's all one water. When one rises, they all rise. When one recedes, they all recede.

And so, it follows: When we open our heart, the heart of humanity fills us. When our eyes are opened by love or suffering, the heart of the world fills us. Everything we encounter is part of the one water we call the common good. We are born in it. We are cleansed in it. Great love and suffering return us to it. We purge ourselves of pain in it. We drink from it. When we honor the one water, we live together differently.

I'm drawn to tell one more story, which comes from Éliane Ubalijoro, a professor at McGill University in Montreal. As a Rwandan, she is working with the generation orphaned by the genocide of 1994. After the mass killings, survivors were confined to refugee camps. In this particular settlement, women had to cross a dark field outside the camp to get water for their children, where they risked being raped by the guards, which happened repeatedly. This horrific situation holds issues that all communities face.

First, as a community, how are we to bring the water to those who need it? A direct solution is always to move the water supply near those who need it. The compassionate solution here would have been to move the water supply *inside* the refugee camp. But why did the guards put the water outside of the camp in the first place? What are the assumptions in this community that allow its men to believe that they are entitled to exploit women? How do we clear the human acequia so that wisdom and compassion can flow from source to village?

At the heart of this atrocity is the courage and love of these women who went into the dark to get water for their children, knowing the violation that awaited them. How can we draw on this deep emotional resource when we need it most?

We could say that compassion flows like water between countries and communities. If this is so, then each of us is a carrier of that water. In a simple gesture that can save the world, we're here to drink from each other, and to ensure that the water of love keeps flowing. We're called to keep the global acequia clear, to embody the workmanlike art of clearing what's in the way and sharing what keeps us alive.

Each day, we face these choices: Will we clear the debris that blocks the flow or be the thing in the way? Will we be a caretaker or a gatekeeper? Will we be the one who flows or the one who hoards? No matter how off course we may be, our humble task and fate is to wake one more time as one of those who would carry the water.

Working our way through obstacles until we can connect all things is what helps move us from being one who hoards to being one who flows.

Unraveling the Knots

If there is anything I have learned about men and women, it's that there's a deeper spirit of altruism than is ever evident. Just as the rivers we see are minor compared to the underground streams ... the idealism that's visible is minor compared to what people carry in their hearts unreleased or scarcely released. [Hu]mankind is waiting and longing for those who can accomplish the task of untying what is knotted, and bringing these underground waters to the surface.

—ALBERT SCHWEITZER

Often our efforts at community are crippled by cynicism: *It's all been tried, why bother?* Or blinded by grandiosity: *We will do what's never been done!* It's hard to hold on to the fact that it's always both. It's crucial to remember that it's simply our turn. What if our purpose in each generation is to inhabit the human struggle on Earth for what the experience does to us? What if the goal is not progress but embodiment, not advancing knowledge but increasing compassion? What, then, is knotted within us and between us, and how can we unravel the knots?

Despite the harshness of reality, survival of the fittest isn't the only rule of nature. Wolves live in social packs up to fifteen strong. They are wild, and they are wired to care for each other and to depend on each other to survive. An old Native American saying observes that there's no such thing as an orphan in the wolf world. Naturalists confirm that wolf pups "are almost universally loved and accepted, even adopted by another female or pack if need be." Similarly, African wild dogs run in large packs that will tend to their weak or ill members. Lions that live in smaller prides will rarely leave a cub. Elephants will circle back hundreds of miles for a lost member of their herd. Dolphins, whales, and elephants commit to lifelong relationships. A widowed whale will swim thousands of miles looking for its mate.

The social impulse of gorillas also demonstrates a yearning to care for each other. Gorillas live in troops as large as thirty and are very affectionate and patient with their offspring. Adult gorillas help each other grieve the loss of young ones and, when the leader of a troop dies, the entire group mourns for days. When in danger, members will defend the entire troop and not just their young. Gorillas clearly are committed to the life of their community.

As humans, we always have a choice: to stand on the neck of the fallen or to lift them to their feet. We can choose whether to dominate and be alone or to cooperate and mate for life.

So, how we approach obstacles and each other matters. The Jewish philosopher Abraham Heschel offers that the aim of any community is not to conquer and possess, but to relate and pass on meaning, to discover and understand.

And toward what end is all our understanding? The Eastern traditions tell us that, more than understanding life, the goal is to experience life. For it's our direct experience of life and each other that makes community possible.

The visionary educator Parker Palmer declares:

> Nothing anyone else can do to us is worse than what we do to
> ourselves by not being who we are, by not remembering our
> birthright gifts and using them in service of the community.

Our direct experience in being who we are, and our direct giving and receiving of care and attention, make empathy possible. And empathy, the felt experience of others, makes our connections visible.

A recent study shows that rats, allowed to roam, prefer freeing caged rats to eating food, suggesting that rats experience empathy. The free rats, hearing distress calls from other caged rats, learned to open the cages and release the other animals. Astonishingly, if given access to a small hoard of chocolate chips, the free rat would usually save at least one treat for the captive. Peggy Mason, the neurobiologist who conducted the experiment, remarked that the experiment shows that empathy "is part of our biological inheritance." Or, as the Native Americans say, care is part of our original instructions.

Neuroscientists have discovered *mirror neurons* in the brain that confirm our biological capacity for empathy and compassion. When one person watches another person have his finger pricked, the same neurological spot lights up in the brain of the person watching as in the brain of the person pricked. At the cellular level, there's very little separating us. When one person is hurt, humanity feels it. When one person is touched, the world sighs, though we may not hear it. This is more evidence of our inherent relatedness, a tremendous resource, as Albert Schweitzer suggests in the opening quote of this chapter.

Withholding this connection can be devastating. In the 1940s, René Spitz documented a compelling study of institutionalized infants, all orphans. The institution was clean and provided the babies with adequate clothing, medical care, food, and shelter. But there was only one nurse for every eight infants, and, except for brief feedings and diaper changes, the babies were isolated in their cribs, the sides draped with sheets to prevent the spread of infection. Starved for contact and affection, these babies suffered severely. Several literally turned their faces to the wall and died. Many didn't survive to the age of two. Those who did survive were physically stunted, highly prone to infection, and often mentally impaired. By three years of age, the surviving children weren't able to walk or talk. They were withdrawn and apathetic. It seems so simple, but without care and attention, we shrivel and die.

In an elemental way, empathy and connection are life-giving. Let's consider how birds sing at the sign of first light. By itself this is remarkable, that light causes the heart to sing. This is also how birds re-map their web of relationship each morning. Like a form of natural radar, their songs bounce off each other and a new geography of birds is established—or re-established—for the day. Their maps and sense of territory stay current. They begin freshly with each appearance of dawn and co-exist by singing their song and acknowledging each other's song. By voicing and receiving their individual songs, birds relocate each other every morning.

Human co-existence also hinges on our commitment as individuals to voice our song at the first sign of light. When we can do this, we, too, can re-map our web of relationship to what is real and true in the moment. Otherwise, we're flying blind and responding to tracers of relationship that no longer exist.

It seems a psycho-spiritual law that when we don't voice ourselves cleanly, then others—*not hearing or meeting our song*—think that their territory is larger than it is. When we muffle our voices, we collude in our own oppression and enable a false sense of entitlement among those who think their songs speak for others. When we go silent—when we withhold our presence—we allow the human community to slip out of balance.

We spend so much time pointing fingers, judging, and accusing, when it's more affirming and effective to simply be honest and transparent about what we experience. If you discount me, I can re-map the web of relationship between us by not hiding what that does to me, by voicing what is true for me. In this way, we can re-map our web of community by sustaining our presence and voice. Like those birds at dawn, one waking presence can meet another in a daily way until our songs, bouncing off each other, announce a new geography of community that is current.

For humans, authentic life involves perceiving and feeling things as they are. When we can see beyond what we want or what we fear, compassion allows us to know the living being before us as it is. Not in the abstract way of an observer, but in the felt way of a participant—as one body of song fluttering before another.

I chanced to meet a Maasai farmer from Kenya, Kuntai Karmushu, who offered that to be a member of the human family means—and has always meant—to care for what is next to you wherever you are. The presence of this gentle soul has stayed with me. I truly think it comes down to what Kuntai points to—that if we're honest, we will feel our connection and simply and fully care for whatever is next to us.

As noble as our efforts can be, we always get entangled along the way. While most of us are good people with integrity, our fears can cause us to slip out of generosity. The real-world practice of community depends on learning how to untangle ourselves from the weeds of our good intentions.

To engage this tangle and to survive it, we need to mature in our efforts to unravel our knots. We need to experience and embody the life next to us in order to bring our deeper spirit of altruism to the surface. And we need to re-map our web of relationship by voicing who we are, so we can lift those who are hidden and be uplifted when we are hidden. Regardless of how much we need to learn, regardless of how much we stumble, we can freely give our care wherever we are.

> The goal is not progress but embodiment, not advancing knowledge but increasing compassion.

Bending or Loving the World

> A great many people think they are thinking when
> they are merely rearranging their prejudices.
> —WILLIAM JAMES

I was at the airport, traveling to New York, waiting to go through security with my passport out, when I noticed for the first time that each page has a quote on it. And two of them, back to back, capture the way we work with and against community in our American culture. On page 20, Lyndon Johnson says, "This is what America is all about . . . Is our world gone? We say 'Farewell.' Is a new world coming? We welcome it—and we will bend it to the hopes of man." On the page before, Dwight Eisenhower says, "Whatever America hopes to bring to pass in the world must first come to pass in the heart of America."

Johnson reveals the dark arrogance of our American will over centuries to bend whatever we encounter toward our desire. Of course, bending by itself is a creative skill and, done with care, has released the potential of the world. But bending others to the point of breaking has led to tyranny and atrocity across history. In modern America, consuming is a form of bending resources till they break. We bend things to innovate; we bend animals to make our labor easier; and we bend people to make ourselves rich. But along the way we've bent and consumed the Earth until it's become dangerously out of balance.

Yet Eisenhower reveals the core of what has made America at its best the beacon of the world: our ability to change the world around us by embodying our values. Gandhi said, "As a man changes his own nature, so does the attitude of the world change toward him . . . We need not wait to see what others will do." When we can let who we meet and what we aspire to pass through the heart of our community, we cooperate with life and relate to things, animals, people, and the Earth—much like the Native Americans who cared for this land before us.

Since our Founding Fathers conceived of a free society while also institutionalizing slavery, America has struggled between bending the world and loving the world. Today, we hide in isolation until we're jarred into letting the world pass through our heart. When we bend things to the point of consuming or breaking them, we manufacture a world of tools and debris and are seldom satisfied. When we cooperate with what we meet, we animate a dynamic world of living things we can love. If blessed to be broken of our arrogance, we can face what's before us humanely and inhabit a deeper sense of security.

Often, the difference between arrogance and humility is whether we insist on our self-interest above all else or accept that our welfare is mutual. Our insistence on self-interest has plagued the human experiment since the beginning. Robert Kegan, a pioneer in the dynamics of adult life development, calls the insistence on self-interest centrism. Centrism of any kind—whether egocentrism, gender centrism, religious centrism, national centrism, or family centrism—can hinder our understanding of others and the world around us. Kegan defines *centrism* as installing what is familiar as true and sacred, accepting what is comfortable as foundational. Then we base our experience of the world on what is familiar and not necessarily true. When we assume that what is familiar is true, we start to push away new experience.

Centrism is the seed of fundamentalism and prejudice. We all have cultivated centrism. It's a psychic habit we need to reform, more than once.

In a modern world in which self-centeredness and competition are brutal driving forces, resistant cancers have proliferated dramatically. No mistake that cancer is a disease of rabid self-interest in which the part (the cell) lives at the expense of the whole (the body). No mistake that in an increasingly impersonal and complex hive of centrism, depression—which can be defined as "learned helplessness"—is more prevalent than ever. No mistake that attention deficit has become a psychological epidemic in a world of seven hundred channels that bombard us with thousands of images with no time to digest just one. Given all this, receiving each other freshly each time we meet, simple as it sounds, is an act of courage.

In our self-centeredness, we often project our struggles onto everything around us. For example, while animals exist outside our need to name them, the names we give animal communities are more revealing about us. In our arrogance to identify solely with the strong, we see a pride of lions. In our dark push to have our way, we see a murder of crows. In our stubbornness, we see a crash of rhinos. In the anxious way we peck at each other, we see a brood of chicks. In our obsession with death, we see a wake of buzzards. In our capacity to exploit those who are weaker, we see a mew of capons. In our want to be deceptive, we see a skulk of foxes. In our need to look, which we often avoid, we see a stare of owls. And in our need to be received by the deep, we see a host of whales. But seldom do we see these qualities in ourselves. Not doing so only leads to false differences between us. As an ancient Greek saying confirms, it isn't reality that divides us but our perception of reality.

Still, we can choose to see things as they are and cooperate with life rather than consume it. Working with her husband in Nicaragua, a young activist was nursing her newborn on a strip of shore along the Pacific where magnificent turtles lumber up from the sea to lay their eggs. Left in the sun, the eggs seemed ready to birth the mysteries incubated in the deep. The young couple was spellbound as these ancient creatures slowly came and went from the sea, leaving their unborn young in sand-nests just out of reach of the surf. And even more astonished to see poor young men steal these magnificent eggs to sell to restaurants as delicacies.

To take inventory of our centrism in any given moment, we can ask ourselves: Am I an egg-collector or an egg-nester? Am I snatching and selling the life I see or helping things be born? Of course, if you're one of the poor young men needing to feed your family, it's not that simple. Desperate enough and we'll do anything to survive.

Though the opposite is also true. It was the kindness of many, which I felt compelled to return, that helped me survive cancer. Since both are true—we *will* do whatever is necessary to survive *and* give all we have left to keep others alive—the more telling questions are: At what point in our suffering are we opened to share whatever we have left? At what point of desperation are we reduced to finding a way together? How close to death before we realize that helping each other—which has more to do with lifting than bending—is the best way to survive? Ultimately, our fear leads us to believe that self-interest will save us, while our suffering lets us discover that we are more together than alone.

This struggle between bending the world and loving the world is archetypal. And long before we could see cancer cells as a biological equivalent of self-centeredness, the coldhearted among us, like Machiavelli, have exploited other life.

From the Hopi tradition, filmmaker Godfrey Reggio coined the term *Powaqqatsi*, which refers to a way of life that bends or consumes the life-force of other beings in order to further itself. This describes the voracious appetite of narcissists to consume everything they meet in order to further their own existence. The Hopi-based term points to our unchecked self-centeredness, which has always been a destructive underside of our humanity.

Slavery, fascism, apartheid, the British domination of India, and the slaughter of Native American tribes—these examples of *Powaqqatsi* speak collectively to the I-It relationship that Martin Buber (1878–1965) describes as the unholy feeding off of others for our own ends.

In his first visit to America, Carl Jung sensed the presence of this bend-to-break ethic in our culture when he wrote that America is a society based on the individual, though it seems to sustain itself by devouring the individual.

In a society so intent on bending, breaking, and consuming everything, we use up an enormous amount of energy, both personally and collectively, over-protecting ourselves. Being constantly on guard, we deplete ourselves. When preoccupied with either personal or national security, we tend to strengthen and thicken our boundaries, whether necessary or not. This inevitably leads to a mistrust that depletes our capacity for cooperation. In such a heightened state of skepticism, we stop letting in other people—and the world.

The more mature versions of personal or national security rely on inter-personal and international bridging, where the focus is on keeping our boundaries permeable and current. This can evoke a curiosity that will stir our creative energy and create a trust that will restore our capacity to live together.

Of course, no one knows quite how to do this, which is why we've struggled with it for centuries. Yet all the great spiritual leaders have challenged us to let the world pass through our heart, another name for love. It seems one profound antidote to centrism—to the heart-less bending, breaking, and consuming of the other—is to fall in love with our enemy.

Since every generation gets lost in the conflicts it inherits, it's imperative that we try to truly behold each other anew. Until, like the poet Eugene Ruggles, we might dream of the day that we can say:

> I have no enemies left,
> Only some friends who are late,
> Come in, there is no lock, hang your coat
> beside the fire and pull up a chair to its edge . . .
> We shall drink tea and clear the path
> leading back to the heart's first address . . .

All the great spiritual leaders have challenged us to let the world pass through our heart, another name for love.

The Courage to Take Others In

Give me your tired, your poor,
Your huddled masses yearning to breathe free,
The wretched refuse of your teeming shore.
Send these, the homeless, tempest-tossed to me,
I lift my lamp beside the golden door!
—WORDS ON THE STATUE OF LIBERTY

I'm sure it began in prehistoric times, when a fire overtook a cave, killing most of a clan but for a mother and child who wandered to the next cave seeking shelter. Were they shut out or taken in?

Life throws others at our door, from orphaned nieces to the 300,000 Japanese refugees who lost their homes in the wake of the earthquake-created tsunami that devastated the main island of Honshu in 2011. No one asks to be uprooted or relocated. And so, the questions are always there for each of us: Will we be shut out or taken in? And will we shut others out or take them in?

Every age has its stories. Between 1881 and 1920, pogroms swept Russia, prompting more than two million Jews to emigrate to eastern Europe and beyond. The Balkan Wars of 1912–1913 caused 800,000 people to flee their homeland. Between 1915 and 1923, one million Armenians left Turkey to escape persecution and genocide. And between 1936 and 1939, thousands of children were evacuated from Spain to escape the Spanish Civil War.

In our current age, Turkey has welcomed more than 1.7 million Syrian refugees, while Pakistan is hosting 1.6 million Afghan refugees. Often our hearts are only opened once something dear has been taken away. Then we know what a fragile miracle it is to have a home and wake beyond catastrophe. The more isolated we are from the river of life, the more we watch and judge.

During the summer of 2014, some of us watched and judged, while others tried to help, as more than 52,000 children, many of them unaccompanied by adults, entered the United States, coming from El Salvador, Honduras, and Guatemala. Most of these children fled because of rampant gang violence fueled by the drug trade in their home countries. Like most refugees throughout history, they were safer leaving than staying. And despite the ethic carved into the Statue of Liberty, most of these children were not received by Americans.

The virulent response included demonstrators chanting "Go back home!" and "USA!" on July 1, 2014, in Murrieta, California, as they blocked three buses carrying homeless children. Yet there were those who never lost sight that these were frightened children without a country. Despite more protests in Texas, Dallas County judge Clay Jenkins viewed this wave of homeless children as a humanitarian crisis and issued a plan for his county to house 2000 of them. Judge Jenkins told the media, "Regardless of your stance on immigration, we cannot turn our back on the children that are already here."

Within a week, about two hundred people, most of them bilingual, volunteered to help care for the children expected to arrive in Dallas. The organization Catholic Charities Fort Worth gathered 130 volunteers as mentors. Another organization offered to provide laundry and shower facilities. Judge Jenkins issued a call for individual families to take children into foster care. Families responded from across Texas, Wisconsin, Pennsylvania, California, Montana, Minnesota, Alabama, and New Jersey.

In another time, children were forced from their homes by the dark clouds of fascism. As the violent months of 1938 unfolded in Germany, 10,000 Jewish children were given up by their parents, who sensed the Holocaust brewing like a storm they couldn't outrun. Secretly and with great sacrifice, they sent their children to England, where British families took them in. This inspiring emergence of kindness is known as the Kindertransport.

Imagine the courage on all sides. Mothers and fathers sending their children away, telling them they would soon follow, but knowing deep down that they would probably never see them again. Imagine the wholeheartedness that opened so many British families, many struggling themselves, to say: *My God, we must take in one of these broken birds.* Imagine the children themselves—nine, ten, eleven—bumping along the European rail and crossing the English Channel, completely on their own, with no understanding of why. Imagine the ten-year-old whose parents in their fear charged her with getting them out of Germany. Imagine her little heart churning in the chill of England. Imagine the old gardener who took her in, giving her a flower every day and saying, "There. There. It will all be over soon."

I imagine the same love and sacrifice surfaced among the thousands of Latin American parents desperate to save their children. We can learn from each of their sufferings and each of their kindnesses. We can learn how to let go of what we love so it might survive. In Germany, one father couldn't bear to send his little girl away, and pulled her from the train window at the last possible moment, only to have her join him in Auschwitz. In our day in Guatemala, a twelve-year-old boy saw his father killed as his mother yelled through her tears for him to run, to never stop running.

And we can learn from those braver than us how to lift our heads from the hardships at hand to somehow make another place at the table for a new life that doesn't even speak our language. And we can learn from the children how to follow the scent of safety till it leads to where life is again possible. These little ones are heroes, not problems.

In the Hebrew Bible, God asked Abraham to kill his only son to prove his faith. But throughout the harsh and sudden storms of history, mothers and fathers have been asked to kill a piece of themselves so that their children might live. I cannot fathom their loss. I only know that since the forces that turn us loose in the world will never end, the courage to let others in will always be needed.

What will you do when it's your turn?

The questions are always there for each of us: Will we be shut out or taken in? And will we shut others out or take them in?

Putting Down the Brick

The threads of these questions around community can be found throughout my work. As I look back, this chapter from *The Exquisite Risk* seems even more foundational in this discussion. And so, it feels important to share it here as well.

> We must love one another or die.
> —W. H. AUDEN

Compassion has always been the key to whether we understand each other or not. Like so many things, this is old medicine, carried in timeless pouches we call stories.

One such story goes like this. In the beginning, everyone spoke the same language. Thousands of years ago in the land of Uruk, which was in what is now Iraq, the early human family, still of one tribe, devoted themselves to building a single tower that would be taller than any structure ever built. Their hope was to create a visible landmark, so that anyone losing their way could simply turn and look to the tower and find their way home.

The entire tribe was united behind this purpose. But it took much longer than anyone imagined. By the time the third generation assumed the task, the tower, still incomplete, was so high that it took a worker almost a year to carry the next brick to its place.

But the grandchildren of the original builders really didn't carry the same devotion for the job. It felt more like a chore for them, having to build someone else's dream. Without their own devotion, it wasn't long before the press of the task consumed them. Finally, one day, a worker carrying the next brick fell, and they mourned the brick over the worker.

165

Of course, the broken landmark was the Tower of Babel, and shortly after this brick-carrier died, the now heartless workers, pressed to finish someone else's dream, decided to loot Heaven, upon which God *confounded* or *confused their tongues*. They instantly lost the ability to understand each other. The tower was never finished, and the human family, no longer able to speak to one another, dispersed across the Earth.

The medicine carried in this story tells us that the moment we value the brick over the person, we lose the ability to understand each other—we lose the privilege of a common language. And the moment we agree to build a dream we don't believe in, for whatever reason, we become enslaved to the task.

We each carry this possibility in us daily. But there is an antidote as well, carried in another story. It seems that, generations after Babel, a mysterious spirit came to Earth, powerful in his gentleness and acceptance of human frailty. His ways were somehow threatening to the conquerors of the time and he was killed, but he had touched the lives of many in his short time on Earth. One of his closest followers felt compelled to keep his master's ways alive, but like the others, he was heartbroken by his master's death. Confused and torn apart, he wandered for days. Then, Peter was stunned to meet Jesus again. He had come back to life. What this did to Peter was inexplicable.

Not long afterward, Peter found himself before a crowd of Jews assembled from all over the world. They spoke more than a dozen languages and there were no translators. But Peter could not be distracted by their differences and devoted himself to telling the profound experiences that had shaped and awakened him. Miraculously, as he spoke humbly and directly from his heart, everyone assembled understood him in their own language. They had, in fact, been touched by and returned to the one original language that all beings share.

The medicine carried in this story tells us that the moment we dare to speak humbly and directly from our heart, we find each other. The moment we speak from the truth of compassion, we speak the same language always waiting underneath our differences. The mystery here is that when we speak from the divine center of things, from our own understanding of God, things become one again. So we carry this in us, too: the possibility of Oneness.

These are the deeper, perennial valuations: how to know when we begin to value the brick over the person; when we begin to get lost in building someone else's dream; when we slip into speaking different tongues; and how to put the brick down, how to make the dream ours again, how to find the one tongue God has given us. These are the things we need help with, again and again.

We carry both possibilities daily. In a moment of stress, in a moment of building a dream we don't believe in—in a moment of being more concerned with the task than the person doing it—we slip out of compassion. In that moment, we lose the ability to understand each other. In that repeatable moment, we lose access to our common, original language.

Yet, in a moment of vulnerability, in a moment of suffering or acceptance, in a moment of letting the truth of things rise within us—in a moment of risking to be who we are in front of others—we can feel the life of others wash over us as we slip back into the sea of compassion. And in that repeatable moment, there is only one tongue.

In a modern world that ever presses us with deadlines and profits, the brick is disguised as a god, which looking to, even briefly, confuses our tongues, and we find ourselves alone. But no matter the language of my trade—whether it be the language of engines or organs or plants or computers or psychological states—when I am drawn to speak or listen with compassion, holding what is living above all that the living make, things become one. Suddenly, I belong again to the one tribe that holds each other at day's end.

So, when we find ourselves speaking a language no one seems to understand—or, more importantly, when we can't seem to understand or feel anyone else—we need to ask, *What brick am I carrying, and has it become too important?* For the first step in regaining our ability to listen is to put that brick down. Then, magically, when not distracted by our differences, the one language will return. For the broken landmark we all recognize, no matter how lost, is not a tower, but an openness of heart that says, *Oh yes, we are of the same tribe. Finally, I am home.*

Close to the one-year anniversary of September 11, the *New York Times Magazine* published a moving article, "The Height of Ambition," by James Glanz and Eric Lipton, an in-depth history of the World Trade Center. The story of the Twin Towers is nothing short of a modern Tower of Babel in which greed, pride, and ego led the builders to value the brick over the worker.

Under the leadership of Guy Tozzoli, the New York Port Authority aspired to create the tallest building ever built, an eighth wonder of the world that would include 220 acres of office rental space. The Detroit-based architect Minoru Yamasaki proposed a 90-story structure, but Tozzoli and his team insisted on a larger building, 110 stories, even though the safety of such a structure was questionable.

Until then, skyscrapers were built using thick, steel girders that crisscrossed the core of a building to give it structural strength. But the use of girders limits the amount of square feet that can be rented per floor. So, Tozzoli insisted that another way be found. Structural engineer Leslie Robertson was eager to devise a new building technology and created a system of thin steel spandrels embedded vertically in the exterior walls, freeing up space at the core of the building. In order to speed along construction, insufficient stress tests were performed. Also, to ensure the most space for rent per floor, the stairwells, which usually drape the perimeters of each floor, were stacked at the core of the building, and were walled with gypsum (Sheetrock) instead of brick.

When the attacks of September 11 happened, the bunched Sheetrock stairwells burst into flame, trapping many people, and the thin spandrels melted, causing the towers to collapse. Had traditional girders and brick stairwells been used, the buildings might have stood longer and more people might have been able to escape.

While stronger, more resilient construction would not have prevented the acts of terrorism, it was greed that compromised the Twin Towers' integrity: the economic greed that prized rental space over safety; the competitive greed that insisted that the buildings be higher than any other; and the ambitious greed that implemented designs and technologies that were not adequately tested. The engineer, Robertson, when interviewed recently, said, "The responsibility for the design ultimately rested with me. Should I have made the project more stalwart? In retrospect, the only answer is . . . yes. Had it been more stalwart, surely 1, 2, 50, 100, 1000 people might have gotten out. It's a big burden. I feel terrible remorse for those who died."

How do we live with these revelations and understand them in terms of our awakening? How do we forgive such greed and guard against it?

Like Robert Oppenheimer witnessing the A-bomb destroying Hiroshima, Robertson joins those who have unleashed forces they didn't quite understand, forces whose misuse or limitations they didn't foresee. And though creating new building technologies is not quite as dangerous as splitting the atom, still, in replaying the archetypal lesson of Dr. Frankenstein, whose innovation exceeded his responsibility, Robertson and his melting spandrels—along with Nobel and his dynamite, and Oppenheimer and his A-bomb—all painfully remind us that we risk great violence and destruction when we dare to value the brick over the worker.

That we continue to relive these ancient struggles is less a cause for pessimism than a confirmation that each generation must take its turn upholding humanity. Ultimately, how civilized and compassionate we really are depends on whether we put down the brick. When we become lost in building someone else's dream, we must take steps to make the dream ours again, and to find the one tongue we share under all our differences.

> The moment we value the brick over the person, we lose the ability to understand each other, and the moment we dare to speak humbly and directly from our heart, we find each other.

Removing the Oldest Wall

Access to knowledge is a major step in deepening community, because it welcomes individuals into the ongoing conversation that is the life of community. A compelling example took place in Hanyang, Korea (now Seoul, South Korea), in 1443, when Sejong the Great (1397–1450) created a phonetic alphabet, Hangul, for the people of Korea. Three years later, Sejong made Hangul public. This extended literacy beyond the ruling class. With the creation of Hangul, knowledge and the conversation it opens became available to everyone. Now everyone had a voice.

This monarch found the courage to go beyond his own frame of reference to empower his people as they had never been empowered. How do we find this courage in ourselves?

A Buddhist by nature and education, Sejong became king when his elder brothers, seeing his gifts, abdicated their chance to rule so that Sejong ascended the throne. He quickly showed his innovation and compassion.

Sejong created a farmer's handbook, to gather and preserve the experience of farmers. He allowed his people to pay more or less tax according to the fluctuations of their prosperity and hardship. When the palace had a surplus of food, Sejong distributed food to the peasants and farmers in need. And he established the Hall of Worthies (Jiphyeonjeon) at his palace, a gathering of scholars, sages, scientists, and physicians charged with furthering specific knowledge in science, medicine, and literature while making these advances available to all.

Moved by the illiteracy of his people, Sejong instructed scholars in the Hall of Worthies to construct a phonetic language that would be easy to learn. The new language, Hangul, was issued on October 9, 1446, in a royal document, the *Hunminjeongeum*, which means *the verbally right sounds meant to teach the people.*

Within days, new practitioners, regardless of their background, were able to read, write, and converse. The gift of language removed the oldest wall between the villages of Korea, the thick wall of ignorance. As a life of exchange spread throughout the country, the culture became animated.

In his introduction to Hangul, Sejong wrote that he was saddened by his people's inability to state their concerns. And so, he charged the educated to help the uneducated, not just by sharing knowledge, but by offering the uneducated the means by which to become equal members of their society. He placed the shared interests and common well-being of his people first, and used his power to distribute opportunity and capital fairly.

He made literacy free and extended the capacity for voice to the Korean people forever. In modern Korea, October 9 is still celebrated as Hangul day, honoring Sejong. His ability to lead by listening affirms that the first cause of community, and the first strength of character for a leader, is to assess the needs of the community and to find the means by which to enhance everyone's capacity.

Sejong had an immense and gentle understanding of life. This is remarkable considering the heartless ambition of his father, Taejong of Joseon (1367–1422). King Taejong was a crude monarch who murdered his own brother to gain the throne. To limit the possibility of rivals, he killed all four brothers of his queen, as well as Sejong's in-laws. Surprisingly, Sejong assumed the throne while Taejong was still alive. What did Taejong see in his son and why did he trust it, after a life of distrust? And what allowed Sejong to rule so differently than his father? How did the compassionate son find and maintain his own identity under the cloud of a ruthless father? This ability to break from the cruel traditions he inherited is important to demonstrate in our own time, where the current leader of North Korea, Kim Jong-un, is only perpetuating the cruelty of his father, Kim Jong-il.

The example of a compassionate king who somehow came from a ruthless father holds one of the keys to enlightened social change. For we are not doomed to the patterns we inherit. Sejong relied on a different kind of authority than his murderous father. Ultimately, the integrity of a community depends on the field of trust that the authority of our kindness makes possible. Few of us will ever be kings or presidents or ministers of state, but to care about the concerns of those we live with, and to strengthen the web of connection between us—rather than tear it down—means we won't be alone in the storms or harvests that come.

The first strength of character for a leader is to assess the needs of the community and to find the means by which to enhance everyone's capacity.

Blind Travelers

Moments of the soul endure even
when banished to the back of the mind.
—ABRAHAM JOSHUA HESCHEL

It takes a particular kind of effort to slow down and sink into the waters that matter, to center and drop into the heart of any moment. When we can, that moment becomes the teacher. But more than ever, it seems the speed of modern life banishes the soul to the back of the mind. A college teacher from Kansas said, "It takes courage to stop and think deeply in a world of such interruption that I can go a whole day without finishing a sentence."

Mindfulness is especially difficult within the noise of 24/7 news and entertainment. Today, we face the added difficulty in trying to stay awake in a society that is increasingly numb and half-asleep. And since we as individuals create and sustain our society, we are responsible to a degree for the dark side of our culture. Still, once awake and living authentically, there is a loneliness that comes from facing the currents of our day. As a piece of graffiti I once saw in a gas station in Georgia read, "Those who don't hear the music think the dancers mad." And for sure, we're all blind travelers, sometimes dancing, sometimes wondering what the fuss is all about. Yet no one person or group is to blame for this estrangement.

The dividedness or harmony of an individual often reflects or mirrors the dividedness or harmony of the society they live in. As early as 1844, Karl Marx told us that an estranged and divided society breeds an estranged and divided citizen. He proposed that an *alien nation* gives rise to personal *alienation*. In fact, Marx thought of *alienists* as those therapists who would tend to the repair of the estranged and alienated individual.

This may be why Confucius believed in the health and well-being of the community at large: because only from a healthy garden can healthy vegetables grow. And yet, the inner state of an individual also tells us a great deal about the community at large. For looking into the heart of an individual is like drawing a blood sample from the body politic. No doubt there will be markers in that sample which will tell us much about the health of the larger bloodstream we call society.

During my cancer journey more than thirty years ago, I was sorely in need of a detective of ills, for I had a rare form of lymphoma that no one seemed able to solve. This led me to a doctor at Columbia Presbyterian Hospital in New York City, who turned out to be a brilliant systems thinker. His diagnosis saved my life. Unfortunately, he was a terrible caregiver and my first treatment administered by him was horribly botched and made me sicker.

As a young man, Karl Marx was also a brilliant systems thinker who diagnosed that the modern world was alienated, which is still helpful medicine for us as we try to reclaim our working sense of community in the twenty-first century. Yet, like the treatments by my well-intentioned oncologist, the application of Marxist thought in the body politic ultimately made society sicker.

Still, there's value in understanding alienation as the separation of people from aspects of their human nature, such as one's sense of self and one's innate regard for others. Marx believed that such alienation is a systematic result of capitalism, of people being treated like parts in a mechanized society. Without going into the brutal conflict between communism and capitalism that ensued, what's important here is to understand that societal patterns, conscious and unconscious, have contributed to the individual and community experience of being estranged from our human nature. These estrangements still stand as impediments to the re-emergence of compassionate communities, and include modernization, urbanization, and the loss of primary relationships such as family bonds in favor of goal-oriented relationships.

Émile Durkheim (1858–1917), a French sociologist, further articulated the concept of alienation (*anomie*) when he observed that values regarding how people should treat each other were breaking down. With less attention focused on relationships, people didn't know what to expect from one another. Durkheim foresaw that as societies become more complex, people are no longer tied to one another and social bonds become impersonal. Periods of drastic social disruption bring about greater alienation and higher rates of crime, suicide, and deviance. He described alienation as a type of social suicide associated with the loss of a more relational way of life.

The age we live in and its technological marvels have complicated the ways we are separate from each other, making the need to repair and reanimate our human nature more important than ever.

It takes a particular kind of effort to slow down and sink into the waters that matter, to center and drop into the heart of any moment. When we can, that moment becomes the teacher.

About to Wake

In every generation, there are those who voice the undefeatable song of humanity and those who shout down everything that is different than they are. In the midst of such shouting, it takes a certain kind of persistence to listen for the unspoken essence that keeps us all connected. In this regard, Carl Jung spoke of artists as those born with an inner persistence to listen. Jung thought of artists as lightning rods of the Collective Unconscious, souls who often, without choice or awareness, carry the rumblings of the collective human story through their innate openness. I recently experienced a powerful example of such openness and listening.

Susan and I were in New York City, eager to visit the renovated Museum of Modern Art. We were not disappointed. Four separate works of art—by Marcel Duchamp, Yves Tanguy, René Magritte, and Jean Marcel—all created between 1914 and 1936—spoke to us. Together they foretold the isolation and alienation that would mark the twentieth century. Together they point to the separations of modern life that we're still dealing with.

In 1914, Marcel Duchamp (1887–1968) created a piece in oil and pencil called *Network of Stoppages*. It depicts an aerial view of a vein-like system, noting the stoppages of flow throughout. It's unclear whether the system is a snapshot of a human being's heart or brain or a city's water system or a nation's compassion. But clearly, Duchamp foresaw blockages within us and between us that would swell, to plague us and prevent us from knowing ourselves and each other.

Then we stumbled upon a canvas called *Extinction of Useless Lights*, painted in 1927 by Yves Tanguy (1900–1955). As if an answer to Duchamp's *Network of Stoppages*, Tanguy's stark image calls out from a dark urban landscape for us to extinguish the distractions, so we can see where the stoppages are, and loosen the restrictions to the flow of life and thought that connect us.

Next, a striking painting, called *The Lovers*, created in 1928 by Surrealist René Magritte (1898–1967), shows two hooded lovers kissing through their hoods. It powerfully depicts our struggle to be intimate while hidden, and conjures the numbness of modern life in which we're always there, but seldom present.

I could feel a truth weaving itself through these long-gone painters. Their work hung on separate walls as antidotes to the pain of alienation. They seemed to be saying—alone and together—that if we have any chance of restoring our humanity, we must remove the hoods we wear when we kiss, put out false lights, and find and open the stoppages that keep us from each other.

This brought us to a jarring sculpture created in 1936, just before the outbreak of World War II, by Jean Marcel (1900–1993). Called *Specter of the Gardenia*, the sculpture depicts a plaster head covered with black cloth, with zippers for eyelids and a strip of movie film forming a choker around its neck. Here, Marcel, in an eerie premonition of the Holocaust, seems to say: If we succumb to the false lights and stoppages, if we resign ourselves to love while hooded, the only way to survive the monster of modernity that we've created will be to close our eyes with zippers and to cover our throats with film. We have done this in dramatic ways. Consider the refusal to accept the Holocaust and other genocides since. Consider the escapism of reality TV and the dull narcotic of shopping. Recall, in the wake of the terrorist attacks of 9/11, President Bush urging frightened citizens to shop.

These prescient works can be read as reflections of our growing isolation in the modern world. They sharply diagnose a world turning in on itself. Together they point to the dehumanizing ethos—which now has a life of its own—that muffles our natural harmonies and human nature. I don't offer this as a dark view of the world, but as a way to confront how we choke our human garden, again and again, with social disruptions, and how we need, in every generation, to prune back the tangles we create so that beauty and compassion can break ground again.

Perhaps the only way to reclaim our humanity is to seed and prune the garden of our soul. In this kind of garden, pruning involves clearing the stoppages that keep us from feeling, putting out the false lights that shield us from truly seeing and being seen, and removing the hoods and chokers that keep us from knowing each other. Perhaps the slow answer to social alienation involves uncoupling the zippers we've closed over our eyes.

Within the sleepiness of every society, there are travelers who have awakened to the social patterns we're imprinted with and they see more than the rest of us. Often these reluctant seers sense what holds us together and what entangles us. We usually discount these seers and their insights or exile them. Sometimes we kill them. Sometimes we discover that we are them.

In truth, we take turns being the sighted and the blind. The courage lies in acting on what we finally see. The compassion lies in how we receive those who see when we do not. The recurring challenge is whether we will live in the light of what unifies us or in the shadows of what entangles us. Sadly, we often miss what brings us together because of our assumptions and preconceptions, many of which are not even ours in the first place.

This dilemma is not new. We only have to go back to Plato's analogy of the cave to find a startling description of awakening to reality. A prisoner in a cave who can only see shadows on the wall breaks free of his chains and finds his way to the surface world where he's stunned by the immense experience of direct light. With his newfound sight, he races back into the cave to share this other reality with the prisoners still staring at the flickering shadows. He declares the glory of the real world that he's tripped upon and invites them to join him and leave the cave. They reject him as a dreamer, insisting that the shadows they watch are the only reality. As he grows more animated, trying to convince them of what he's seen so they can become free, too, they grow more frightened and kill him.

Sometimes we're the seer and sometimes the slayer. Sometimes we have to shut down the noise of the alien nation that clouds our senses in order to truly hear and see. Often, it's not about physically staying or leaving the life we find ourselves in, but more deeply about the quiet courage to stay awake long enough to let every day be a new, direct experience that is yet to be interpreted or understood. Often it's as close as turning around and facing each other and the light.

Life in the shadows can traumatize us and separate us from what it is to be human. This alienation can deepen into an abiding, impoverished mental state, which can take many forms, one of which is schizoid personality disorder. In this chronic condition, alienation becomes an involuntary way of life in which a person lacks interest in social relationships, tends toward a solitary lifestyle, and becomes secretive and emotionally cold. It's interesting to note that the word *schizoid* derives from the Polish *Schizotymik*, which means *a person immersed and lost in themselves.*

It's also interesting to note that the origin of the word *idiot*, from the Greek *ídiotēs*, means *a citizen not involved with their community, a person who doesn't care about others.* The word *ídiós* refers to *a person collapsed into themselves.* Being an idiot was a sorrowful condition, not a stupid one. It implies a walking state of disconnection and isolation, one which we suffer today in mass.

We tend to create mirrors of our inner states. I recently learned that impenetrable nano-threads are used in the fabric of shirts. You can spill red wine on them and they won't absorb it. Is this what we've become, impenetrable threads in the social fabric? Are we now indestructible and incapable of absorbing anything? I look around and it seems true: nothing sticks.

We need to open our eyes so we can recover from life in the shadows. Plato describes this liberation from the cave into the light as our journey into the true nature of things, which he calls *the ascent of the soul.* It's akin to the Buddhist and Hindu notion of stripping away illusion to experience things as they are.

Seeing reality is a vital means by which we can enliven our attempts at living together. After the genocide in Rwanda of the Tutsi people by the Hutu army in 1994, the common greeting among survivors became *Mwaramutse,* which means, *Did you wake?* We would do well to greet each other this way. For don't we all suffer the restlessness of feeling separate? And each time we reach out, it's not clear whether our spirit will be muted into a shadow of itself or whether we'll wake next to each other in the fragile miracle of being here at all.

We take turns being the sighted and the blind. The courage lies in acting on what we finally see. The compassion lies in how we receive those who see when we do not.

Grown over Centuries

From 750 to 1492 in southern Spain, Muslims, Jews, and Christians forged a strong and integrated culture. The Jewish tradition had a Golden Age there and thrived in one of the most open-minded and welcoming communities in history.

This remarkable epoch can be seen as a 742-year moment of community. It bears much more attention than one chapter can provide, and yet any inquiry into community must honor this period of extraordinary, if complicated, harmony between peoples. Within this span of history, I want to focus on the height of this civilization from 936 to 1010, and on the mind-sets that made this remarkable community possible.

These people lived together despite their long histories of difference. This capacity seemed to rest largely on their willingness to allow contrary views to exist without one view dominating another. The importance of this can't be overstated. The ethic of leaning into each other while withholding judgment is crucial to lasting relationships, whether they are personal or societal.

In this culture of tolerance and openness, creative community in all areas of knowledge was ripe and dynamic. This fertile culture gave rise to a renaissance of remarkable individuals who learned from each other and furthered the art of civilization on Earth. This enlightened unfolding occurred in southern Spain at a time when the rest of Europe was enduring a dark, illiterate age.

The cosmopolitan center of the Muslim Empire was the city of Córdoba, which, with 500,000 people, was the largest city in the world from 935 to 1013. Three renowned philosophers were born in Córdoba: the Roman stoic Seneca, the Muslim Averroës, and the Jewish physician-philosopher-rabbi Maimonides. During this era, the Muslim Empire in Spain became racially and ethnically integrated

181

through intermarriage. Abd ar-Rahman I, the first emir of Córdoba, was himself half-Berber and half-Syrian. Within the first decade of Abd ar-Rahman I's rule, Jewish and Christian communities were deeply influenced by Arab custom. Like cross-pollinated plants, the variety of custom and tradition made the culture of southern Spain lush and healthy.

There were complaints from conservatives who wanted the faithful of each culture to stay with their own, but the unprecedented merging of ways had an irrepressible life of its own, which was particularly evident in the progressive city of Córdoba. Arab diarists of the time marveled at the diverse beauty of the city. In 948, the geographer Ibn Hawkal exclaimed, "The amount of coins in circulation! The variety of crops grown! The people! The textiles! The gardens! The mosques!" Indeed, at its height, Córdoba had more than 1000 mosques and 600 public baths.

The German nun Hroswitha of Gandersheim wrote in 955 that Córdoba was

> the brilliant ornament of the world . . . a noble city . . . known for its pleasures and resplendent in all things . . . especially for its seven streams of wisdom . . .

Aqueducts and libraries were abundant. The library of the caliph, one of seventy libraries maintained across the city, contained almost four hundred thousand volumes. Yale historian María Rosa Menocal reports that

> in those libraries was a series of attitudes about learning of every sort, about the duty to transmit knowledge from one generation to another, and about the interplay between the very different modes of learning that were known to exist—modes that might contradict each other, as faith and reason did, and do now. These sat happily in those libraries, side-by-side, unafraid of the contradictions.

But the jewel within the jewel was the palace-city of Medina Azahara, which means "the shining city." Set on the outskirts of Córdoba, and built in 936, Medina Azahara is considered the Versailles of the Middle Ages, both in architecture and its intellectual and artistic community. Once completed, Medina Azahara became the capital of Al-Andalus, the Arabic name for the Iberian Peninsula. Eventually, after almost a hundred years of exquisite integration of knowledge and culture, Medina Azahara was sacked in 1010 by Islamic purists from North Africa who considered the Muslim culture in Spain not devout enough in its interpretation of the Koran. A thousand years later, we're experiencing the same violent fundamentalism in the Middle East.

Though the highly civilized center of the Andalusian Empire was destroyed, the populace of integrated cultures remained strong. Muslims who remained under Christian rule, known as Mudejars, scattered to live alongside Mozarabs, Jews who, while unconverted to Islam, adopted the Arabic language and culture. But eighty-five years later, Pope Urban II launched the First Crusade in 1095 against the "infidel" Muslims. A hundred years later, Pope Innocent III, who was anything but innocent, extended the Crusades within and beyond Europe.

Despite the destruction that followed this golden era, the salient features of this remarkable period can help us today. We, too, can exercise our capacity to hold contrary views in the open without insisting on one over another. We, too, can lean into each other while withholding judgment. We, too, can embrace an acceptance of contradictions in order to stay in conversation. We, too, can engage an interest in all knowledge.

Over time, these dynamics of community allowed people of different backgrounds and faith to fall in love with each other. And falling in love over time blended these cultures through intermarriage. And multicultural family life led to the synthesis of the gifts of each culture as visionaries and craftsmen were born, and aqueducts, libraries, and architectures were created. A luminosity shone among the blended people that frightened the orthodox of each original faith. Then the shining city was destroyed, only in time to be built again.

We struggle with these expansions and contractions to this day, among our families, our communities, and our nations. Today, as in the beginning, we're called to resurrect a valiant effort to meet fear with truth and ignorance with love. Today, we're jarred to ask each other: In which community do you live, where our differences weave a tapestry or where our threads form a rope to pull anything different down?

> When standing in who we are without insisting on one view over another, creative community in all areas of knowledge becomes ripe and dynamic.

Building Things Together

Bees can teach us how to work together. Though each hive has a queen, bee colonies create an unfailing collective that self-organizes without relying on any singular leader. Instead, the working movement of the hive shapes the colony's destiny. Bee colonies are highly social: they allow several generations to live in the nest at the same time, they cooperate in caring for offspring not their own, and they inhabit a division of labor that makes the hive flourish.

Female bees are queens and workers and, over a five- to seven-week life span, worker bees trade jobs and serve different functions, including cleaning out dirty honeycombs, feeding larvae, building new honeycombs, receiving food from incoming foragers, guarding the hive, removing corpses, and foraging for nectar, pollen, and water.

When comparing honeybees and bumblebees, it's clear that there's strength and longevity in hives that have a greater division of labor. The larger, more interdependent honeybee colonies can last for many years, while the smaller, less diverse bumblebee colonies are annual.

In *Honeybee Democracy*, Thomas D. Seeley, a leading professor of neurobiology, tells us that

> indeed, there is no all-knowing central planner supervising the thousands and thousands of worker bees in a colony. The work of a hive is instead governed collectively by the workers themselves, each one an alert individual making tours of inspection looking for things to do and acting on her own to serve the community. Living close together, connected by the network of their shared environment... the workers achieve an enviable harmony of labor without supervision.

This description could have been written about the communal Native American ethic, which upholds one's place as an active, devoted member of the tribe over any particular trade or skill. Sharing the work and being willing to do anything that is needed is valued over specialization. In winter one might make arrows, and in summer one might plant corn.

The harmony of bees demonstrates what can arise from the hardworking, unconscious commitment to share the work before us. By devoting ourselves to working together, like honeybees, we can evoke a form of collective intelligence. People immersed in common causes and committed to athletic teams discover this harmony when their members get involved beyond each person being the star.

Our involvement in the world evolves through a desire to care for others and to fix things that break, like the fishing boat that was smashed when the river flooded. While fixing the boat, we lift our head and look upstream and see the causes of the flood. We realize that fewer people will drown or need to be saved if we can build a dam. Now we have to show others the cause and effect. Now community action begins. Now there's resistance when someone who saw a different cause wants to use the resources and labor available to fix other things.

This timeless genesis of action and counter-action is the healthy friction of democracy. Yet, it's the personal that always sparks the communal. It's the fact that someone we loved drowned in that river that awakens our commitment to do something about it. Compassion strengthens everyone involved. Then we're moved to hold an injured person, failing dream, or fading tradition like a broken plate, pressing the pieces together until the bond sets. In essence, holding the brokenness in people until the bond sets is the atom of all community action.

Without this awareness of heart, even good causes become mechanical. And we're sorely challenged when someone is hurt while building a dam or orphanage, and we're so caught up in the cause that we miss the chance to help those right in front of us, which is what prompted our urge to fix and build in the first place.

But toward what end do we build and fix? What good is a house if it never becomes a home? What good is a ship if those on board are never lifted by the immensity of the sea? Abraham Heschel speaks to the larger home that community can become, if we can sustain our common inner life. Then, we can find "spiritual substance . . . compassion, justice and holiness . . . in the daily life of the masses."

The early Persian city of Gondēshāpūr was built to be a home for the immensity of life, which in itself was seen as a resource as important as water. Under the reign of Khosrau I (531–579 A.D.), Gondēshāpūr became an innovative center of learning and medicine. With these resources, Khosrau I created one of the earliest and most important medical schools, the Academy of Gondēshāpūr, which was responsible for transforming medical education by beginning clinical training in a hospital setting. Rather than apprenticing with just one physician, medical students were required for the first time to work in a hospital under the supervision of the *entire* medical faculty. Learning and working together became the path to practice healing.

How we repair our personal connections when trust is broken is as important as repaving a road to a hospital or rebuilding a bridge that's come down in a storm. In the Democratic Republic of the Congo in 1998, there was great ethnic tension throughout the country. Five African armies and three rebel movements were fighting each other in what U.S. secretary of state Madeleine Albright called "the first African world war."

To defuse the tension, Governor Kanyamuhanga Gafundi created the Baraza Inter-Community Forum. The governor hoped to appeal to the common reverence for ancestors as a way to open dialogue. Every ethnic group was represented in the Governor's Forum and, over time, it became part of the Congolese way of life. The purpose of a *baraza* (Swahili for *council* or *public meeting place*) is to maintain an open, safe forum where frank conversation can surface as a way to lessen conflicts before they erupt, and to restore trust.

In 2006, the forum changed its name to Baraza ya Wazee (Swahili for "the forum of the elders") and opened its doors to all people in the community, so they can meet to discuss problems. The *Baraza* has become a gathering place where everyone has a voice and a say in the life of the village.

The structure of the *Baraza* goes back to when the ancestors would gather under a big tree in the village to attend tribal issues. Today, the meeting place might be in an open field outside the chief's office or in a church or mosque. Given the corruption of local authorities, the *Baraza* has become an informal system of justice where the poor and the rich are heard under one community roof. The conversations in the *Baraza* have led to community development projects as well.

Baraza has also come to mean a stone bench placed in front of a house as an open invitation for visitors to come and talk. *Baraza* is also used as a metaphor for any meeting place and people have begun to use it in naming restaurants or cafés as friendly places to gather.

In the contemporary Hispanic community, *conocimiento* means "to nurture connection by sharing knowledge of each other." There's no English equivalent for this word. It's a principle of unity brought about by building relationships in order to embark on common tasks together. Before you can build in the world, you must build the bonds that will be strong enough to endure the labor necessary to make things that will last in the world.

Conocimiento goes back to the pre-Colombian tradition of educating future leaders. Now *conocimiento* is a process for deepening team-building by honoring commonalities and differences. *Conocimiento* is about creating connections. Giving each person in the community a chance to be seen for who they are leads to shared values. When we understand each other, we make a greater commitment to the work we can do together. And with trust and true understanding, there's more creative power together than alone.

Community expert Roberto Vargas describes the process and impact of *conocimiento*:

> The real connection occurs when you take time to meaningfully get to know each other . . . actively sharing about ourselves to create connection . . . I am doing *conocimiento* when I meet a new person, extend my hand, share who I am, and ask several questions to invite him or her to similarly share . . . I am also doing *conocimiento* when I sit down with my mother or daughter and ask, "What's going on in your life?"

What we build visibly in the world depends on what we build invisibly between us. People across history have always known this. In the innovative center of Gondēshāpūr in sixth-century Persia, one of the first teaching hospitals wove knowledge and practice together in order to heal. In the Congo, the forum of elders opened a space where trust had to be restored before villages could be rebuilt. And in contemporary Hispanic communities, you have to know each other first before you can build anything together that might last.

Weaving knowledge and practice to heal, maintaining a safe, public place where truth can be voiced, and creating deep personal connection in order to build together—these are tools that have no visible handles. Yet these forms of kinship are necessary if there's to be substance in our everyday existence. Toward what end do we build, unless to inhabit what we build together?

As a way to endure our problems, we shelter each other and huddle together. What then are the lasting forms of huddle? The Sufis speak of *shared inwardness* as a basis for compassionate community. And in poor rural tribes in Kenya, they say, "We push our problems into the center of the circle and lift them up together with love."

Regardless of where we come from or where we're going, we all fall like emperors forced to huddle in each other's ordinary care. The wellness group I was a part of when suffering through cancer was such a huddle. We'd meet once a week, and whoever was chilled by the closeness of death would be warmed in the center. Then we'd take turns. This is what it means to be civilized: that we huddle around whoever is most chilled, and then we take turns. No one is left out in the cold. At the core of our deep want to build is our deep want to hold and be held, which we in our troubled lives often forget.

In essence, holding the brokenness in people until the
bond sets is the atom of all community action.

QUESTIONS TO LIVE WITH

+ Bring three friends together and invite two new people into your group. In conversation, have each of you describe a time when you turned from being a caregiver to a gatekeeper. How did this happen? What did you learn from this experience? In the next three weeks, identify a caregiver and a gatekeeper in your community and begin a conversation with each.

+ Bring three friends together and invite two new people into your group. As a group, discuss the notion of an acequia and how it is cleared each spring of all its debris so the mountain water can feed the village. Then, have each of you describe the debris of thought and feeling you carry and how you might go about clearing the acequia of your mind and heart. In the next three weeks, identify an acequia or common channel in your community that needs communal clearing, and begin the process.

+ Bring three friends together and invite two new people into your group. In conversation, have each of you tell the story of a time when you insisted on your own view and where that insistence led. Then tell the story of a time when you withheld your judgment and welcomed a view other than your own. Where did that openness lead? In the next three weeks, convene a community conversation on an issue important to you with those who hold an opposite view from you, and see if you can understand each other.

+ Bring three friends together and invite two new people into your group. In conversation, have each of you tell the story of one way you are self-centered and one way you are other-centered. How does being self-centered and other-centered affect your relationships? What might you do to expand your circle of viewpoint and concern? In the next three weeks, make an effort to inquire into someone else's life.

✦ Bring three friends together and invite two new people into your group. In conversation, have each of you tell the story of a time when you were shut out and a story of a time when you were taken in. Where did you learn how to meet the misfortune of others? In the next three weeks, take a step to let someone you don't know into your life.

✦ Bring three friends together and invite two new people into your group. In conversation, have each of you tell the story of someone you know whose prime way in the world is to conquer and possess. Compare this person to someone you know whose prime way in the world is to discover and understand. How are these people different? Which way of knowing is prominent in you? Discuss the kind of community you live in.

✦ Bring three friends together and invite two new people into your group. In conversation, have each of you tell the story of something you created or built with another person and what this process felt like. How did this co-creation affect your relationship? What would you say to a child about the nature of building things together? In the next three weeks, work with another to create, build, or repair something in your community.

HOW WE MEET ADVERSITY

What is to give light must endure burning.

—VIKTOR FRANKL

M any have argued whether the inner life or the outer life is our home; the reflective saying that the outer world is but an illusion while the pragmatic say that all the meditation you can muster won't feed you. Each has its lineage. Socrates said, "The unexamined life is not worth living." And Berthold Brecht said, "Hunger is understood in any language." Yet, in moments of great love or suffering, in moments of great crisis or wonder, there is no inner or outer—there is only one life. In moments of searing connection, there is no individual or community—there is only one life. And in the crucible of living, we have yet to learn the wisdom of that fleeting Oneness that empowers us to keep going.

Without the inner life, we peck at each other like chickens with no eyes. Without the outer life, we grope for each other like medics with no hands. The truth is that in the face of adversity, the tool is only as useful as the hand that lifts it. And the hand is only as useful as the mind and heart that guide it. In any given moment where love becomes visible, mind and heart and hand and tool are one. How do we learn this? How do we teach this? How do we preserve this?

Beginning Again

You our father can build a church that you grow up praying in. You can watch the children of your friends and enemies come of age there. And one day, while praying with your eyes closed, you can be stabbed in that same church. While bleeding, you can watch your brother die. In the starkness of your grief, you can hang those who betrayed you. And you can begin again, trying to make sense of a world where we can be killed where we pray.

You can carry the loss around for years like a pill you're supposed to take but don't. Until one day, you swallow it all and open your home to the greatest minds of your time. You can seek out the greatest artists you can find and bring them home to live with you, and give them everything so they might build a better world.

This is the story of Lorenzo de' Medici (1449–1492) of Florence, who seeded the Renaissance, that two-hundred-year expansion of mind and heart that changed the world. His great lesson is that we don't have to become what is done to us. His great warning is that we're always capable of both, of destroying the world out of vengeance and of creating a new world out of loss.

Lorenzo's great-grandfather was born in poverty and started a bank. After two generations, the Medici family was among the wealthiest in Europe. As a boy, Lorenzo was tutored by the humanist Marsilio Ficino (1433–1499). When his father died in 1469, Lorenzo, at the age of twenty, became the head of the family and all its affairs.

With the pope's support, rival papal bankers in Florence began to plot against the Medici family. And so, the Pazzi conspiracy was set in motion. On Sunday, April 26, 1478, during High Mass at the Duomo Cathedral in Florence, the Medici brothers were attacked before a crowd of 10,000. Giuliano, who was twenty-five, was stabbed nineteen times by Bernardo di Bandino Baroncelli and Francesco de' Pazzi. As his brother bled to death on the cathedral floor, Lorenzo escaped with serious wounds.

The assassins were caught and within the hour, 120 conspirators were captured, and, at Lorenzo's command, eighty were hanged. Jacopo de' Pazzi was tossed from a window. From the crowd, a twenty-seven-year-old Leonardo da Vinci sketched the hanged conspirator Baroncelli.

The horrific loss had Lorenzo re-examine what to do with his life and his wealth. He discovered that the journey is both grace-filled and bloody. But how we respond to brutality is what saves the world.

At the time of the Pazzi conspiracy, the Renaissance was beginning to bloom, though many Florentines were opposed to the progressive trends of humanism. At this turning point in history, Lorenzo's grief led him to use his wealth and power to protect the artists and thinkers of the time and support their work, in hopes that they might create a better world. And so, in 1488, the Medici Circle was created, becoming the first art school in Europe.

More than a formal school, the Medici Circle was a crucible of innovation and dialogue. Lorenzo used his own collection of art for students to study while maintaining an open house where philosophers, writers, and artists were free to come and live and work. He went to great lengths to purchase Greek and Latin manuscripts and have them copied. His brilliant literary circle included Angelo Poliziano, Marsilio Ficino, Luigi Pulci, and the genius Giovanni Pico della Mirandola.

Pico was at the heart of the Medici Circle. At twenty-three, he spoke sixteen languages and proposed a conference to explore the unity of religion, philosophy, nature, and magic, for which he wrote nine hundred theses. These essays formed his *Oration on the Dignity of Man* (completed 1486, published 1496).

The Medici Circle included artists such as Botticelli, Leonardo da Vinci, and Michelangelo, who, at fourteen, came to live and work in Lorenzo's sculpture school. Other Renaissance artists included Ghirlandaio, Verrocchio, Vasari, Volterra, and Raphael.

The innovation of the Medici Circle led Europe out of the Middle

Ages. In thirty-seven years of patronage and public service, during and after his lifetime, Lorenzo the Magnificent, as he was known, and his estate spent more than 663,000 florins (approximately $460 million) on the arts, architecture, and charity.

Pico, Ficino, Botticelli, Michelangelo, Leonardo, Raphael, and others would never have been able to birth their extraordinary gifts without Lorenzo protecting the gestation of their talents from the difficult aggressions of the world. Yet, Lorenzo didn't shield them from the harsher realities. Because of his losses, he wanted the full paradox of life to inform their work.

One of the most compelling functions of community is to let the fullness of life, harshness and all, shape our sensibilities while protecting each other from the difficult aggressions that surround us. At its best, community serves as a trellis on which the delicate flowers of humanity can grow and blossom.

Years after Lorenzo was stabbed in church and saw his brother die, Pico paused in reflection, in the center of the circle Lorenzo had created. Trying to make sense of all we're given and all that's taken away, the young thinker looked at Lorenzo and said, "Friendship is the end of all philosophy."

> We're always capable of both, of destroying the world out of vengeance and creating a new world out of loss.

The Bell of Nagasaki

Located on the southern tip of Japan, Nagasaki was a small fishing village until the Portuguese landed there in 1543, after which it quickly grew into a diverse port city. By the start of World War II, Nagasaki was the largest city on the southern island of Kyushu.

A week before the atomic bomb was dropped, Nagasaki withstood severe attacks, including six incendiary bombs that destroyed the Nagasaki Medical College and hospital. At the time, Nagasaki was home to 263,000 people, including 9000 Japanese soldiers and 400 Allied prisoners of war.

August 9, 1945 would change the world. Just before dawn, Major Charles Sweeney lifted off in a B-29 from Tinian's North Field with the A-bomb on board. He headed for Kokura, but the city was too clouded to make a clear sighting. And so, because of a shelf of clouds, Nagasaki became the target. Twenty minutes later, Major Sweeney was flying over Nagasaki, waiting for the clouds to clear there. Growing short of fuel, Sweeney circled one more time, when the clouds opened. The A-bomb was dropped from about 1650 feet. Fifty-three seconds later, at 11:02 a.m., the bomb exploded over the city's Urakami Valley. Within a second, the north of the city was annihilated. More than 70,000 people were killed instantly, while others suffered long, incendiary deaths.

So devastating was the blast that people were instantly cremated. In the memorial today, there's a slab of stone with a shadow on it, except there is no light casting this shadow. It's a human shadow; that is, the permanent shadow on the stone is the stain of human lives incinerated by the bomb—their remains fixed in the stone. Others would die later of radiation poisoning.

It took days for the heat to dissipate, but the radiation lingered. One survivor would later declare, "With all my might, as I once cried out for water while crawling among the charred bodies on that fateful day, I cry now for peace."

In the rubble, only one column of Urakami Cathedral remained standing. The story is that in the terrible aftermath, someone crawled his way to strike a broken piece of the cathedral bell. And the ringing of a broken bell in the midst of all that devastation was a signal to begin again. Hearing that bell, those who survived somehow inched their way back into what were their streets. And dazed by their pain, a few cleared small pieces of rubble. Then others did the same. The sound of stones and debris being pushed aside became a dark and muffled music. The human story was beginning again.

Each day, for months, the Bell of Nagasaki was rung in the morning and the survivors knew it was safe to come out and continue rebuilding. Is this crazy or noble? It seems that no matter the devastation, there's a resilience within us to rebuild whatever has been destroyed. Whether this story is true or not, we need to have such a story, so we can believe there is a way out.

Let each story in this section of the book serve as a ring of that bell. The story of Nagasaki tells us that while it's incredibly hard, it's possible to make peace with the truth of almost anything—to accept the unalterable fact of reality. This is not resignation but the courage to see what is there. In order to proceed, we must: feel the injustice where it burns; feel the loss and what it's taken; grieve so as not to unknowingly perpetrate the same injustice on others; and unlace the cruelty in order to keep it from happening again.

Though forgiveness is possible, some cruelties are unforgivable. If I had been one to survive Nagasaki, I don't know if I could ever forgive the Americans for dropping the bomb or Emperor Hirohito for being so ruthlessly stubborn in provoking the Allies to drop it. Recently, I stood before the ovens at Terezín, an hour north of Prague, stared into the bed of ash where 30,000 Jews were burned, and walked by the Ohře River in which the Nazis threw tons of body ash to eliminate the evidence. I stood there and felt every emotion burn till I was left with a somber and stark acceptance.

These sites are unspeakably dark, the human ash of the Holocaust and the incinerated lives of Nagasaki. Yet though heinous acts happen when we eclipse our humanity, the world is not a dark place. Nor is the human heart. In our response to adversity, there is always one more hand that gives than takes, one more voice than all those silenced, and one more slip of moonlight that we can feed to those broken of hope.

My time at Terezín helped me understand that reconciliation is not about reparation or compensation or resolution. It is the difficult journey of meeting the truth of what-is in a way that allows those who are hurt to be whole again. It is the inner task of coming to terms with the truth of what has happened and what is still possible between the violated and the violator. But more importantly, between the violated and life. Accepting the truth does not minimize the need for justice. But whether justice is possible or not, reconciliation is necessary. This call to meet truth is how we reconcile what has happened to us with our larger understanding of life.

There's always a bell to be rung that tells us it is safe to come out and try again. Often, it's the bell of understanding that rings through our being when the nerve of life is struck. Even when everything is taken, there's something in us that will twitch its way back into the light.

> No matter the devastation, there's a resilience within
> us to rebuild whatever has been destroyed.

The Road Before the Temple

Mahatma Gandhi (1869–1948) is widely revered for his strength of spirit (*mahātmā* is Sanskrit for *Great Soul*) and his nonviolent struggle for Indian independence from the British Empire. But he also stood up to his own people in order to challenge the unequal and closed-minded treatment of other Indians in the caste system. Moreover, Gandhi stood *for* a deeper truth between the living, which often required his standing *against* others numbed by tradition or prejudice from seeing or feeling that deeper truth.

The heart of Gandhi's philosophy centers on what we in the West call nonviolent resistance. But Gandhi's understanding is more encompassing. While nonviolent action is the visible stem that breaks ground, it grows from a strong set of roots that thrive out of view. Gandhi called this deeper root system *Satyagraha*.

Satya is Sanskrit for *truth* and *graha* is Sanskrit for *to grasp or hold*. Together they imply *grasping or holding the truth*. In 1920, Gandhi described Satyagraha this way:

> Its root meaning is "holding on to truth," hence truth-force. I have also called it love-force or soul-force. In the application of Satyagraha, I discovered in the earliest stages that [the] pursuit of truth [does] not [allow] violence [to be] inflicted on one's opponent but that he must be weaned from error by patience and sympathy. For what appears to be truth to the one may appear to be error to the other. And patience means self-suffering. So the doctrine came to mean [the] vindication of truth, not by [the] infliction of suffering on [one's] opponent, but on oneself.

Gandhi was committed to grasping and holding this core sense of truth-force, love-force, and soul-force in the face of real situations among the living. And while his strength of conviction was legendary, so was his humility about how truth might manifest in the world. Truth for Gandhi was a lifelong inquiry. In fact, he called his autobiography *The Story of My Experiments with Truth*.

Gandhi's notion of Satyagraha was influenced by the concept of Ahimsa in the Hindu Upanishads. *Ahimsa* is a Sanskrit term meaning *to cause no harm* or *nonviolence*; *himsa* literally means "doing harm" or "causing injury." Ahimsa is based on a harmlessness of thoughts as well as actions, and as such prohibits the killing or injuring of living beings. Gandhi described the social meaning of Ahimsa as *intercommunity harmony*, affirming more what it is than defining it solely by what it is not, nonviolence.

This brings us to a remarkable moment of community that occurred in Vykom, India, during 1924 and 1925, when Gandhi was fifty-five years old. Gandhi had been trying to persuade other Indians to abandon the caste system, which has been such a harsh feature of Indian society for thousands of years.

In Hinduism, four castes exist in a hierarchy. Anyone who does not belong to one of these castes is an *outcast*. Each caste has certain duties and rights and members of each have specific occupations. The highest caste, *Brahmin*, are priests and the educated. *Kshatriya* are rulers and aristocrats. *Vaishya* are the landlords and businessmen. The lowest caste are *Shudra*, peasants and working-class people who labor in non-polluting jobs. Below these castes are the outcasts, the untouchables, who toil in jobs considered degrading, such as cleaning and removing sewage.

Despite the reverence for life that permeates the Hindu tradition, the untouchables were seen as polluting peoples and had almost no rights in society. The treatment of untouchables was often punishing. Their dwellings were kept at a distance. They were not allowed to touch people from the four castes or enter their homes or use the same wells. They were not allowed to enter any temples. In public, they were compelled to sit at a distance from others. In some regions, even contact with the shadow of an untouchable was seen as polluting.

If an outcast touched the belongings of a caste member, what they touched had to be washed. In some cases, untouchables who associated with castes were beaten and even murdered.

In 1924, when high-caste Hindu reformers came to Gandhi, he was eager to help them take a stand. In Vykom, in Travancore, India, one of the states ruled by an Indian maharajah instead of the British, untouchables had been forbidden for centuries to use a certain road leading directly to their quarter because it passed an orthodox Brahman temple of the highest caste.

The high-caste reformers gathered with untouchable friends and without announcement or fanfare walked together down that road and stopped in front of the temple. Orthodox Hindus attacked them and some of the demonstrators were arrested and put in prison. To everyone's surprise, thousands of volunteers gathered from all parts of India to support the Satyagraha that was happening in Vykom. The maharajah ordered the police to set up a barricade to keep the large number of reformers from entering the road.

The reformers walked up to the barricade and stood in prayer, asking the police to let them pass. They faced each other in silence. Neither would budge. Both groups organized day and night shifts. The reformers quietly pledged to stand in prayer until the Brahmans honored the right of untouchables to use the road before the temple. This went on for days.

The moment of urgency and confrontation had come and gone. And there on the street, the untouchables with their high-caste friends stood in prayer facing the maharajah's police, the barricade between them. They all quietly and tensely held their ground. Everyone began to suffer the long watch, the ache of standing long hours in prayer, the ache of holding guns poised for days. Spirits rose and fell and both sides became weary, irritated, and vulnerable. They forgot and remembered what they were doing and why. Some volunteers went home. Others replaced them. A good many stayed the course.

Months went by this way. Gandhi himself wrote at the time, "At the present moment, over fifty volunteers stand or squat in front of the barricades. They remain there at a stretch for six hours." That very day he gave a talk to those standing weary in prayer. He encouraged them not to blame the police or the Brahmins for upholding their beliefs, but to stand firm in their own. He said, "Three-fourths of the miseries and misunderstandings in the world will disappear, if we step in the shoes of our adversaries and understand their standpoint." Gandhi himself stayed behind the scene. He also sent away sympathetic foreigners, claiming that such good intentions would matter little compared to Hindu facing Hindu. He said, "The silent loving suffering of one single pure Hindu will be enough to melt the hearts of millions of Hindus."

They continued to stand and face each other. Then the rainy season came and the maharajah thought that the harsh cleansing waters of India would wash all this away, the way anthills disperse in a downpour. But the volunteers stood before the barricade in their weary shifts despite the rains. In time, the road was flooded. Those standing in prayer had to shorten their shifts to three hours. At its worst, the waters rose to their shoulders. The police had taken to boats. The waters swirled and passed between them.

When the waters receded, the reformers continued. It was becoming less and less clear who was keeping who from what. Those in quiet prayer grew weak and strong at the same time, as did the police now sitting on their guns. Somewhere along the barricade, a tired policeman began to weep and another passed a bit of food to those praying. One of those praying, his lips swollen from the heat, blessed the man weeping and sitting on his gun. After enough patience and sympathy, they had lost track of the world that others had built for them. They began to reach across the barricade and feel each other's pain.

At last, the maharajah ordered the barricade to be taken down, allowing the untouchables to pass. Piece by piece, the police hauled it away. But those who had stood in prayer for so long would not move. They quietly declined to walk down the now open road until the orthodox Hindus changed their attitude. The reformers said, "Your permission is not enough. You need to understand that we are the same." Receiving word of this, the Brahmins were angered and stunned and frustrated and the vigil continued.

Finally, after sixteen months of suffering the firm prayer of their beliefs, without taking up arms, without imposing their wills or ideas on anyone, their simple and unwavering presence drew the orthodox Brahmins from their temple. No longer waiting behind the power of the maharajah, the Brahmins came to the open road where the barricade had stood. They came to the suffering reformers, still standing in open prayer, and said through their own suffering, "We can no longer resist the prayers that have been made to us. We are ready to receive the untouchables."

How do we begin to feel and understand such a moment? How do we begin to grasp the transforming power of unwavering patience and sympathy? How do we find and enter such moments, sitting before the barricades we face until those upholding them start to understand that the wall is in our minds? How do we melt the heart of those who build walls? Or disarm the wall builder in ourselves? How do we stop giving, withholding, and asking for permission? Or begin to feel in our heart of hearts that we are the same?

Can you right now admit to a barricade you are maintaining? Can you grasp and hold on to why? Who are you treating as an outcast and why? Can you starve the wall builder you feed within? Can you melt your own heart? Can you burn the barricade with your presence to warm those kept on the outside for so long? I don't know how to do this. But I want to learn. I need to learn. Can we sit together long enough to find a way? Can we outwait the barricade? Can we teach each other? Aren't we all untouchable and touchable in our own way? Don't we all sit through the rains with one hand on the prayer and one hand on the gun?

After enough patience and sympathy, we lose track of the world that others have built for us. We begin to reach across the barricade and feel each other's pain.

Helping Each Other Up

Pain marks you, but too deep to see.

—MARGARET ATWOOD

In the grisly battles of the Civil War, more than 620,000 lives were lost and 476,000 soldiers and civilians were wounded. To give a sense of the enormity of the loss, consider that 420,000 Americans died in World War II. But during and after the Civil War, the North and South made monumental efforts to heal the wounded.

As soon as the Civil War was under way, the urgent need for care was incomprehensible. When the Confederates fired on Fort Sumter in South Carolina on April 12, 1861, America had no system to transport wounded soldiers, no field hospitals in place, and few established hospitals in its cities.

By August of 1862, Jonathan Letterman, the medical director of the Army of the Potomac, had created a system of ambulances and trained stretcher-bearers enlisted to evacuate the wounded as quickly as possible. In addition, large infirmaries were developed to treat animals too sick or fatigued to be of use. A staggering one million horses died during the Civil War.

In his second inaugural address, President Lincoln asked the nation to care for those who had borne the burdens and horrors of the war. The creation of the National Home for Disabled Volunteer Soldiers was one of the last pieces of legislation Lincoln signed before he was assassinated. Fifteen soldiers' homes would be established around the country.

While both sides were brutally maiming and killing each other, there was an almost invincible undercurrent of care, a determination to help each other up. In truth, this drive to care for the fallen has been there throughout the ages, regardless of the conflict.

In the midst of this living hell was a forty-year-old woman from Oxford, Massachusetts, who worked as a hospital nurse on the front lines. She was at the battles of Cedar Mountain, Second Bull Run, Antietam, and Fredericksburg. She was cleaning field hospitals, applying dressings, and serving food to wounded soldiers. While dressing the wound of one poor man, a bullet ripped through her sleeve, missing her, but killing the young man. She came to be known as an angel of the battlefield. Her name was Clara Barton (1821–1912).

After the war, Barton ran the Missing Soldiers Office, where she and her assistants wrote over 41,000 replies and helped to locate more than 22,000 missing men. Her work with the Civil War wounded and their families shaped her as a humanitarian and she later founded the Red Cross in the United States. One hundred and thirty years later, the mission of the Red Cross is still "to alleviate human suffering in the face of emergencies by mobilizing the power of volunteers." In 2013, the Red Cross helped 100 million people in seventy-three countries. We must never underestimate what one act of care can grow into, long beyond the life that authored it.

Yet what does helping each other look like when there's no way out? To understand this, we must go to Kovno, Lithuania, a dynamic center of Jewish culture in eastern Europe from 1850 until its liquidation by the Nazis in July 1944.

On July 7, 1941, the Germans arrived in Kovno. The Jews were herded into a ghetto and the killing began. By August 15, barbed-wire fences—erected by the Jews of Kovno at gunpoint—were in place and the city was now sealed off from the rest of the world. The Germans demanded that a head Jew be chosen to interface with the Gestapo. In panic and frenzy, the elders gathered. The only one they could agree on was a respected sixty-two-year-old physician, Dr. Elkhanan Elkes (1879–1944). And so, Dr. Elkes reluctantly became the leader of the Council of Elders in the Kovno Ghetto. He would have to meet regularly with the Gestapo and try to save as many Jews as he could.

Toward the end of that summer in 1941, the same summer Ted Williams hit .406, a notice was posted in the Kovno Ghetto saying there was work for educated Jews. The same summer Joe DiMaggio hit safely in fifty-six consecutive games, hundreds assembled at the gate to the ghetto—musicians, scholars, rabbis, elders, architects, writers, lawyers, engineers, doctors. And on August 18, while Boston played New York in a doubleheader, the educated of Kovno crowded the gate waiting for work, and as Ted doubled off the right-field wall, a gray truck pulled up and a squad of expressionless Germans shot them all.

With despair mounting, Dr. Elkes tried to re-create a community within the walls of the ghetto. Under his leadership, the Jews of Kovno convened secret schools, for which they risked execution if discovered. Quietly, the ghetto organized lectures, art classes, and a literary circle. There were even art exhibits within the barbed-wire fences.

Avraham Tory, a survivor of the Kovno Ghetto, writes:

> The Nazis aimed to destroy the cultural and intellectual strength of the community, targeting schools, synagogues, cultural centres, and the Ghetto intelligentsia. The Ghetto immediately began to rebuild, however, and several illegal schools, a hospital, a religious network and several musical and theatre groups were established. In the summer of 1942, the Ghetto orchestra came into existence. Made up of thirty-five instrumentalists and five singers, the orchestra was led by the conductor Michael Hofmekler. Over the course of the Ghetto's existence approximately eighty concerts were performed.

The power of art can remind us of our humanity; it can stall war. As Lenin said, "If I keep listening to Beethoven's *Appassionato*, I won't finish the revolution."

In the summer of 1944, Dr. Elkes was informed by the Gestapo that the ghetto would be terminated. Those who had survived to this point would now be shipped to the work camps at Dachau. Immediately, Dr. Elkes organized plans for escape, for as many as possible, including tossing children over the walls of the ghetto in potato sacks. In addition to all the practical urgencies, he instructed the ghetto orchestra to prepare a concert in which they would play

Beethoven's *Ode to Joy*. In the midst of certain doom, this practical yet hopeful elder told his tired people that, with nowhere to go, they would look to Heaven as it exists between them. They would stand their ground and honor the beauty of life for as long as they could. Imagine those who were left, a week before they were box-carred to Dachau, standing in the filthy square within the barbed-wire fences, listening to their musicians. Imagine the force of Beethoven's music filling their gaunt and bony frames.

Dr. Elkhanan Elkes was sent to Dachau, where he went on a hunger strike, refusing to perform medical experiments on his own people. In late 1944, he died, a testament to finding what matters in the midst of all that doesn't, to seizing the inch of light that won't go out in the midst of so much darkness, and to putting a stake in the ground for joy while knowing death is near. This was the legacy of the Kovno Ghetto.

Camp survivors have talked about the long walk at Auschwitz. Without a word, they were suddenly taken by a guard, alone or with others, not sure if this would be the last walk. The field between the barracks was always muddy, sometimes to the ankle. Exhausted and in pain, filled with fear or wrung out of all emotion in a detached numbness, waiting for death, they found it easier to walk in the steps of others, a small comfort to feel the firmness where others had gone before. This, too, is how we help each other up.

> We must never underestimate what one act of care can grow into, long beyond the life that authored it.

Let the Trauma Speak

Trauma is an experience that ruptures the sense of self. We
lose our understanding of who we are. And so, something
remains unfinished within us. There is a lapse in our story.

—PUMLA GOBODO-MADIKIZELA

There are two ongoing choices in response to adversity and trauma.
We may unconsciously re-enact our pain, reinforcing it, or we may
work through it, by consciously unraveling the pain, breaking apart
our pattern of suffering, and returning to a fresh perspective. The
work, for both the individual and the community, is to face these
questions: How do we find the lapse in our story caused by adversity
or trauma? How do we finish what is left unfinished in us?

In the Western model, therapy is chiefly a one-on-one affair,
which has tremendous benefits. But most indigenous traditions,
including the Native American tradition, have ceremonies and rituals that function as communal therapy. This opens another level of
healing and transformation.

Alone or together, this is the journey before us all: to live well and
love well, and to find each other. Finding each other through truth
and kindness connects the individual's journey with the journey of
the community.

This reminds me of a public learning ground in our time, South
Africa. It was Nelson Mandela who said, in the midst of his twenty-
seven-year captivity on Robben Island, "We will make a university
of our suffering." And in 1996, President Mandela created another
experiment in what Gandhi called Satyagraha (grasping or holding
the truth), which our world is still trying to understand. He launched
the Truth and Reconciliation Commission (TRC), in which those
responsible for the atrocities of apartheid would publicly confess

to enable the healing of their nation. And so, on April 15, 1996, the South African National Broadcaster televised the first two hours of live hearings. The rest of the hearings were presented on television each Sunday from April 1996 to June 1998 in hour-long episodes. The TRC was a community experiment in restorative justice.

In the words of Pumla Gobodo-Madikizela, who served on the commission, this was and is the work of "making public spaces intimate." I raise this because this is the kind of education we're not given in school. I raise this because, in the lineage of heart-givers and truth-seekers, it's our turn to make public spaces intimate, so we can explore how truth and kindness are the eternal initiations into making our deeper kinship known.

In our modern American culture, *The Oprah Winfrey Show* created a tradition of making public spaces intimate in an effort to educate and heal aspects of our society. For twenty-five years, the show convened authentic public space and served as a common ground for honest questions, open public dialogue, and the exploration of those things unfinished within us and between us, from racism to addiction. Whether hosting a town hall conversation in Williamson, West Virginia, in 1987 around the mayor's closing of the public pool because Robert "Mike" Sisco, a gay man living with AIDS, went swimming there, or convening two hundred men in 2010 who were sexually abused as children, Oprah has been steadfast in her untiring effort to publicly educate all our tribes about trauma and compassion.

Yet we in America largely fear community healing. We can see this in how we treat our war veterans. Psychotherapist Edward Tick, an expert on veteran trauma, reminds us that the word *anathema* comes from the Greek *ana thema*, meaning *against the theme of life, against the order of life, against the way of life.* Tick says that all war is *ana thema, against the way of life,* that such trespasses don't end when the physical violence is over. The war continues inside those who have chosen or been forced to take life. Yet, in our fear of what they've done and been through, we turn away from our veterans when they come home.

Tick describes how community-centered cultures work with veterans:

Indigenous cultures . . . watched over their warriors after their return. For example, among the Papago people of the American Southwest, after a warrior had his first experience of combat, they held a nineteen-day ceremony of return . . . [using] purification techniques to cleanse him, and also storytelling techniques . . . The war dance wasn't what Hollywood portrays it as: a bunch of savages whipping themselves into a frenzy before battle. It came *after* battle and was a dramatic reenactment of the conflict for the tribe . . . [So i]nstead of having a parade and going shopping, we could use our veterans' holidays as an occasion for storytelling. Open the churches and temples and synagogues and mosques and community centers and libraries across the country, and invite our veterans in to tell their stories.

Another indigenous example of community therapy comes from the Kaluli people of New Guinea. After the death of a family member, the holy ones are invited to dance and sing to help the grieving process their grief. This ritual dance is called Gisaro. As they mourn, those who can't stop crying and those who can't cry at all wait for the holy ones to come to their village. Once there, the holy ones learn about the life of the person who has died. Then they dance and sing stories about that person so the family can release their feelings. As a sign of gratitude and kinship, the mourners scar the Gisaro dancers, so they will carry the truth and pain of the loss for the tribe. Isn't this what we do for each other in the dance of deep friendship? When truly by the side of those who are grieving, aren't we scarred anyway in the crease of heart where we hold them?

These public rituals work because the truth once put in the open binds us, while the truth kept secret separates us. Consider this powerful story. From 1474 to 1778, Portugal was colonizing four countries in Africa: Angola, Cape Verde, Guinea-Bissau, and Mozambique. The Portuguese explorer Diogo Cão first landed in Angola in 1483. Like most European conquerors, their rule was oppressive. In an act of rebellion, a band of Angolan warriors kidnapped a ship of Portuguese soldiers once they came ashore. But instead of killing them, they took the soldiers deep into the jungle, tied them up, and told them the full story of their oppression—their pain and degradation and unnecessary losses. Then, without harming the soldiers, they let them go. This band of warriors did this several times. Several years later, a coup was staged to free the Angolans living under Portuguese rule. But it was the Portuguese soldiers forced to hear those stories who rose up to free the people they had abused.

In how they tied up their oppressors and forced them to listen to the effects of their oppression, these Angolan warriors can be seen as ancestors of the TRC in South Africa. The power of truthful storytelling brought out in the open can't be underestimated. These warriors didn't seek revenge, but bravely told their oppressors the truth of what their actions caused. In so doing, they deepened what it means to be a warrior.

Another, more contemporary example of pubic healing also comes from Africa. Libby Hoffman, a former political science professor, founded a non-profit organization called Catalyst for Peace (CFP). In the spring of 2008, CFP worked with John Caulker and the African human rights organization Forum of Conscience (FOC), to launch a project in Sierra Leone called Fambul Tok, which is Creole (Krio) for *Family Talk*.

In the aftermath of the brutal civil wars that took place in Sierra Leone from 1991 to 2002, the people—maimed, wounded, orphaned, and widowed—were ready to talk and listen to each other. So, on March 23, 2008, on the very day the war started seventeen years earlier—in the village of Kailahun, where the first shot was fired—thirty villagers gathered in a circle of chairs set out in the open. After a significant silence, a man with one arm began telling his story. After another silence, the one-armed man was asked if the person who cut off his arm was there. He nodded and pointed across the circle. After yet another silence, the man who lived near him came over, fell to his knees, and asked for forgiveness. Then, in their own way and in their own time, they began to ask each other, *What went wrong?* Such a simple and indispensable question: *What went wrong?*

Fambul Tok has had a lasting impact in the villages of Sierra Leone, because following the truth-telling ceremonies, activities are organized so the newly reconciled individuals can strengthen their connection by working together for the good of the community. They partner in projects like radio-listening clubs, football games, and village-initiated community farms. It's important to note that Fambul Tok is not rooted in Western concepts of blame and retribution, but in the African need for communities to restore wholeness, with each member playing a role.

We're beautifully born whole, though no one can escape the journey of trauma that undoes us. Yet, in time, we can be put back together, if given the chance to know and be known thoroughly. Putting ourselves back together, by finishing what is unfinished within us and between us, allows community to form. But each of us must find our own way to listen to what we've done to each other in order to make a university of our suffering. Each of us must find our own way to make public spaces intimate so we can help each other release our feelings. Each of us must find the lapse in our story and figure out what went wrong. This is work worth doing.

After years of grief and loss, the villagers in Sierra Leone define *peace* as being able to eat from one bowl, as one family. This is something to work toward.

The truth once put in the open binds us, while
the truth kept secret separates us.

When to Stand Up

The next two chapters explore what happened at Masada in 73 A.D., at Babi Yar in Russia, and during the Warsaw Ghetto Uprising in Poland, the last two taking place during World War II. The responses revealed in these confrontations live inside all of us: fighting to the death like those in the Warsaw Ghetto; or the numb, compliant walk of terror into the ditch at Babi Yar, just waiting to be shot; or the dreadful integrity with which those at Masada took their lives as a community rather than be enslaved by the Romans. I recognize these impulses—to fight, to be numb and compliant, or to leave. Like everyone who ever lived, I'm vulnerable and capable of each, not sure what leads me to one or the other.

Let's begin with Masada, an ancient Judean fortress perched on top of an isolated rock plateau, 1509 feet high. The natural approaches to the cliff are sheer and almost impossible to scale. The fortress has many towers. Within the encampment is a palace supported by barracks, storehouses for food, and cisterns for rainwater. Three narrow, winding paths lead to fortified gates.

Almost all we know about Masada and what happened there comes from the Jewish Roman historian Flavius Josephus (37–100), who had become a Roman to save his own life. Originally fortified in the first century B.C., the fortress fell to Herod the Great, a Roman king of Judea, in a power struggle that followed the death of his father. In 70 A.D., the Roman general Titus invaded Jerusalem. When the Jews wouldn't surrender, he destroyed the city. Many of the surviving Jews fled a burning Jerusalem to settle on the mountaintop at Masada.

In 73 A.D., the Roman governor of Judea, Flavius Silva, had had enough of the Jewish resistance and lay siege to Masada with the Tenth Roman Legion, along with auxiliary troops and Jewish prisoners. Surrounding Masada with 15,000 troops, the Romans settled into eight camps, and over three months built a wall around the base of the mountain as well as a 375-foot assault ramp with a battering ram. At first, the rebels of Masada threw stones at those building the ramp. But when the Romans put enslaved Jews to work on the ramp, the rebels stopped their attacks. Eventually, the Romans used the battering ram to break through the stone wall of the fortress and burned the interior wooden wall. Flavius Silva then ordered his troops to rest before the final assault the next day, when they would enter Masada. During the night, Elazar Ben Yair, the leader of the Jewish rebels, persuaded everyone among them that it would be better to die by their own hands than to be slaves to the Romans.

With testimony gathered from the few survivors, Josephus reconstructed part of Elazar's speech, "We were born to die, and we bore our children to die, and even the happiest and most content man cannot escape death. However, a man is not doomed to slavery and disgrace or to watching his wife and children suffer . . . Our hands are not yet tied . . . we can grasp the dagger. Let us bring our own salvation and kill ourselves before we fall as slaves in the hands of our enemies."

No one knows what kind of conversation followed. But once accepting Elazar's call, the rebels drew lots, and ten among them were chosen to kill the others. Then lots were drawn among those ten, and one was chosen to kill the other nine. The last Jew would then set fire to the fortress, leaving the wells and food storerooms full, as evidence that their death was not a result of hunger or thirst. With everyone gone, the last Jew was to drive a sword through his own heart.

According to Josephus, when Roman troops entered the fortress in the morning, they discovered 960 bodies. Only two women and five children, who had hidden in a cave, survived.

Josephus ends his account with this: "And when the Romans found the dead Jews, they did not rejoice in the death of their enemy, but were astonished by their great spirits and powerful deed."

What are we to make of this, today, in our modern lives? Was this tragic loss of life truly a great and powerful deed? What would we find impossible to live with? What would we as fiercely live for? And what might we as fiercely build together that could bridge our differences?

Almost 1900 years later, on September 29 and 30, 1941, the Nazis massacred 33,771 Jews at Babi Yar. Before those fall days in 1941, Babi Yar was known as a magnificent ravine in the Ukraine, near Kiev. The Russian novelist Anatoly Kuznetsov described the ravine as "enormous, you might even say majestic: deep and wide, like a mountain gorge. If you stood on one side of it and shouted you would scarcely be heard on the other." But it can only be known now as the site of one of the most brutal and heartless mass executions in history.

After bombing Kiev for eight days, the Nazis captured the city, which was home for 175,000 Jews. Within two weeks, the decision was made by Nazi officials to kill the Jews of Kiev. The executions were sanctioned by the military governor Major General Kurt Eberhard, SS officer Friedrich Jeckeln, and Commander Otto Rasch. The order was carried out by Colonel Paul Blobel.

The Germans posted public orders throughout the city. In Russian, they read:

> All Yids of the city of Kiev and its vicinity must appear on Monday, September 29, by 8 o'clock in the morning at the corner of Mel'nikova and Doktorivska streets (near the cemetery). Bring documents, money and valuables, and also warm clothing, linen, etc. Any Yids who do not follow this order and are found elsewhere will be shot. Any civilians who enter the dwellings left by Yids [to] appropriate the things in them will be shot.

With brutality and deception, thousands of Jews were gathered that morning near the cemetery, which was close to Babi Yar. They waited for hours, moving slowly toward what many imagined was a train. But once it was clear what awaited, there was little resistance. It's inappropriate to judge these victims, who were beaten and terrorized en route to their deaths, but we need to try to understand what unfolded.

Eventually, those in line could hear machine-gun fire in the distance. What must have been going through their frightened minds: *What was that? It's not for us. Or is it? Should we stay? Should we run? Should we fight? Will fighting make it worse? There's very little time! What should we do?!*

The crowd was so large that most of the victims didn't know what was happening. And yet the killing went on for two days. The 34,000 Jews vastly outnumbered the German soldiers, but there was no rebellion or effort to escape during the night. If they had tried to flee en masse, how many might have lived? Others have asked this question, from the safety of the war's end, but it's impossible to know or judge the reactions of a starving people, traumatized, and depressed by the bombings and the war.

After passing through the gate of the cemetery, they were forced to leave their baggage. Many wondered when they would get their belongings back. The soldiers herded the masses closer together. More machine-gun fire could be heard ahead. Some realized what was happening but it was too late to escape. The Germans formed a barricade and checked papers.

At the front of the line, groups of ten were led through a gauntlet of soldiers, who started beating those who walked by. There was a perverse frenzy to how the Germans were hitting innocent people. Led onto a ridge overgrown with grass, those nearest the ravine were told to undress. Those who hesitated were kicked and stripped with sadistic fury.

Naked and terrified, they were forced into the ditch and shot. Then, more rows of ten were forced to lie on top of those shot before them. Again and again. There was no way out and yet there was less and less resistance. Layers upon layers of dead bodies filled the vast ditch. We can see why the Jews at Masada took their own lives.

How do any of us know when to stand up and when to give up? At a very weak and painful point in my journey through cancer, my former wife took my hand and said, "If it gets to be too much, it's okay." I'd never thought of giving up, but realized there might come a time when giving up was the right thing to do.

Very few survived Babi Yar. Those who did, though badly wounded, managed to crawl from under the corpses and scurry into hiding once the Germans left. One survivor remembers how she looked down from the edge of the ravine before being shot, and her head began to swim. Beneath her was a sea of bodies covered in blood.

These terrible things happened: at Masada, at Babi Yar, and elsewhere. You would think something as horrific as the annihilation of the Jews by the Nazis would be the end of depravity. But genocides have continued to happen. There was the cruelty of the Khmer Rouge in Cambodia in the 1970s, the ethnic cleansing in Bosnia and the Rwanda genocide in the 1990s, and the slaughter in Darfur in the early 2000s. And more recently there has been the bombing and poisoning of Syrians by their own president.

As we look on all this from the safety we're blessed to have, there's a responsibility for those of us not in line to speak up and keep the violence from growing. In 2006, sixty-five years after Babi Yar, Yisrael Meir Lau, the chief rabbi of Tel Aviv, spoke at a memorial conference in Kiev, calling for us to stop being silent. Rabbi Lau—who, at seven years old, was found hiding under a pile of corpses at Buchenwald by a U.S. Army chaplain—said at the memorial service:

> Maybe Babi Yar was a test for Hitler. If . . . Babi Yar [could] happen and the world did not react seriously . . . [he could kill more].
> So a few months later in January 1942, near Berlin in Wannsee, a convention was held with a decision [to go ahead with] a final solution to the Jewish problem . . . Maybe if the world's action had been a serious one, a dramatic one, in September 1941, here in the Ukraine, the Wannsee Conference would have come to a different end . . .

How do any of us know when to stand up and when to give up?

Facing Evil

The Warsaw Ghetto Uprising, the largest single revolt by any group of Jews during World War II, took place in Nazi-occupied Poland from April 19 to May 16, 1943. Though there was no way out, and perhaps because there was no way out, the Jewish resistance persisted for three months, finally erupting into full-scale armed conflict with the German SS. Unlike their ancestors who killed themselves at Masada, and unlike their contemporaries who were herded into the ditch at Babi Yar, the Polish Jews were determined to fight, knowing they couldn't defeat their captors.

In 1939, the Germans had crowded more than three million of Poland's Jews into ghettos set up in captured Polish cities. The Warsaw Ghetto was the largest, densely packing almost 400,000 people in a 1.3-square-mile area. Within months, thousands of Jews died from disease and starvation.

In September 1942, the German resettlement commissioner, SS officer Hermann Höfle, met with the leader of the ghetto's Jewish Council, Adam Czerniaków, and ordered 7000 Jews a day for resettlement to the East. Believing his people were being relocated, Czerniaków cooperated. In the months that followed, almost 300,000 Jews were sent to the concentration camp Treblinka, where they were murdered. When Czerniaków discovered the truth, he committed suicide.

As the truth spread throughout the ghetto, there was outrage and despair and widespread terror. In the midst of the chaos, a Jewish resistance movement began to organize a revolt. For the first time in captivity, there was a growing sentiment that it was better to fight to the last than to quietly board the death trains. Let's pause here to imagine the internal difficulty for everyone in that ghetto, resisting or not. There would never be a fear-free moment again. There was only the suppression of fear and the search for a resolve that might guard the flicker of dignity that some still believed was there under the degradation and terror.

In secrecy, resisters began to gather weapons any way they could. They bought, stole, and traded food and personal belongings for revolvers, machine guns, rifles, hand grenades, and bags of ammunition. The Germans weren't used to meeting resistance. The German commander of Warsaw, Jurgen Stroop, wrote in his dispassionate report:

> When we invaded the Ghetto for the first time, the Jews and [some] Polish bandits succeeded in repelling participating units, including tanks and armored cars, by a well-prepared concentration of fire . . . One such battle group succeeded in mounting a truck by ascending from a sewer on Prosta [Street] . . .

In response, the German task force would swell to more than 2000 men armed with mine-throwers, medium artillery pieces, and more than 200 machine guns. The Nazis sent in an additional 800 paramilitary soldiers. All to silence 1000 Jews who had endured their fear until it peeled away into a fearless desperation.

On the morning of January 18, 1943, the Germans swiftly and brutally entered the Warsaw Ghetto by surprise, demanding Jews report for deportation. But now, the Jews of Warsaw knew where they would be taken and for the first time they refused to report voluntarily. Only a small number acquiesced to the German calls to file into the streets with their papers. The Germans started snatching people where they could.

That day, a group of resisters was caught, but as they were being led away, others who were armed dispersed among the crowd and, on Mordechai Anielewicz's command, attacked the Germans. One of the first actions of fighting back that day came from a young girl of seventeen who attacked a German soldier with a knife. Though she was killed, she made it visibly clear for the first time that the Germans weren't invincible. They could bleed, they could fall, they could be afraid, they could die.

All the Jewish fighters gathered that day were shot. Only Mordechai Anielewicz survived. Elsewhere, another group of Jewish resisters ambushed German soldiers as they burst into Jewish homes. For the first time in the history of the ghetto, Germans had come to physical harm. There were German casualties.

The events of January 18 led hundreds of people in the Warsaw Ghetto to join the fight. This included women and children sparsely armed with handguns and gasoline bottles. Most of those fighting didn't think their actions would save them. Rather, they were now battling for the honor of the Jewish people and to protest the world's silence.

In his diary that night, Shmuel Winter wrote:

> Had we but resisted, at least as much as we resisted during the last deportation, the Nazis would not have succeeded so easily in destroying such a large Jewish community. If the Jews had at the very least not gone of their own free will, but stubbornly hidden as they have been doing in the last few days—then the deportation would have lasted for months on end. One shudders to think that it required a quarter of a million Jews to give their lives, for the remainder to understand the reality of the situation . . .

For the next three months, there was an endless skirmish between the Jewish resisters and the infuriated Germans. On April 19, 1943, the ghetto erupted. The SS forces violently entered the ghetto. They were planning to deport every Jew within three days. But the Germans were ambushed by a well-prepared Jewish force tossing hand grenades and Molotov cocktails from alleyways, sewers, and windows. Stunned by the assault, the Germans retreated. Two of their armored vehicles were set on fire. The next day, police commander Ferdinand von Sammern-Frankenegg lost his post.

That day, two ghetto boys climbed on the roof of a building in the square and raised the red-and-white Polish flag and a blue-and-white Jewish banner. The flags remained highly visible for four days. The German commander Stroop noted after the war:

The matter of the flags was of great political and moral importance. It reminded hundreds of thousands of the Polish cause. It excited them and unified the Jews and Poles. We all knew that. Himmler bellowed into the phone: "Stroop, you must at all costs bring down those two flags!"

On April 22, Stroop issued an ultimatum to the Jews of Warsaw to surrender or be annihilated. Knowing they would be annihilated anyway, the Jewish resisters rejected the ultimatum. Stroop then ordered his soldiers to systematically burn the houses in the ghetto block by block using flamethrowers and fire bottles, blowing up basements and sewers. The only surviving uprising commander, Marek Edelman, recalled in 2003:

The sea of flames flooded houses and courtyards . . . there was no air, only black, choking smoke and heavy burning heat radiating from the red-hot walls, from the glowing stone stairs.

Yet, in a letter to a friend, Mordechai Anielewicz wrote:

What happened [yesterday] exceeded our boldest dreams. The Germans fled twice from the ghetto. One of our companies held its position for forty minutes, while the other one lasted—upwards of six hours . . . I can't describe to you the conditions in which the Jews are living. Only a handful will survive. All the rest will succumb, sooner or later. Their fate has been sealed. In almost all of the bunkers in which our friends are hiding one cannot even light a candle at night, for lack of air. Goodbye my friend. Perhaps we will see each other again. The main thing is this: My life's dream has become a reality. I have seen the Jewish defense of the ghetto in all its strength and glory.

Stroop's burning of Warsaw would last an entire month. Eventually, the organization of the resisters weakened and collapsed. Thousands of Jews fled into the sewer system and hid within the ruins of the ghetto. The Germans brought in dogs to search the ruins and dropped smoke bombs to force people into the streets. They flooded the sewers and then exploded them.

On May 8, the Germans discovered the remaining leadership of the Jewish resistance. But rather than be captured, most of the leaders, like their ancestors at Masada, committed mass suicide. Along with their chief commander, Mordechai Anielewicz, they ingested cyanide. Two days later, his deputy Marek Edelman escaped the ghetto through the sewers.

On May 10, a member of the Polish government in exile, Szmul Zygielbojm, received word in London of the destruction of the Warsaw Ghetto. Distraught, he committed suicide in heartfelt protest to the world's inaction in the face of the Holocaust. In his suicide note, he wrote:

> I cannot continue to live and be silent while the remnants of Polish Jewry are being murdered . . . I belong with them . . . By my death, I give expression to my profound protest against the inaction in which the world watches and permits the destruction of the Jewish people.

The uprising officially ended on May 16, 1943, when Stroop personally pushed the button that exploded the Great Synagogue of Warsaw. The ghetto was now leveled and 13,000 Jews had been killed during the uprising. Most of the remaining 50,000 Jewish civilians were sent to concentration camps. The Germans recorded a total of 110 casualties—17 dead and 93 injured—though by Edelman's count, the Nazis suffered about 300 casualties. Stroop was later captured by Americans in Germany, convicted of war crimes, and executed by hanging in Poland in 1952.

In 1968, on the twenty-fifth anniversary of the Jewish resistance, one of the survivors, Yitzhak Zuckerman, was asked what military lessons could be learned from the uprising. He replied:

> I don't think there's any real need to analyze the Uprising in military terms. This was a war of less than a thousand people against a mighty army and no one doubted how it was likely to

turn out. This isn't a subject for study in military school . . . If there's a school to study the human spirit, there it should be a major subject.

At the web page Voices from the Inferno: Holocaust Survivors Describe the Last Months in the Warsaw Ghetto, you can listen to survivors of the uprising testify to what they went through. Listening to their voices, in Polish, Yiddish, and German, you can hear the indestructible resolve that lives in all of us, whether you understand what they're saying or not. In their worn but vibrant faces, you can see the strength that comes from being cut to the bone. You can see the fragility that comes from surviving what's unspeakably evil. This will touch you in a place I hope you and I never have to access. Though we must know this place and honor these survivors for their raw resurgence of dignity.

You may have already been asking yourself, *What would I have done?* It's a necessary question that can't possibly be answered until we're on the edge between life and death. Yet ask it we must. One thing is clear: it's not where we're going that matters, but how we are while we are here.

> There was only the search for a resolve that might guard the flicker of dignity that some still believed was there under the degradation and terror.

In the Middle of the Storm

We think we make choices, but no one in the history of the world has chosen how they love, any more than an orchid chooses its color or the degree to which it opens. And no one chooses to be straight or gay or bisexual or transgender. We root in the earth and grow into the light and open completely if given enough time. Yet the lesbian, gay, bisexual, and transgender (LGBT) community has been demonized, criminalized, and persecuted for centuries.

Despite this harsh history, same-sex relationships have a long and healthy lineage. For centuries, the Etoro and Marind-anim tribes of Papua New Guinea were built on same-sex relationships. In fact, they viewed heterosexual relationships as odd and sinful, though their demonization of the straight life was no less insidious than the long prejudice against same-sex relationships.

Prior to European conquest, the indigenous peoples of the Americas, including the Aztecs and Mayans, engaged in same-sex relationship freely. Outraged by what they found, the Spanish conquerors stigmatized this peaceful way of life as sodomy and attempted to banish it by brutalizing the indigenous peoples they met in the Americas. In 1513, the Spanish explorer Balboa burned gay indigenous tribal members and had them torn to pieces by his dogs. Their horrific tortures were far worse than any imagined moral trespass.

Indigenous same-sex relationships developed over hundreds of years. A bisexual child was recognized at an early age as a Two-Spirit individual. Allowed by their parents to discover which path was natural for them, Two-Spirit individuals were considered wise and precocious. They were viewed as shamans, capable of mystical powers.

In China, same-sex relationships were prevalent as far back as 600 B.C., and in Japan and Thailand for over a thousand years. The ancient Greek poet Sappho, who wrote passionately about both sexes, was born on the island of Lesbos, which became the namesake for lesbians.

In Europe, Sigmund Freud held that neither heterosexuality nor homosexuality was inborn and that bisexuality was the normal human condition, thwarted by society out of fear and neurosis. The analytic terms *homosexual* and *heterosexual* were only coined in the nineteenth century, the term *bisexual* brought into usage in the twentieth century. Each seems to have been voiced by those outside the LGBT experience, in much the way that intuition is often characterized as irrational or even demonic by those unfamiliar with it or afraid of it.

Persecution of homosexuals and other non-heterosexual people was coarse and widespread throughout Europe. Hitler arrested close to 100,000 gays and lesbians, of whom 15,000 were tortured and killed in concentration camps. And though same-sex marriage is now legal in the United States, vestiges of pernicious prejudice still infect America and the rest of the world, just as racism lingers, though mandated segregation is illegal. Hard as it is to comprehend, same-sex intercourse still carries the death penalty in several modern nations: Uganda, Saudi Arabia, Qatar, Iran, Iraq, Mauritania, Nigeria, Sudan, Somalia, the United Arab Emirates, and Yemen. Yet, it is how we cast what we fear as unnatural and evil that is insidious and dangerous.

Within this long history of persecution, I want to tell you about one small group's heroic response to adversity. In New York City in March 1987, playwright and novelist Larry Kramer was asked to speak at the Lesbian and Gay Community Center in Greenwich Village.

The film director David France describes that spring:

The gay ghetto was a tinderbox by March 1987. Ten thousand New Yorkers had already become sick with AIDS; half were dead. Along Christopher Street you could see the dazed look of the doomed, skeletons and their caregivers alike. There was not even a false-hope pill for doctors to prescribe.

Then the posters appeared. A small collective of artists had been working on a striking image they hoped would galvanize the community to act. Overnight, images bearing the radical truism SILENCE = DEATH appeared on walls and scaffolding all over lower Manhattan. The fuse was set—and then the writer and activist Larry Kramer struck a match.

Without anyone realizing what was unfolding, that meeting birthed the AIDS Coalition to Unleash Power (ACT UP), a movement of tender, raw souls who by caring for each other and fighting for their lives with dignity would save future generations from the plague of AIDS.

Frustrated by the federal government's slow response to the AIDS crisis, ACT UP organized protests and demonstrations. Though none of their members had scientific training, the core of ACT UP helped to identify promising new drug treatments and they encouraged patient trials. Even as these first AIDS activists were dying, their tireless engagement and hard work over many years finally made AIDS a manageable condition.

The peak of ACT UP's work from 1987 to 1996 is a remarkable example of a self-organized community brought into existence because their lives were in danger. Because they were grossly mistreated at every turn, gay men had to create their own society within the larger society.

From 1992 to 1995, 8.5 million people died from AIDS. And though under siege by both disease and exile, ACT UP served as a bedrock of hope, empowerment, and steadfast compassion. As stars can only be seen in the dark, these spirits were their brightest during the plague years in which AIDS decimated the gay population and frightened the world. The capacity of these brave men and women to stand authentically in their situation, while many of them were sick, models the raw power of democracy. They became a creative collective, learning out of necessity to become their own researchers, educators, medical advocates, media strategists, and government lobbyists. Early on, Mark Harrington created a glossary of AIDS and its Pandora's box of evolving treatments, which was distributed freely. ACT UP then challenged the FDA and drug companies and developed their own sound and humane AIDS research agenda, detailing where and how to begin. Their protocol was finally adopted by the FDA.

Scientists finally learned that the AIDS virus itself doesn't kill but compromises the immune system, opening all the doors in the body for opportunistic infections to come streaming in. Collaborating with members of ACT UP and the FDA, chemists at the drug company Merck discovered protease inhibitors, which, in combination with other drugs, became the breakthrough treatment to arrest the development of the virus in HIV-infected individuals.

Many of the early pioneers in ACT UP died. Discriminated against in schools, hospitals, businesses, and at every level of government, they were treated like the lepers of their time, though they endured as bodhisattvas of our age.

In February of 2004, the mayor of San Francisco, Gavin Newsom, ordered the city-county clerk to issue marriage licenses to same-sex couples. Jubilantly, thousands poured into the streets to celebrate their right to love. A month later, the California Supreme Court overturned Newsom's directive, yet on June 26, 2015, the United States Supreme Court legalized gay and lesbian marriage throughout one of the largest countries on Earth.

When I stop to take in what all these brave souls endured and accomplished, when I stop to put down my assumptions and conclusions—when my hands are empty and my heart starts to open—I am returned to our natural kinship with each other, no matter our path. Then I can see the man or woman wandering the streets, not as homeless but as a human being without a home. Then I can see the one just out of prison, not as an ex-convict but as someone who made a mistake. Then I can see the one born with both sexes, not as an aberration that needs to be pruned into male or female, but as a rare and beautiful flower in the human garden.

When I dare to listen, not knowing what I will hear, the differences that parade between us evaporate and it's just *us*, breathing the same air. Then I'm reminded that no one knows what being alive is like or where this life will lead. Any sense of what's normal is just an illusion.

We all need the courage to be vulnerable with each other, no matter how different our experience may seem. When we encounter difference, we need to resist the fear that wants to make everything we meet just like us. Such sameness is crippling. Instead, we need to open our histories and listen, so we can be made whole by the parts of life we lack.

Today, being a global citizen requires the courage to stay truthful about our experience *and* the courage to be touched and shaped by the faces of humanity we meet and help along the way.

> When I stop to put down my assumptions and conclusions—when my hands are empty and my heart starts to open—I am returned to our natural kinship with each other, no matter our path.

Turning Fire into Light

David Anderson Hooker is a leading peace-builder who teaches at the Kroc Institute for International Peace Studies at the University of Notre Dame. As a boy, he returned in 1973 to Moultrie, Georgia, where his family had lived before he was born. In the center of that southern town, the Hanging Block, erected for public lynchings in the 1800s, had been replaced with a Liberty Bell. For white children who never knew of the Hanging Block, the change had little significance, but to Hooker, an African-American, the substitution was both freeing and suspect.

Moultrie is a small town originally situated within the colony of Georgia, which was founded in 1732 and named for England's king, George II. In the 1830s, a wave of immigrants sailed from England to America, and a few landed just sixty miles from the Florida coast to settle in what would become Moultrie. Thousands of acres of fertile Georgian land were cleared there, tilled, and seeded by African slaves for the lucrative harvest of corn, tobacco, peanuts, and cotton. In 1879, the city of Moultrie was chartered and named after a Revolutionary War hero, General William Moultrie.

Lynching in America was named for Charles Lynch, a Virginia planter turned militia officer, who organized the unauthorized punishment of criminals, including public whippings and hangings, as early as 1780. In time, lynching became the execution of an individual without due process of law. After the Civil War, a domestic genocide of African-Americans took place. Lynching in Southern states became so common, it was impossible to keep accurate records. The *Chicago Tribune* reported that between 1882 and 1903, 3,337 blacks were known to have been lynched by white mobs.

The following is an account of a lynching that took place in Moultrie, Georgia, on July 15, 1921, described by an eyewitness for a local newspaper:

Williams was brought from Moultrie on Friday night by sheriffs ... Saturday court was called ... The trial took half an hour.
Then Williams, surrounded by fifty sheriffs armed with machine
guns, started out of the courthouse door toward the jail ... 500
[whites] rushed the sheriffs, who made no resistance ... They
tore the negro's clothing off... The negro was unsexed, as usual,
and made to eat a portion of his anatomy ... The negro was
chained to [a] stump ... The pyre was lit and a hundred men ...
women, old and young, grandmothers among them, joined
hands and danced around the negro while he burned.

The legacy of this inhuman, despicable part of our American history endures today. And Dr. Hooker's questions for Moultrie strike at
the heart of what all communities need to face in order to transform:
What made white people erect the Hanging Block in the first place?
What made them celebrate the mutilation and murder of a fellow
human being? What made people from the same town fifty-two years
later finally take down that wretched Hanging Block? What did they
do with it once they dismantled it? What made them replace it with
a Liberty Bell? Did this change truly signal a new era of equality and
freedom, or was the Hanging Block secretly reassembled somewhere
else? If the next generation has awakened to the history of its own
brutality, by what process might they make restitution and reclaim
their humanity?

Thirty-five years after the Hanging Block was dismantled in
Moultrie, Georgia, Barack Obama became the first African-American
elected president. His inauguration took place on the steps of the
U.S. Capitol, which were constructed by slaves in 1793. Like many, I
was moved to believe that we had endured a significant healing with
regard to race in our country. Yet, in the 2016 presidential election, I
learned that, while we have made progress, racists have grown more
virulent in the face of President Obama's dignity and achievements,
which clearly eclipsed their own. Like dinosaurs rearing and flailing
at the press of their extinction, white male supremacists are rearing
and flailing as they struggle against the mainstream of decency and
equality.

It's within this context that I speak of the tragedy and mysterious healing that took place in Charleston, South Carolina, in the summer of 2015. For the past twelve years, I have gone every spring to Charleston to teach at the Sophia Institute, and have become close friends with the founders, Carolyn Rivers and Henk Brandt, and the poet–praise-singer Kurtis Lamkin. They have introduced me to many good people in Charleston, black and white. We've walked many times past the storied Emanuel African Methodist Episcopal Church—"Mother Emanuel"—just two blocks away, a focal point of the civil rights movement of the sixties.

On June 17, 2015, a twenty-one-year-old white supremacist murdered nine beautiful souls in that legendary church, after sitting with them for an hour as they prayed. He was calculating and remorseless and his act devastated the community. He wanted to start a race war, to stir anger and retribution. He wanted his worst to bring out the worst in everyone else. Yet, within twenty-four hours, the captured killer stood in court before the loved ones of the slain. Several forgave him for his heinous acts while telling him how deeply he had hurt them.

There were no riots in Charleston, no looting, no vandalism. People gathered from all over the country in raw support. More South Carolinians than ever before questioned the Confederate flag flying above their capitol building as a stubborn remnant of a white hierarchy that built its fortune on slavery and oppression. Instead of instigating more violence, the tragic murder of these nine kind souls only highlighted their goodness, empowering thousands to reveal their own goodness.

Later that month, on June 26, 2015, after the Supreme Court legalized same-sex marriage, President Obama offered a eulogy in Charleston for Reverend Clementa Pinckney and the others who had been murdered just a week before. He affirmed that in a true nation, everyone is welcome and everyone has inherent dignity.

Having come of age in the sixties, when many of those who we admired were assassinated, I am grateful to have seen a president of true greatness in my lifetime. With the compassion and acumen of FDR and the humanity of Lincoln, President Obama led our nation with many unique gifts. In his eloquence, he can turn fire into light. Yet it's the depth of his soul that makes him a great man. His depth of soul shows us our own, and his courage to stand in the open holds our flaws in the light of our possibilities. I am also grateful for the dignity of the five Supreme Court justices and the generations who have risked their safety to stand for both civil rights and gay rights. In so doing, they have crested the oldest of walls, prejudice, and have solidified and extended freedom for us all.

> In a true nation, everyone is welcome and
> everyone has inherent dignity.

Reclaiming Our Humanity

Some day man will see
the entire light of this planet
through the window of a tear...
—León Felipe

How do we move from playing out our unacknowledged pain on others to facing our own suffering? How do we undo our obsession with vengeance and begin to soothe each other with the music that rises from our broken places? What are the incremental steps by which we lose our humanity and the steps by which we regain it? Whether victim or perpetrator, how do we recover from our isolation enough to live together with integrity and compassion? While I have no answers, I believe that asking and listening enliven our ability to live together. The art of facing our dark side and the courage to own how we hurt others are not objects we can hold in our hand, yet they can determine whether we can truly hold anything at all.

Often, extreme stories of trespass and cruelty can bring to light underlying truths. In 1994, one month after the terrible genocide in Rwanda, Athanase Hagengimana received word that one of his Tutsi sisters had been murdered. He was living in Nairobi and felt compelled to return home to try to find her remains. En route, he was intercepted by a nun who warned him not to go back, because one of his other sisters, an elected senator in Rwanda, was part of the Hutu State that had authorized the killings. He would not be safe.

He turned around and flew back to Nairobi, grief-stricken at his one sister's death and feeling guilty that his other sister was capable of such cruelty. He remembered his Hutu sister as lovely and kind. It was she who had paid for his schooling. Now wanted by the International Court of Justice, she was probably hiding in the rain forest of the Congo, if she were still alive. The tension of his feelings for his sisters is what shaped Dr. Hagengimana's work as the only psychiatrist in that war-ravaged country.

For five years after the genocide, Dr. Hagengimana trained counselors while working with those who had suffered through the mass atrocity. It was like picking up the bloodied shards of a thousand pots and trying to piece them back together. It was impossible. He could only work to round the edges and piece together something new.

As part of a yearlong experiment funded by the John Templeton Foundation, Dr. Hagengimana attempted to break the bitterness between the surviving Hutus and Tutsis. Though efforts were made to have both sides listen to one another, their deep wounds wouldn't permit them to hear each other. Hutus would congregate away from the Tutsis at every meeting. Tutsis would turn their backs and refuse help from any Hutu. So when talking stalled, mixed groups of survivors were asked to build things together.

Over the course of a year, one group was given a small shop to erect and open for business. Another group was given a field to cultivate and harvest, and asked to sell the produce and split the profits. A third was introduced to animal husbandry. Others were invited to rebuild homes. No one was forced to participate. And slowly, though not in all cases, survivors showed up to work together on simple common goals. This joint effort toward building small things somehow enabled an unspoken acceptance to rise between those who were scarred and those who did the scarring.

In time, when a Tutsi would fall as he carried the weight of a two-by-four, a Hutu would help him up. No words were exchanged. Another man, a Tutsi, was seen bringing water to Hutu workers who were tired. Life went on. Ten years have passed since this experiment and Dr. Hagengimana, who is doing research on the power of apology, remarks, "It is rewarding to go back and see a few Hutus and Tutsis clear the burned ground in order to clean a place where they can marry each other."

A quiet lesson in this story, useful to us all, is that *healing is hidden in the act of building small things together.* For there is something profound and bonding in lifting the fallen tree that blocks our way—

together. Something ineffable yet binding in nailing a roof after the storm—*together.* Working with another to make it through the day is a medicine too often ignored.

Even when the sting of our wounds and our sense of outrage prevent us from being kind, something deep within us is ready to betray our injustice and be kind nonetheless. We often try to quiet this humane impulse. If lucky, our unconditional kindness wins and we keep the world going, a human inch at a time.

The family of Pumla Gobodo-Madikizela had been brutalized by the methodical technicians of apartheid in South Africa. After all her loss, she served on the Truth and Reconciliation Commission (TRC) in 1996 as a committee member on the commission's human rights violations committee. And after all her suffering, she found herself charged with interviewing Eugene de Kock, the officer of state who sanctioned apartheid death squads. Charged with eighty-nine counts of murder, assault, and kidnapping, de Kock was not allowed to apply for amnesty and was sentenced to 212 years in a maximum-security prison in Pretoria.

Gobodo-Madikizela found herself sitting in a concrete room at a simple table, opposite this man known in the streets as "Prime Evil." As they spent hours together, de Kock began to shake and show remorse, as if he were suddenly awakening to the horrors he had authored. Instinctively, she reached to comfort him and placed her warm African hand on his cold white forearm. She was alarmed at her own gesture. How could she comfort the one who had murdered so many? But through her irrepressible kindness, the secret of the oppressed showed its gentle, unshakable truth: it is the kindness that endures, that keeps the brutalized from becoming brutal, that keeps the soil of tomorrow soft enough for things to grow in it. Gobodo-Madikizela couldn't help herself. Through her uncontrollable compassion, she witnessed how de Kock was evil and yet still human.

The ethical terrain uncovered here is neither "Turn the other cheek" nor "An eye for an eye," but keeping the heart soft and open. We all participate in this, like it or not. By facing evil with an open and strong heart, we give no amnesty to our inhuman impulses, but demand that the inhuman become human again, that we pick up what we have broken, look squarely at what we have done, and mend what we can and ourselves.

And so, in the nationally televised TRC hearings, a surviving African man from Soweto faced the Afrikaner who tied a plastic bag around his head and beat him for days, looked him in the eye, and, with the dignity of the ages, said, "What kind of man are you?" And his strong human stare into his perpetrator's numb face with the world watching transformed the brutalizer in a different way than twenty years in prison would. That man began to weep at what he'd done.

Such things as clearing burned streets together in Rwanda and making South African perpetrators look long into the wounds they inflicted are daring in the landscape of spiritual justice. These unprecedented efforts at restoring humanity have implications for us all. They do not replace accountability. They deepen it.

To understand some of these implications, we need to return to Dr. Hagengimana's work in Rwanda. Compelled to understand the conditions that allowed ordinary people to be able to kill, he discerned that such individuals must assume a state of mind in which they stop "being themselves," a state of mind in which they no longer see the people they hurt as human. In Rwanda, he could trace four attributes that contributed to this dehumanized state: assuming masks, initiating violence in the dark, wearing a uniform, and acting under the sanction of a larger authority, such as the government.

Covering your face and acting in the dark—where you can't clearly see who you hurt and where your violent actions can't clearly be attributed to you—make it easier to step outside of your normal self. Similarly, wearing a uniform and assuming another role lessens the barrier to inflicting harm. Soldiers in uniform more readily fire weapons than those in street clothes, because it is expected that soldiers are supposed to maim and kill. Likewise, when a government sanctions killing as patriotic and necessary for the good of the society, this suspends the more universal taboo against killing and makes violence permissible. Not surprisingly, hate groups, such as the KKK and the Nazi street gangs in Germany, have historically worn uniforms and masks and worked in the dark under the encouragement of a larger authority.

In Rwandan, the word *gacaca* (*ga'-cha-cha*) means *being on the grass and listening to the stories of those who have been wounded*. The atrocities in Rwanda were so widespread that when the rule of law was restored there weren't enough magistrates and courts to hear over 130,000 cases. So *gacaca* courts were instituted and hundreds of citizens were enlisted as official witnesses to hear the expressions of sorrow in an unprecedented practice of *communal listening*. But how can we do this for each other before the atrocities begin?

Repeatedly, we are called to face the fact that we are kept from becoming evil by small choices. If we don't keep our hearts open and stay awake, we will inch our way toward being cruel. The prevention of atrocity starts in our daily lives, *before* we stop being ourselves, when nothing seems to be at stake.

And staying awake means dropping our masks when we realize we have strapped them on. It means moving back into the open when we have somehow started to operate in the dark. It means taking off the clothes or costume that others would have us wear and work in. It means staying as naked as possible, unadorned as we can bear. It means honoring the sanctity of life that is natural and abiding, no matter the temporary injunctions that rail at us from the powers of the day. It means instilling these simple values in our children. It means holding a mirror to each other each time we stray. It means helping each other find the courage to give up our illusions and look within ourselves. It demands that, through kindness, the inhuman become human again, so we might clear the burned ground, one more time, in order to build small things together.

By facing evil with an open and strong heart, we give no amnesty to our inhuman impulses, but demand that the inhuman become human again.

Questions to Live With

+ Bring four or five friends together. In conversation, have each of you describe someone you admire for how they face adversity. What can you learn from them about how to work with what you're given? In the next three weeks, help someone discover their own way of meeting adversity. Encourage each person in your small group to convene a similar group on their own to explore the same questions.

+ Bring four or five friends together. In conversation, have each of you describe something you have worked on and cared about that you had to build again. How did you face this? How did you do it? What did you learn from this experience? In the next three weeks, identify something in your community that needs to be built again. Encourage each person in your small group to convene a similar group on their own to explore the same questions.

+ Bring four or five friends together. In conversation, have each of you describe what you might say to a child about the nature of hardship and obstacles, their role in our lives, and how to best meet them. In the next three weeks, begin to work with a hardship or obstacle that has been difficult for you and your community. Encourage each person in your small group to convene a similar group on their own to explore the same questions.

+ Bring four or five friends together. In conversation, have each of you tell the story of a time when you were moved to help another person though you didn't know them well. What made you get involved and help? Was it a life-giving or life-draining experience? Will you get involved again? In the next three weeks, be open to helping a stranger. Encourage each person in your small group to convene a similar group on their own to explore the same questions.

+ Bring four or five friends together. In conversation, have each of you describe a value or pattern of inherited behavior that you're struggling to free yourself from. Why do you want to change this? What kind of resistance are you facing? In the next three weeks, identify one pattern of inherited behavior in your community that needs to change and convene a conversation about this. Encourage each person in your small group to convene a similar group on their own to explore the same questions.

+ When faced with fear, we have these impulses: to fight, to go numb and compliant, or to leave. Bring four or five friends together. In conversation, have each of you describe a time when you experienced each impulse and where each led you. Without judgment, how do you value these impulses and what would you like to learn next in how to face fear? In the next three weeks, identify a place of fear in your community and begin a conversation on how you and others might face it. Encourage each person in your small group to convene a similar group on their own to explore the same questions.

+ Bring four or five friends together. In conversation, have each of you explore what it means to you to reclaim your humanity. Describe a situation in which you felt that you lost some of your humanity and how you went about repairing who you are and becoming whole again. In the next three weeks, support a project in your community that supports the reclaiming of our humanity. Encourage each person in your small group to convene a similar group on their own to explore the same questions.

Our Interests Are the Same

Man did not weave the web of life,
he is merely a strand in it.
Whatever he does to the web,
he does to himself.
—CHIEF SEATTLE

M artina Whelsula, a Native American from the Seattle area, shared that when she came of age she was handed a bundle of sacred objects. She was then charged to be kind and gentle in her life. This is an ancient Native instruction which we can only inhabit by living. For isn't the heart of our journey to discover how what is sacred can help us be kind and gentle? Isn't this the perennial task of community? We are constantly being asked, "What is in your sacred bundle and how can you pass it on?"

Each of the stories in this book and the lives they represent is part of the sacred bundle we know as community, and each mirrors what is possible between us. If we listen under all our politics, we can hear the elders of all traditions. Can you hear them? Their voices mix in the wind before we wake. They plead and demand that we open what is sacred, within us and between us, and make good use of it. In family, in friendship, in town halls, in synagogues, in mosques, in churches, in elder circles, in diplomacy and treaties, what is there to do but place what is sacred in a bundle and pass it on?

When We Understand

When you understand, you belong to the family;
When you do not understand, you are a stranger.
—THE GATELESS GATE

I began this book with a quote from the great historian Howard Zinn, which came from a long conversation we had in the fall of 2005. I asked Howard where we might turn to study examples of people working well together, no matter how fleeting. I want to share his response:

"People are not told about those early months in 1936 in Spain at the very beginning of the Spanish Civil War, described by George Orwell in his book *Homage to Catalonia*. This was a period in which you might say that the anarchists of Catalonia took over the city of Barcelona. Took over but not in a controlling or dominant way, but rather they took over in a different sense. In those months in Barcelona, there was no over-reaching authority. There was no police state. People policed themselves. There was virtually no crime. People shared things. There was no stark inequality. People traded goods and services and took care of one another. And Orwell describes it in such a beautiful way in his book. When you have things like that happen, even for a brief period, it suggests that it could happen for a longer period.

"I'm reminded of a brief moment in French history in 1871 when the Commune of Paris was formed. People really acted in common, in community, for themselves. They created an amazing, though short, period of equality and justice in Paris, where people gathered together every day and talked with one another. No one would accept salaries much higher than anybody else. One of the first things they did was to float hot-air balloons over the countryside, and those in the balloons dropped leaflets to the French peasants, and the leaflets had a very simple sentence on them: 'Our interests are the same.'

"I think this is the most important message we can address to one another. We are all human beings. Our interests are the same. Our problem is to discern which interests have been artificially drummed into us: like the interest of accumulating a lot of money, or the interest of being a stronger country than any other, or even the interest of being more beautiful than anyone else. These false, artificial interests have been inculcated. I can't think of anything more important to do than to be able to resist these false interests and to declare our common interests . . ."

When the Paris Commune came into power, the citizens of Paris were separated from those living in the rural provinces by a blockade. The idea of reaching those in the provinces via hot-air balloons was, in fact, risky. In all, sixty-five balloons were launched. With very little ability to navigate, many ended up in Belgium, Holland, Germany, and Norway, behind enemy lines, or in the sea. Carrier pigeons were also sent. Of the 302 carrier pigeons released only 59 got through. All these efforts to simply say, "Our interests are the same."

In the early months of 1936 during the Spanish Civil War, the people broke the hold that the rich had on the poor, and the revolutionaries had not yet asserted their own hold. There was a spot of time equivalent to the eye of a storm where all is calm and possible. Perhaps we're destined to move between these oppressive extremes of different groups in power, but we can learn from the brief and hopeful place in the middle.

In order to explore this moment of community, we have to move beyond the common, dangerous sense of the word *anarchy*, which refers to a state of chaos. In contrast, social anarchism is a philosophy that sees individual freedom as being dependent on mutual aid. Social anarchism emphasizes community and social equality while resisting the oppression of a dictator or dispassionate ruling class.

In the written history of the Spanish Civil War, social anarchists are seldom acknowledged for their brave resistance to General Francisco Franco and fascism. The anarchists preferred to call their movement the Spanish Revolution, as they rose up in response to the military threat of General Franco to take over the government. Franco would ultimately defeat the revolution in 1939 and rule as a dictator in Spain until his death in 1975.

In the spring of 1936, Prime Minister Santiago Casares Quiroga was given evidence of an impending military coup, but chose to look away and planned to step aside. When Franco's coup began in July 1936, the workers armed themselves and organized detachments to seize barracks and arsenals before the military could do so. A self-organized militia comprised of millions of Spanish workers beat the fascists and, for a time, took control of Spain.

Augustin Souchy, a German journalist who witnessed the revolution, wrote from Barcelona in 1937:

> The [workers] did not want to conquer power for themselves, nor did the unions seek to establish a dictatorship... The smashing of the military coup was like the bursting of a dam, releasing a surging human tide of imagination and creativity.

Within the first few months of the uprising, seven million workers took over their workplaces and the land. Streetcars, cinemas, department stores, factories, and farms were all run by their employees. A form of barter kept Barcelona residents fed for the first part of the war. In some places, money was abolished and shopping was done with vouchers.

Gaston Leval, a member and historian of the revolution, wrote in 1938 about the farm collectives of Aragon:

> In the short space of a few years the small peasants and agricultural laborers demonstrated that, far from chaos, anarchism was an efficient, desirable and realizable method of running things. There were unprecedented levels of voluntary collectivization throughout the land on the anti-Fascist side.

This self-organized movement challenged fascism, just months before World War II erupted. In the midst of the upheaval and suffering, the Spanish people lived together with respect and equality. In spite of some unsuccessful strategies and misguided problem-solving, a brave goodwill came forward to meet oppression while caring for each other.

Later in life, Eduardo Pons Prades, who as a youth fought against Franco, recalled:

> At the time, it seemed impossible to solve [our] initial difficulties, but looking back, people really showed a lot of common sense. Everything was improvised. You could call it a miracle, despite the religious meaning of the word. It was a miracle achieved by the ordinary people.

Time and again, fear and greed get in the way and then, when we suffer enough, we rediscover our kindness. If we could only sustain our kindness without having to suffer. But it seems we can't. That's why moments of community—even when they don't work—matter. Because, often, falling down humbles us to open to each other. Like those trying to help one another in Spain in 1936, and those wide-eyed workers in Paris in 1871 dropping leaflets from the sky. The Dalai Lama wonders profoundly about this tension between turning to and from kindness:

> Right from the moment of our birth, we are under the care and kindness of our parents, and then later on in our life when we are oppressed by sickness and become old, we are again dependent on the kindness of others. Since at the beginning and end of our lives we are so dependent on others' kindness, how can it be in the middle that we would neglect kindness toward others?

It seems we're always asked to expand our heart-view after experience and catastrophe constrict it. Depth psychologist Bill Plotkin offers four ways to expand our heart-view if we are to care for the soul of the Earth, our largest community: defending and nurturing the innocence and wonder of children; mentoring and initiating adolescents; guiding the evolution or transformation of our culture;

and maintaining a balance between human culture and the greater
Earth community.

When we understand that there are many ways to live together,
peace begins. A deep call for our involvement comes from an anonymous letter attributed to a Hopi elder from Oraibi, Arizona. The
excerpt pertains to any age, but especially to our own:

> You have been telling the people
> that this is the Eleventh Hour.
> Now you must go back and tell them
> that this is *the* Hour!
> And there are things to be considered:
> Where are you living?
> What are you doing?
> What are your relationships?
> Are you in the right relation?
> Where is your water?
> Know your garden.
> It is time to speak your truth.
> Create your community.
> Be good to each other.
> And do not look outside yourself
> for the leader.
> This could be a good time!

We're always asked to expand our heart-view after
experience and catastrophe constrict it.

Our Global Body

If you succumb to the temptation of using violence in the
struggle, unborn generations will be the recipients of a
long and desolate night . . .

—MARTIN LUTHER KING, JR.

Violence is one of the most fun things to watch . . .

—FILMMAKER QUENTIN TARANTINO

Dear friends recently returned from Bali, where it is illegal to own
guns. While they and their sweet children were away, the United
States Supreme Court ruled that a ban of handguns in Washington,
D.C. was unconstitutional.

Without romanticizing one or demonizing the other, what does
this say about what each culture holds sacred? Is it by accident that
these two communities are on completely opposite sides of the
Earth?

Despite the 2002 terrorist bombings in Bali, there is still virtually
no personal violence in Bali, while the incidence of personal violence
in the United States is astronomic. While the contrast between Bali
and the United States is stark, the epidemic of violence is worldwide.
Even more troubling is how the long and desolate night that Martin
Luther King, Jr. predicted not only has arrived, but that within it violence is perceived as fun, a perverse and indirect way to feel.

In 2002 the World Health Organization issued its first *World
Report on Violence and Health*. In the sample year 2000, about 1.6
million people in the world lost their lives to violence. Twenty
percent of these deaths were the result of armed conflicts, one-third
were homicides, but almost 50 percent were from suicide. In other
words, more people worldwide die by their own hand than by war.

Close to 750,000 people are in such pain and so dissatisfied with life that they kill themselves. In 2000 the equivalent of the entire population of Manhattan was killed by violence, and the equivalent of half of Manhattan took their own lives. What does this say about modern life on the planet?

The Centers for Disease Control also report that in one year (1997), firearms killed no children in Japan, 19 in Great Britain, 57 in Germany, 109 in France, 153 in Canada, and 5,285 children in the United States. More recently, a study done in 2014 by Everytown for Gun Safety reported that two children die almost every week in unintentional shootings. In most of the deaths, the shooter is a child playing with a gun.

The aim of the WHO report is not to enervate us further with this stark reality, but to shift the way we look at violence: not as inevitable but as a social disease. Frances Henry, a leading doctor devoted to violence prevention, speaks of violence as a psycho-social germ:

> Dr. Louis Pasteur advanced germ theory in the mid-1860s and proposed inoculation to build up antibodies and immunity to infectious disease. Scientists took another hundred years to develop successful public vaccines, but by the turn of our millennium, medicine offered vaccines for all eleven of the major childhood killers like smallpox and polio, measles and mumps. Today, ninety-nine percent of the sicknesses that would have been caused by those infections are prevented ...
>
> And so it is with violence. Violence travels like the microbes that cause disease—in the news, in the movies, in the home, and in each other. And it strikes like a disease—spread from one person, group, or country to another in an endless cycle of hurt ...
>
> What would a vaccine for violence look like?

While biological inoculation builds up antibodies and immunity to disease, individuals and communities are challenged to discover a social inoculation by inhabiting practices that keep us awake to the precious unrepeatable quality of life. Such practices from all traditions build up our immunity to the isolation and numbness that enable violence. And just as some diseases require booster shots to keep the body immune over time, we must inhabit the deeper practices of being human or else we will fall back into the disconnection that breeds violence.

On February 20, 2016, there was a mass shooting where I live in Kalamazoo, Michigan. It was heartbreaking. Random people were shot and killed in parking lots across from where we have coffee. In the aftermath we, like everyone else in the world, must now choose between caring for each other and striking out at each other.

Charles Dickens began his novel *A Tale of Two Cities* with the sentence, "It was the best of times, it was the worst of times . . ." Every era, every generation, every day, is the best of times and the worst of times. It is up to us to choose, as those before us chose, between love and fear.

If we look at humanity as one global body, then, like in every human body, there are healthy cells and toxic cells. Health in the world abounds when there are more healthy individuals than toxic ones. And every time we meet in kindness and truth, we strengthen the immune system of the global body. Since everything is connected, everything matters, and every time you strengthen a heart, you lessen fear and violence somewhere in the world. This is the challenge of our time: to strengthen our hearts and to lessen our fear and violence. We are all in this together, no matter where we live.

> Like everyone else in the world, we must now choose between caring for each other and striking out at each other.

If Another World Is Possible

We must prepare the hearts of the children
for the conflicts they will inherit.
—ROBERT ENRIGHT

How do we prepare ourselves inwardly to
participate in the oneness of humanity?
—VINCENT HARDING

If another world is possible, what is
your role in making it happen?
—CYNTHIA CHERRY

Psychologist Clarissa Pinkola Estés tells the story of an old man who on his deathbed calls all his loved ones to his side. He gives each a short, sturdy stick and instructs each to break it. They do so with ease and he remarks that this is how it is when the soul is alone. He then gives out more sticks and asks them to put their sticks together in a bundle. Then, he asks them to break the bundle. They can't, which causes him to smile and say, "When we stay together, we can't be broken."

This is one way to live the questions offered in the quotes that start this chapter, which ask how we can stay together in life and death. I also cited the quote by Robert Enright in the preface to this book. After all we've discussed, it helps to hear it again. For our children need our will to live and love, not our conclusions and precautions. We have to prepare those who will come after us, so they can be more tolerant and compassionate than we are. We have to instill a greater tenderness and resolve than we've been able to manage.

A perennial challenge in community is to stay open to more than our own opinions so we don't wall out what might save us. We're called to open our minds and hearts beyond the limits of our assumptions and conclusions. We're asked to trust in our common good, beyond our personal wounds and preferences.

Whether it's a soldier carrying a wounded brother to safety or a fireman carrying someone from a burning building or a daughter paying her elderly mother's rent, the impulse to rescue and tend to each other is native to all living things. Consider the Costa Rican leafcutter ant. Leading holistic veterinarian Barbara Royal offers this:

> Each leaf-carrying ant carries, for miles, an ant friend on the leaf, who is preparing the leaf for cultivation. [The leaf-carrying ant] will also defend the line if needed. How they learned, why they chose this method to survive, and what makes them keep going are still a mystery to us all. They continue on, over, under, through, and around. They get there ... I see health in their own form of tenacity, loyalty, productivity, altruism, tenderness, and I believe even an ant form of hope and love.

Next to humans, leafcutter ants form the largest and most complex of animal societies on Earth. In a few years, the central mound of their underground nests can grow to more than a hundred feet across, containing eight million individual ants, all working at their part in building and maintaining the nest.

It's important to realize that where ants, penguins, albatross, and gorillas are innately content to do their part for their colony, nest, or troop, we as human beings need to keep the common good in our consciousness. Without a covenant with the life around us, we can become petty in how we face the tasks before us. I think this is one reason we have the gift of consciousness: to be constantly aware of the common good we are a part of and which we work toward enlivening.

Historian James MacGregor Burns (1918–2014) defined human leadership as the effort to "engage in transforming each other for the greater good," which involves preparing the common ground for communities to go where we as individuals can't go. This reminds me of the Roman Seneca's invocation, "We are members of one great body, planted by nature in a mutual love and fitted for a social life. We must consider that we were born for the good of the whole." And the whole always includes those beyond the group we belong to.

Preparing a life for our descendants that is more welcoming and diverse than our own depends on:

- recognizing that the whole is greater than the sum of its parts
- investing in a humility that lets us see beyond ourselves
- believing that truth resides in more than one capacity, in more than just the mind, the heart, the intuition, or the gift of questioning
- believing that the path to peace resides in more than just one person, organization, way of thinking, tradition, or generation
- educating ourselves and our children in the sacred skills of listening, dialogue, and collaboration, and
- committing to create environments, systems, and institutions that are greenhouses for awakened leadership and respectful community engagement.

But we have to begin with our own self-correction and self-education. Buddhist teacher Chögyam Trungpa speaks about self-liberation as the ground on which an enlightened society rests, if such a society is at all possible:

> In Tibet ... there are stories about a legendary kingdom ... governed by wise and compassionate rulers ... This place was called Shambhala ... [A]mong many Tibetan Buddhist teachers, there has long been a tradition that regards the kingdom of Shambhala, not as an external place, but as the ground or root of wakefulness and sanity that exists as a potential within every human being ... [T]he first principle of Shambhala vision is not being afraid of who you are. Ultimately, that is the definition of bravery: not being afraid of yourself ... The premise of Shambhala vision is that, in order to establish an enlightened society for others, we need to discover what we inherently have to offer the world.

To find what waits underneath all our trouble and misunderstanding, we're called in each generation to rediscover how to participate in the oneness of humanity. And if another world is possible, I believe that it's this one remade and revealed through our efforts to find the common good that waits in the truth of our individual journey. Such important tasks begin with unstitching the knots we've tied along the way. Such important work begins by surfacing what we've been carrying within us that can help repair the world.

In 1998, six descendants of the Sahtu Got'ine tribe from the northwestern United States made a pilgrimage of reparation. In the 1940s, their fathers, desperate for work, had hauled heavy loads of ore from the mines near their village to the barges on the coast. Long after their fathers died of cancer, the tribe learned that the ore they had hauled was uranium, used to make the bombs that were dropped on Hiroshima and Nagasaki. Fifty-three years later, this small group of elders made amends to the Japanese people for their part in their pain. When the descendants of those who unwittingly helped make the bombs crossed the Pacific Ocean to say they were sorry, some part of the dead was put to rest, and a dark, callous part of the heart of humanity was reclaimed.

As the poet-president of the Czech Republic, Václav Havel (1936–2011) said in his poem:

It Is I Who Must Begin

Once I begin, once I try—
Here and now,
Right where I am,
Not excusing myself
By saying that things
Would be easier elsewhere,
Without grand speeches and
Ostentatious gestures,
But all the more persistently—
To live in harmony

With the *voice of Being* as I
Understand it within myself—
As soon as I begin that,
I suddenly discover,
To my surprise, that
I am neither the only one.
Nor the first,
Nor the most important one
To have set out
Upon that road . . .
Whether all is really lost
Or not depends entirely on
Whether or not I am lost . . .

If another world is possible, it's this one remade and revealed through our efforts to find the common good that waits in the truth of our individual journey.

The Seeing Place

Partialities are not false, just limited.
The way branches never lie.
They're just not the whole tree.

The word *theatre* comes from a Greek word meaning "the seeing place." It implies a fundamental law that we often resist: that wisdom is accessible only when we live out the drama of our experience. This embodied path is the seeing place from which, through which, we can know the secrets of living, and living together. We can only go so far by conceptualizing or watching. The truth is that we must live what we're given, singly and together, if the heart is to find and inhabit its place in relation to other life.

Biologist and philosopher Humberto Maturana says, "Love is the only emotion that opens intelligence and expands awareness." We often forget that, when we love, we expand. As we reduce our participation in life, we distance ourselves from this truth. In modern times, we have muted ourselves into a society of critical watchers.

Larry Braskamp, who taught at Loyola University in Chicago, suggests that, in a culture of criticism, we have become obsessed with analyzing and dissecting, which leaves us unable to integrate and generate. In our daily quest for meaning and community, each of us has to swim with or against the powerful undercurrents in our society. Do we interrogate, dissect, dismiss, and say no? Or do we inquire, enjoin, embrace, and say yes? Do we minimize what is difficult and move it far away? Or do we hold what is difficult until it expands our deeper intelligence?

Spiritual elder Raimon Panikkar, an ordained and practicing Catholic priest, Hindu priest, and Buddhist monk, said: "Our call is to appreciate, not classify; to understand, not synthesize; to love as a way of reasoning." But what does this look like in the messiness of life?

Here is one story of how love as a way of inner reasoning expands our intelligence. An oncologist who grew up in Hyderabad in south-central India tells of being an intern in a clinic where an old man came to be treated for a swollen left eye. He had walked thirty-five miles, shoeless, because his eye was so enlarged that it was almost bulging out of its socket, the result of a botched local remedy for a cataract. He didn't know what a cataract was, but he knew that when your eye went cloudy, you could go to a barber who, for a price, would push on the center of the eye with a pointed instrument. You would feel a painful pressure, then a pop, and you could see again—at least for a while. With this illegal procedure, the barber was pushing the filmed part of the lens into the eye itself. Once out of the way, sight was again possible, briefly, but the risk of infection was high.

As a young doctor, the oncologist helped take out that old man's eye. But when the old man was told that he could put the barber who cost him his sight in jail, he rubbed his forehead above where his eye used to be, shrugged, and said, "Who will feed his children if he is in jail? He meant well. And I can see with one eye as well as with two."

The old man embraced intent over result and accepted only that which can add to the world and not take more away. But what if the old man had lost both eyes and gone blind? Would he have pressed charges then? And what if the barber hadn't meant well?

The oncologist says, "The point is that through compassion we see the world and its situations differently." It makes me wonder what petty form of seeing the old man shed by losing his one bad eye. What was taken from him that allowed him to be so loving? What sort of seeing place was uncovered in him? What do I need taken from me so that love can expand my intelligence?

In his work with veterans and their struggles with post-traumatic stress, Ed Tick has witnessed, again and again, that if we take an eye, we must restore an eye. In leading healing journeys back to Vietnam, he has seen remarkable reawakenings of damaged souls. Consider Stan, an American vet who has been numb and depressed for thirty years. Ed helped him find his way back to the village he helped destroy. There, Stan met a disabled Vietnamese vet whose family was homeless. After months, Stan wound up paying for and helping to build a home for his counterpart. When the home was finished, Stan was welcomed to their table and the two wept and broke bread. Only then was Stan able to feel that he was part of humanity again. Only through such honest restitution can we return to the seeing place and come alive.

In a story from ancient China, Lo-Sun, a blind boy, prays for sight and is answered by a spirit in a dream. The spirit shows Lo-Sun how to be his own healer. In the dream, Lo-Sun is instructed that each time he is kind, no matter how small the gesture, a little light shall enter his blindness. As his kindness expands, the scales that have kept him from seeing will fall off and his sight will be restored. If, instead, he should soil his heart by being cold and indifferent, then his eyes will be sealed tighter.

This parable says plainly that the reward for kindness is sight. Of course, it is never quite this simple. There is the rightful need for justice and accountability as well as restitution. Yet how might we stay long enough in the seeing place to drop below the false dualities which have us choose between justice and kindness? How do we stay there together, long enough to uncover the paradox of how they inform each other?

Through such acts of holding the truth with compassion—or Satyagraha, as Gandhi termed it—we can gain access to the seeing place and, like the blind boy Lo-Sun, restore our connection to everything. In essence, though it is hard to understand and harder to live out, the simplest and most direct way to reduce our blindness is to be kind. When we turn softly to our center, we know this to be true. When we can live from the seeing place, we reduce our blindness every day, struggling to let kindness widen our eyes.

We must live what we're given, singly and together, if the heart is to find and inhabit its place in relation to other life.

QUESTIONS TO LIVE WITH

✦ Martina Whelsula, a Native American from Seattle, was given a bundle of sacred objects as a child and told to be kind and gentle wherever she went. Bring three friends together and invite two new people into your group. In conversation, have each of you name three things in your sacred bundle that help you stay kind and gentle. How can you pass them on? In the next three weeks, make an attempt to be kind and gentle to others in your community. Encourage each person in your small group to convene a similar group on their own to explore the same questions.

✦ In 1871, the leaders of the Commune of Paris dropped leaflets from hot-air balloons across the countryside which read: "Our interests are the same." Bring three friends together and invite two new people into your group. In conversation, have each of you identify a common interest that is life-giving, as well as a common problem you are facing. In the next three weeks, explore two ways you can work together in your engagement of both. Encourage each person in your small group to convene a similar group on their own to explore the same questions.

✦ Bring three friends together and invite two new people into your group. In conversation, have each of you describe how you are affected by the epidemic of violence in our society today. Are there ways you are violent in your daily life? How can you stop being violent? In the next three weeks, take a step toward stopping the epidemic of violence in your community. Encourage each person in your small group to convene a similar group on their own to explore the same questions.

+ Bring three friends together and invite two new people into your group. In conversation, have each of you describe your experience of self-interest and serving the common good. How does your self-interest show up in your days? And how does serving the common good affect your relationships? In the next three weeks, identify one place in your community that serves the common good and support it. Encourage each person in your small group to convene a similar group on their own to explore the same questions.

+ Bring three friends together and invite two new people into your group. In conversation, have each of you tell the story of a time when the courage of another opened you beyond your own assumptions and conclusions. In the next three weeks, do one thing in your community that will make it more inclusive. Encourage each person in your small group to convene a similar group on their own to explore the same questions.

+ Bring three friends together and invite two new people into your group. In conversation, have each of you tell the story of an experience of love that expanded your intelligence. In the next three weeks, do something loving in your community. Encourage each person in your small group to convene a similar group on their own to explore the same questions.

+ Bring three friends together and invite two new people into your group. In conversation, have each of you describe one way that family, friends, or community have helped to deepen your empathy. In the next three weeks, do one thing to expand the presence of compassion in your community. Encourage each person in your small group to convene a similar group on their own to explore the same questions.

The Peacemakers

I do not want the peace which passeth understanding,
I want the understanding which bringeth peace.
—HELEN KELLER

It's often a small but courageous pause that lets the fire of our vengeance go out, so that a re-examination of what matters can ignite our compassion.

This is the story of the five Iroquois Nations, known as "the people of the longhouse." They include the Mohawk, Oneida, Onondaga, Cayuga, and Seneca. These tribes have lived for generations in the southern Great Lakes area, extending into Canada, and along both sides of the Allegheny Mountains into Virginia, Kentucky, and the Ohio Valley. For decades, these tribes were in vengeful conflict with each other. It was the most violent period in Iroquois history, with one brutal act leading to another.

Legend has it that the Great Spirit contemplated beginning again, the way God in the Western tradition sent Noah to survive the great flood. Instead, the Great Spirit sent a peacemaker to forge a lasting truce among the nations. This took place around 1570.

The first person to accept the peacemaker was a kind woman, Jikonsahseh. Her home was a safe place for anyone, no matter the blood on their hands. Tired warriors would leave their weapons outside and she would bathe them and feed them till they forgot why they were fighting.

Then there was Tadodarho, an evil warrior who resisted the peacemaker with his entire being. Nothing could persuade Tadodarho to accept the notion of peace. Finally, the peacemaker gathered forty-nine true warriors and together they worked on opening the mind of Tadodarho. Eventually, the dark warrior couldn't resist and he accepted the notion of peace. It was then that the peacemaker offered Tadodarho a special role in the years to come. Because he knew the heart of violence so intimately, Tadodarho was asked to watch for the signs of violence growing in others. And Tadodarho was asked to guard the fire of peace and to keep it burning on behalf of the five nations. With his heart fully opened, Tadodarho agreed.

This part of the story represents the eternal argument between the peacemaker within us and the vengeful, hurtful one, the Tadodarho within us. Often, we need a safe place to put down our weapons, so we can summon the forty-nine voices of love to work on the vengeful one who lingers in our darkness.

Once Tadodarho agreed to be the firekeeper of the peace, the peacemaker gathered the chiefs and warriors of the five nations. He saw how hard their hearts were as they gripped their bloodied weapons. So he brought them to the oldest tree he could find. It was an ancient white pine. And with the help of the Great Spirit, he uprooted the tree without harming it and told all the chiefs and warriors to bury their weapons in the unearthed hole of the ancient tree. They all resisted until Tadodarho put his weapons in the hole first. Then one by one the chiefs and warriors followed.

The peacemaker then replanted the tree over the buried weapons and placed an eagle to live atop the white pine, so no one would forget the Great Tree of Peace. In time, the muscular roots grew into place around the decomposing weapons, not letting them surface back into the world. In time, the mulch of the buried weapons fed the roots of peace. And Tadodarho, the evil one turned firekeeper, spent the rest of his days watching over the Great Tree of Peace.

Each time around, we need to bury our weapons under our common roots. Each time we're tempted toward vengeance, we need to listen to the forty-nine voices of love until they turn the vengeful one within us into a firekeeper of peace.

Out of this lasting peace, the League of the Iroquois was formed as the oldest democracy in North America. When the Founding Fathers of the United States looked for models of liberty and community, the peaceful governance of the Iroquois Nations was close at hand. By the time the Declaration of Independence was signed, the League of the Iroquois had been practicing a balanced form of tribal democracy for two hundred years.

The Iroquois tribal system involved three councils among the five nations. The first was the Council of Chiefs, whose members were known as *sachems*. They were elected by the women of noble families. There were fifty sachems, who served life terms unless deposed by the women who selected them. The second council was the Pine Tree Chiefs, chosen on merit by the worthiest warriors. And the third council was the Firekeepers, comprised of the Onondaga chiefs who served as a moderating body.

To this day, the League of the Iroquois remains active. Its capital sits in Onondaga County, just south of Syracuse, New York. The Onondaga Firekeepers still host meetings of the League of the Iroquois.

We're all firekeepers struggling to keep our roots wrapped around our weapons, trying to keep the centuries of violence at bay. It's the forty-nine voices of love that keep justice from turning into vengeance. And only strong, common roots can turn our weapons into dust.

We need a safe place to put down our weapons, so we can summon the forty-nine voices of love to work on the vengeful one who lingers in our darkness.

Eight Worldviews and Practices

Since prehistoric hunters had to work together in order to survive, people have had to learn how to share both the workload and the harvest, and the problems and the joys. Through the centuries, traditions have formed and complexities have grown. But the health of all community depends on how we treat each other.

I'd like to explore eight worldviews and the practices they offer. Each can help us stay wholehearted, authentic, and in true relationship to life and each other.

The Native American notion *All My Relations* views all of reality and life as related and interconnected. Every aspect of life is seen as part of one intrinsic family. In the Blackfoot tribe, when people meet, they don't say "How are you?" but *"Tza Nee Da Bee Wah?"* which means, "How are the connections?" If the connections are in place, we must be all right. If the connections are not in place, then we need to tend them first. Inherent in the Native American view is that our well-being is based on how everything goes together. There can be no lasting individual health unless there is a working harmony among all living things. The practice that grows from this worldview is the need to discover, name, and repair the connections that exist between all things. This is considered sacred and necessary work.

The African ethic of ubuntu is often translated as *I am because you are, you are because I am.* It implies that we find our humanity in each other. *Ubuntu* literally means *a person is a person through other persons.* This heartfelt tradition concentrates on the irrevocable connectedness that exists between people. Based on this fundamental commitment to human kinship, there is no word for orphan in the African continent, because each tribe automatically assumes a lost child as part of its larger family.

At work here is the belief that in our very nature, we rely on each other to grow. As quarks combine to form protons and neutrons, which then form atoms, which then form molecules, individuals innately form families, which then form tribes, which then form nations. Our strong need to interact stems from the irreducible nature of love. In fact, all the worldviews we're discussing are manifestations of our innate need to join. The practice that comes from the notion of ubuntu is the vow to water our common roots by which we all grow and to honor our strong need to join.

The Hindu view takes us through our self and beyond our self into the interdependent mystery, where we find ourselves in each and every living thing. This is what the holy phrase *Thou Art That* means. The notion comes from the story in the Chandogya Upanishad of a humble father Uddalaka and his precocious son Svetaketu, who at an early age is chosen to study with the holy Brahmins, the priest class in India who study spiritual knowledge. As soon as he begins to study, Svetaketu has no use for his father. He looks down on his simple father and never asks him a question. One day, his father interrupts him, and Svetaketu impatiently asks, "What do you want, Father?"

Uddalaka says, "I want you to come with me." He leads his son to the foot of the great Nyagrodha tree. He picks a fruit and asks his son to hold it, then asks him, "What do you see?" His son curtly answers, "Nothing. I see nothing." His father asks him to break open the fruit, which Svetaketu does, and they can see the seeds inside it. Again, his father asks him, "What do you see?" Again, his son says, "I see nothing, Father. Nothing!" Uddalaka takes a seed, which is hollow in the center, and puts it close to his son's face, and says, "Thou Art That, my son, thou are that nothing."

More than putting his son in place, Uddalaka jars him to feel the great truth that out of that unseeable center, we all come to be. We all grow from this great nothing, even the massive Nyagrodha tree. And so, the practice we're compelled to learn here is how to face and feel a life of compassion that honors that we are at heart the same.

The notion of I and Thou, discerned by the philosopher Martin Buber, holds that God only appears in the unrehearsed, authentic dialogue between two living centers. When we see ourselves as the sun and everyone we meet as planets in our orbit, we are trapped in the I-It relationship, objectifying everyone we meet. But when we can meet others as equal living beings, each with their own center, then we live out the I and Thou relationship, through which the Mystery manifests as a vital life-force between us.

Buber discovered the notion of I and Thou while walking in a field at dusk as a storm was approaching. Leaning on a walking stick, he stopped near a huge oak tree. Lightning appeared, and he could see everything about him clearly. In the darkness that followed, he could only tap his way blindly until his walking stick touched the thick bark of the oak before him. In that moment, he could feel the tree through his walking stick, though he wasn't directly touching it. The walking stick became a symbol for the authentic dialogue that lets us feel life in the honest speech we offer. The practice that arises from this worldview is to stay committed to the life of honest conversation.

The Lebanese greeting, "Ya Ayuni!" literally means "Oh, my eyes!" or "Oh, my darling!" Implicit in this ancient greeting is the recognition that we need each other to see, that one view is insufficient. Empowered by the presence of each other, the Lebanese people say, "Oh, my eyes! You're here! Now we can see!" This custom reminds me of how Native American elders meet in a circle, not just for equity, but so that each elder will have a direct view of the Center. The belief at the heart of this worldview is that the Center and the Whole are not comprehensible by any one person alone. Therefore, we need everyone's view to glimpse the enduring truths of life. And so, we gather meaning, we don't choose it.

Like the Chien, the mythic bird of ancient China that has only one eye and one wing, we must find each other in order to see and fly. "Ya Ayuni!" "Oh, my eyes! You're here! Now we can see!" The joyous practice of this custom—that we sorely need to enliven today—is to welcome other views in the belief that we need each other to be complete.

The next notion of connection comes from the early Christian mystics, the desert fathers of the third century, who gave us the metaphor of *the Great Spoked Wheel*. Imagine that each soul on Earth is a spoke in an Infinite Wheel and that no two spokes are the same. The rim of that Wheel is our living sense of community, and each spoke does its part to hold up the rim. But the common hub where all spokes join is the one Center where all souls come from.

As I become myself out in the world, I discover my unique gifts and find the one particular place on the rim of the Great Wheel that is mine to uphold. And so, as I move into the world, I live out my uniqueness. But when love and suffering cause me to go inward, I discover the common Center where we are all the same. When I dare to look into my core, I come upon the one common core where all lives meet. In our becoming, which grows outward, and our being, which grows inward, we live out the paradox of being both unique and the same.

The image of the Great Spoked Wheel shows us how we need each other. If any of these parts are removed, the wheel falls apart. Remove the rim, which is community, and humanity goes nowhere. Remove any of the spokes, which are the individual souls that make up life, and the wheel doesn't turn. Remove the Center, which is God, and there is no wheel. The practice offered here is to embody the paradox of our uniqueness and commonness by which the Great Wheel of Humanity turns.

The Danish notion *Hygge* (pronounced *hue-gah*) comes from a Norwegian word meaning "well-being." The word first appeared in Danish writing in the eighteenth century. The Danish word suggests coziness. As a practice of community, *Hygge* refers to the atmosphere we create between us. The Danish practice of Hygge invites us to create well-being, connection, warmth, and a sense of belonging. In Denmark and Norway, *Hygge* refers to "a form of everyday togetherness," "a pleasant and highly valued everyday experience of safety, equality, personal wholeness, and a spontaneous social flow."

The final worldview comes from a greeting offered by African Bushmen. For centuries, the Bushmen have affirmed each other with resolve. When one becomes aware of his brother or sister coming out of the brush after hunting or gathering, the one at home exclaims, "*I See You!*" and then the one returning rejoices, "*I Am Here!*"

This timeless gesture of bearing witness is both simple and profound. We all need to be seen and heard, recognized and verified. This is the emotional lifeblood of all relationship, which in our busyness and pain we often forget. The wholehearted acknowledgment of each other's journey is at the heart of all therapy. The practice enjoined here is to be present and bear witness to each other and other life. Whether someone is filling your glass with water at a restaurant or taking your change at a gas station, no one is invisible. By being alive, we're enlisted to affirm each other by saying, "I See You!" in whatever way we can.

In summary, the eight worldviews and their practices are:

- *All My Relations* from the Native American tradition.
  The Practice: To discover, name, and repair the connections that exist between all things.

- *Ubuntu* from the African tradition.
  The Practice: To water our common roots by which we all grow and to honor our strong need to join.

- *Thou Art That* from the Hindu tradition.
  The Practice: To face and feel a life of compassion that honors that we are at heart the same.

- *The I and Thou Relationship* from the Jewish tradition.
  The Practice: To stay committed to the life of honest conversation.

- *Ya Ayuni!* from the Lebanese tradition.
  The Practice: To welcome other views in the belief that we need each other to be complete.

- *The Great Spoked Wheel* from the early Christian mystic tradition.
  The Practice: To embody the paradox of our uniqueness and commonness by which the Great Wheel of Humanity turns.

- *Hygge* from the Danish tradition.
  The Practice: To create well-being, connection, warmth, and a sense of belonging.

- *I See You! I Am Here!* from the African Bushmen tradition.
  The Practice: To be present and bear witness to each other and other life.

How we personalize these ancient worldviews and their vibrant practices is for each of us to discover. What does it mean for you: to repair the connections, to water our common roots, to face a life of compassion, to stay in honest conversation, to welcome other views, to honor our uniqueness and commonness, to create a sense of belonging, and to bear witness to each other? These are not concepts but living tools by which tribes and cultures have sustained human growth on Earth. How can you make good use of these tools today? By figuring out how to enact these practices in our daily life, we can strengthen the human community, one relationship at a time.

The health of all community depends
on how we treat each other.

The Highest Ethic

Community is like a large mosaic . . . a fellowship of . . .
people who together make God visible in the world.
—HENRI NOUWEN

I slept and dreamt that life was joy.
I awoke and saw that life was service.
I acted and behold, service is joy.
—RABINDRANATH TAGORE

Shared values are not the same thing as *shared humanity*. Shared
values are based on agreements that come from the head. They form
the basis of culture. But it's our shared humanity that is the basis of
community. Our shared humanity is rooted in the honest and caring
acknowledgment of our firsthand experience. In truth, the ways in
which we meet without pretense are the ways we strengthen the
bonds that hold us together.

For example, in the support rooms, and waiting rooms, and treatment rooms I was a part of during my cancer journey, we seldom
spoke of our religious backgrounds or our politics or worldviews.
We were only there to keep each other company, with sensitivity and
honesty, so that as many of us as possible could make it through our
world of treatments. The highest ethic has always been the courage
to be with each other in our pain and to honor each other's journey.
This is what it means to stand in compassion.

During the recession of 2008, banks were foreclosing on homes
nationwide, making thousands of families homeless. In Chicago,
most of the people being evicted were diligent renters who had no
knowledge that their landlords were delinquent with the banks.

In Chicago's Cook County, law enforcement officers were scheduled to evict residents affected by more than 4700 foreclosures. This was when Cook County sheriff Thomas Dart put a moratorium on all foreclosure evictions. Sheriff Dart couldn't support taking the law into his own hands, but, at the same time, he couldn't put innocent families on the street.

Sheriff Dart said, "It's one of most gut-wrenching things we do, seeing little children put out on the street with their possessions. And the hard part is that these parents played by all the rules, and they're being traumatized."

In deciding not to evict these people, Sheriff Dart was using the power of his office compassionately rather than being blindly punitive. This is an example of shared humanity guiding an officer of the court, rather than a dispassionate obedience to arbitrary rules. Sheriff Dart reached a moral boundary he couldn't in good conscience cross. This uncrossable moral boundary isn't always definable though it's always knowable. We know when we're about to do harm, even under the guise of propriety. While ideas help us understand values, stories help us understand each other.

This leads to another story from modern-day Uganda. In 1996, in northern Uganda, the government placed 1.5 million Ugandans in "protective villages" which were really containment camps. Many Ugandans still live there in small huts about eight to ten feet apart with eight waterholes per 30,000 people.

A painful part of their twelve-year civil war has been the massive abduction of children, turning little boys into young soldiers, in some cases sent to kill their own parents, and turning little girls into sex slaves. John Bryan is part of a refugee resettlement organization called Alliance for African Assistance. He's met several times with the Ugandan elders who are restricted to these camps. Now that there's a truce in Uganda, many young girls are returning with small children born during their ten years of abduction. On his last trip, John asked the elders, "What will happen to the young girls coming home?"

One elder quickly said that if a girl had run off and returned pregnant, she would be cast out of the village. This was their tribal law. But the question was put by one Ugandan elder wizened by his captivity: "And what will we do when ten thousand of our children, abducted and abused, return with a generation of our grandchildren fathered by our enemies?" One of the elders stared off, another cried. And in the incubation of that painful silence, a new form of thinking arose that would bring the children home. In this painful opening lies the hope of humanity.

Strangely, a decade of exhaustion from all the suffering has made the warring Ugandans one reluctant family. Mysteriously and painfully, when we deny that we're of one human family, we're forced in time to reconstruct our principles in order to embrace and love those who have suffered and survived. This is the bedrock of a shared humanity that places the care of each other as the highest ethic, no matter the hardships we encounter.

These aging chiefs have become reluctant pioneers, because they've been forced to widen centuries of tradition in order to welcome the unimagined offspring of a suffering no one thought possible. By facing this challenge, the northern Ugandans have added to the growing knowledge of truth and reconciliation explored by the ethical leaders in South Africa. The Ugandan elders serve as a profound example of the moral tension that can exist between our traditional values and our shared humanity.

By accepting a generation of children born of war, the northern Ugandans began to reclaim their stolen humanity. They soon began to create schools for the children who were returning. Today, in the district of Kitgum, a hundred children meet daily in a small hut with one teacher and one book. God bless that teacher, but what is that one book? And what does it attempt to teach? And what do these children of war and containment dream about? How do those born of abuse make sense of how their fathers and grandfathers were enemies? How do any of us make sense of such things? But this is our charge, the charge of every generation: to rediscover with courage and care our shared humanity.

From the sheriff of Cook County to the weary Ugandan elders, these are examples of human beings living out of the highest ethic: the ethic of compassion by which we step in to prevent disaster or to recover the innocent ones who have been trampled by evil.

In Africa, the great Baobab tree grows in the center of certain villages. An ancient myth says that the gods planted the first Baobab trees upside down so the roots would grow in the open. It's believed that ancestor spirits live inside the Baobab tree. The long fruit grows from the roots and has a sweet fiber. It's believed that if you eat the fruit of the Baobab when in pain, you will feel our connection to everything. Every spring, the elders of the village make pilgrimage to sit in the hollow of the Baobab tree to hear the voices of the ancestors. Some say this is where the stories go to live once they are told. And those who find the courage to sit in the hollow of the Baobab tree are filled with the truth and heart of all who have come before.

On an elemental level, a level of necessity, spiritual courage involves facing our humanity, with all its messiness and frailty, without turning away, until, like those who sit in the hollow of the Baobab tree, we begin to experience the common source of all humanity. Then we do not *sort* who will or will not belong to our community, we *enlist* everyone.

And enlisting everyone is how we live wholeheartedly—individually and in community. It's a difficult covenant to put into practice. Such commitment brings to mind the notion of *priyankar*, which is Sanskrit for *one who must both do good for others and endure others*. This ethic of goodwill rests on upholding our faith in our deeper capacities, of believing in each other while holding each other accountable for our lesser selves.

The truth is that the heart is like the great Baobab tree. Through the heart's open-air roots we grow our consciousness, and through the heart's fruit, we sweeten the world. When we do good, our capacity for connection reveals itself. When we endure others without subjugating ourselves to abuse or violence, we create a larger home in which all are welcome. Being wholehearted, we are strengthened by the mysterious fact that we are all that we touch and all that enters us, matured by each.

The highest ethic has always been the courage to be with each other in our pain and to honor each other's journey. This is what it means to stand in compassion.

A Small Boy

I'm always on the edge of silence as I near the end of a book. Like a conductor three bars from the last note, I'm winded and exhilarated, unsure exactly how we got here, hoping we've played what needs to be played.

I leave you with one more image. It's a heartbreaking and inspiring image of our capacity to respond to adversity, captured in a photograph by American photojournalist David Seymour, widely known as Chim. UNESCO commissioned Chim to photograph the orphans and children who survived World War II. His travels in Europe during 1947–48 resulted in a sixty-two-page classic called *Children of Europe*, published by UNESCO in 1949.

This photo was taken in 1948 in Rome. I came across it while wandering in the International Center for Photography in New York City. It centers on a blind boy, eight or nine, who lost his arms in World War II. At an outdoor table in the sun, his small head is pressed against the pages of a large book of Braille. In the rubble, he's learning to read by rubbing his lips across the raised dots on the page.

This is more than a sad photo. It's more than poignant. It's emblematic of all that is human. I began this book by looking for the essential stories that might bring into view the indelible nature of our kinship to each other and life. After years of research, of looking for stories across history about the DNA of community, I keep returning to the image of this boy torn by war.

After all this way, I land in this moment in the ruins of Italy in 1948. What happened to this little boy is tragic, but his want to learn how to read is a testament to how the human spirit continues to glow after the life that carries it is broken. Unable to see or turn the pages, the boy is immersed in *feeling* the raised words against his lips. He's becoming the words. It's a moment of unmitigated living.

Blind, Armless Boy Reading with His Lips, Italy, 1948, Chim.

I couldn't move from the wall on which this photo hung. Like a brilliant sunset, made more beautiful and compelling because of the dark silhouette of trees it bursts through, the resilience of the human spirit alive in this little boy, bursting through the dark silhouette of his losses, remains brilliant, beautiful, and compelling.

From the lips of a war-torn child comes the irrepressible impulse to keep going. Beyond all principle and philosophy, beyond all religious codes, this is the human seed which only knows to wait and sprout. This is the indestructible life-force we are born with, though all our labors to access it are understandably great, given the unspeakable things we meet over time. The moment seems to say, if we could just kiss what we're given, our difficulties would show us how to read the signs of life.

But there's more in this telling moment. Starkly, we are responsible for *everything* in this photograph. Deeply, we *are* everything in this photograph and *capable* of everything in this photograph. We are the dark ones who create the war. We are the strong ones who clean up the ruins. We are the exhausted who keep rebuilding the world after we destroy it. And we are the bewildered boy born into a world beyond his control. And we are the violent ones who cause him to lose his arms. And the determined ones who create the Braille. And the kind ones who set up the worn table in the ruins that he comes to. And we are the compassionate who turn the pages. And we are the relentless witness traveling vast distances to photograph all that is human.

We contain and grow these destinies: to be creative, to be destructive, to be resilient, and to bear witness. Over and over, we create and destroy and resurrect against all odds. In each generation, everything depends on what we choose while here. This whole book is about the necessity of choosing love over fear, of choosing the big raft over the little raft, of accepting that we are interdependent creatures who, given the chance, will make honey of our suffering. I keep saying it like a prayer I don't quite understand: we are more together than alone.

In the heart of it all, we are both irrepressible and uncontainable, compelled to find our way into the sun, even when we've lost the ability to see, and compelled to help each other through. Perhaps, the best of community comes down to this: taking turns being blind and sighted as we tumble through all life has to offer, surviving the ruins, clearing the rubble, and learning to read the signs of life as we help each other up, again and again.

Online Community Guide

If anything in this book has moved you, I invite you to explore this online community guide, which includes guidelines for gathering in small groups, a page on Facebook where you can share and pass on your own stories of community, the "Questions to Live With" that appear in the book, and a suggested reading and film list (which is also included in the following pages). I encourage you to enter these conversations, activities, and resources with a friend or loved one, and in time, with someone you don't yet know. For community grows when a kindness is given and a voice is heard, and when something is built together that can't be built alone.

http://threeintentions.com/more-together
-than-alone-online-community-guide.

Suggested Reading and Films

BOOKS AND ARTICLES

Awakening Earth: Exploring the Evolution of Human Culture and Consciousness by Duane Elgin. New York: William Morrow, 1993.

Better Together: Restoring the American Community by Robert D. Putnam and Lewis M. Feldstein with Don Cohen. New York: Simon & Schuster, 2003.

Birth of a Global Community: Appreciative Inquiry in Action by Charles Gibbs and Sally Mahé. Bedford Heights, OH: Lakeshore Publishers, 2004.

Bowling Alone: The Collapse and Revival of American Community by Robert D. Putnam. New York: Simon & Schuster, 2000.

Community and Growth by Jean Vanier. Mahwah, NJ: Paulist Press, 1989.

"Comprehensive Compassion: An Interview with Brian Swimme" by Susan Bridle, in *What Is Enlightenment?* 19 (Spring–Summer 2001).

Confucius: The Secular as Sacred by Herbert Fingarette. New York: Harper & Row, 1972.

The Connect Effect: Building Strong Personal, Professional and Virtual Networks by Michael Dulworth. San Francisco: Berrett-Koehler, 2008.

Cosmic Consciousness: A Study in the Evolution of the Human Mind, edited by Richard Maurice Bucke. Mansfield Centre, CT: Martino, 2010.

Cultivating Communities of Practice by Etienne Wenger, Richard McDermott, and William M. Snyder. Boston: Harvard Business School, 2002.

Defiant Gardens: Making Gardens in Wartime by Kenneth I. Helphand. San Antonio: TX: Trinity University Press, 2008.

Dr. Elkhanan Elkes of the Kovno Ghetto: A Son's Holocaust Memoir by Joel Elkes. Orleans, MA: Paraclete Press, 1999.

The Earth Is the Lord's: The Inner World of the Jew in Eastern Europe by Abraham Joshua Heschel. Woodstock, VT: Jewish Lights, 2001.

The Expansion of Consciousness by Ralph Metzner. Berkeley, CA: Green Earth Foundation and Regent Press, 2008.

The Great Transformation by Karen Armstrong. New York: Alfred A. Knopf, 2006.

The Guide for the Perplexed by Maimonides. A mix of Jewish thought and Sufi mysticism, and Islamic mystics.

Hardwired to Connect: The New Scientific Case for Authoritative Communities, sponsored by the Institute for American Values, the YMCA of the USA, and the Dartmouth Medical School. www.american values.org.

Healing the Heart of Democracy: The Courage to Create a Politics Worthy of the Human Spirit by Parker J. Palmer. San Francisco, CA: Jossey-Bass, 2011.

Heart: A Personal Journey Through Its Myths and Meanings by Gail Godwin. New York: William Morrow, 2001.

Homage to Catalonia by George Orwell. N.P.: Benediction Classics, 2010.

Honeybee Democracy by Thomas D. Seeley. Princeton, NJ: Princeton University Press, 2010.

Humanity and Self-Cultivation: Essays in Confucian Thought by Tu Weiming. Berkeley, CA: Asian Humanities Press, 1979.

"The Importance of 'Reculturing': Case Studies in Mining the 'Mother Lode of Leverage' for School Change" by Scott Thompson, in *Education Week* 25, issue 25 (March 1, 2006), pp. 30–31, 44. https://www.edweek.org/ew/articles/2006/03/01/25thompson.h25.html.

In the Vale of Soul-Making: A Dialogue between Rupert Sheldrake and Matthew Fox, August 2005. Originally published in *Resurgence* magazine in 1999.

The Journey from Knowing About Community to Knowing Community by Sally Z. Hare, March 2005.

Leadership and the New Science: Learning About Organization from an Orderly Universe by Margaret J. Wheatley. San Francisco: Berrett-Kohler Publishers, 1994.

Left to Tell: Discovering God Amidst the Rwandan Holocaust by Immaculée Ilibagiza (with Steve Erwin). Carlsbad, CA: Hay House, 2006.

Lev Tov (A Good Heart). A book of Jewish custom and ritual regarding community.

Life in a Crowded Place: Making a Learning Community by Ralph Peterson. New York: Heinemann, 1992.

Life Together by Dietrich Bonhoeffer. New York: Harper & Row Publishers, 1954.

Man's Search for Meaning by Viktor Frankl. Boston: Beacon Press, 2006.

The Medici Effect: Breakthrough Insights at the Intersection of Ideas, Concepts, and Cultures by Frans Johansson. Boston: Harvard Business School Press, 2004.

Mind in Society: The Development of Higher Psychological Processes by L. S. Vygotsky; edited by Michael Cole, Vera John-Steiner, Sylvia Scribner, and Ellen Souberman. Cambridge, MA: Harvard University Press, 1980.

The Moral Imagination: The Art and Soul of Building Peace by John Paul Lederach. New York: Oxford University Press, 2010.

"The New Science of Leadership: An Interview with Margaret Wheatley" by Scott London, 2006. http://www.scottlondon.com/interviews/wheatley.html.

The Ornament of the World: How Muslims, Jews and Christians Created a Culture of Tolerance in Medieval Spain by María Rosa Menocal. Boston: Back Bay, 2003.

The Politics of Non-Violent Action (three volumes) by Gene Sharp. Boston: Harvard University, 1973. A history of nonviolence and how it works. Vol. I: Power and Struggle; Vol. II: The Methods of Nonviolent Action; Vol. III: The Dynamics of Nonviolent Action. See http://www.peace.ca/genesharp.htm.

The Power of Collective Wisdom: And the Trap of Collective Folly by Alan Briskin, Sheryl Erickson, John Ott, and Tom Callanan. San Francisco: Berrett-Koehler, 2009.

Rights and the Common Good: The Communitarian Perspective by Amitai Etzioni. New York: St. Martin's, 1995.

Spiritual Ecology: The Cry of the Earth, edited by Llewellyn Vaughan-Lee. Point Reyes, CA: Golden Sufi Center, 2013.

Surviving the Holocaust: The Kovno Ghetto Diary by Avraham Tory, edited by Sir Martin Gilbert. Boston: Harvard University Press, 1990.

Teaching Community: A Pedagogy of Hope by bell hooks. New York: Routledge, 2003.

"Parker Palmer's Thirteen Ways of Looking at Community (. . . with a Fourteenth Thrown in for Free)" by Parker J. Palmer, in *Inner Edge* (August/September 1998). Online at Center for Courage & Renewal. http://www.couragerenewal.org/parker/writings/13 -ways-of-looking-at-community.

"Using Emergence to Take Social Innovations to Scale" by Margaret Wheatley and Deborah Frieze, 2006. http://www.margaretwheat ley.com/articles/emergence.html.

War and the Soul: Healing Our Nation's Veterans from Post-traumatic Stress Disorder by Edward Tick. Wheaton, IL: Quest Books, 2006.

What's Going On in There?: How the Brain and Mind Develop in the First Five Years of Life by Lise Eliot. New York: Bantam, 2000.

What Is Life? by Lynn Margulis and Dorion Sagan. New York: Simon & Schuster, 1995.

Where Do We Go from Here: Chaos or Community? by Martin Luther King, Jr. Boston: Beacon Press, 1968.

The Wisdom of Crowds by James Surowiecki. New York: Doubleday, 2004.

FILMS

Following Sean (2006). This documentary by writer-director Ralph Arlyck begins with a conversation with four-year-old Sean Farrell, the son of free-spirited parents living in 1969 in San Francisco's Haight-Ashbury neighborhood. Arlyck revisits Sean and his parents thirty years later, reflecting on his own life journey along the way.

Frederick Law Olmsted: Designing America (2014). A film by Lawrence Hott and Diane Garey. An excellent PBS documentary on Olmsted's struggles and genius.

Grace Is Gone (2007). Director James C. Strouse tells the story of an ex-military man trying to find the courage to break the devastating news to his two daughters that their mother has died while serving in Iraq. The film won the Dramatic Audience Award at Sundance 2007.

Grave of the Dragonflies (1988). Named Best Animated Feature at the 1994 Chicago International Children's Film Festival, this 1988 film by director Isao Takahata is a compassionate tale of orphans Seita and Setsuko as they struggle for survival in post–World War II Japan.

How to Survive a Plague (2012). This Oscar-nominated documentary by David France is the story of two coalitions—ACT UP and TAG (Treatment Action Group)—whose activism and innovation turned AIDS from a death sentence into a manageable condition. Despite having no scientific training, these self-made activists infiltrated the pharmaceutical industry and helped identify promising new drugs, moving them from experimental trials to patients in record time. See http://surviveaplague.com.

John Adams (2008). The PBS miniseries based on the book by the Pulitzer Prize–winning historian David McCullough.

The National Parks: America's Best Idea (2009). Legendary filmmaker Ken Burns's unfolding of this extraordinary part of America's history. Viewing anything by Ken Burns is helpful in understanding the evolving community that is America.

The Pianist (2002). This remarkable film by Roman Polanski is an adaptation of the autobiography of Władysław Szpilman, a famous Polish Jewish pianist working for Warsaw radio, who sees his whole world collapse with the outbreak of World War II and the invasion of Poland in September 1939. The story chronicles his life in hiding and his eventual witnessing of the Warsaw Ghetto Uprising of 1943.

The Qatsi Trilogy, produced by Godfrey Reggio. This is a landmark film trilogy. The first film is *Koyaanisqatsi* (1982), which is Hopi for life out of balance. The second film, *Powaqqatsi* (1988), combines two notions, *powaq* (sorcerer) and *qatsi* (life). It refers to a way of life that consumes the life-force of other beings in order to further its own life. The third film is *Naqoyqatsi* (2002), which is Hopi for a life of killing each other.

Shakespeare Behind Bars (2005). A documentary film by Hank Rogerson portraying the prison theatre company *Shakespeare Behind Bars*, founded by Curt Tofteland.

Gratitudes

They say it takes a village to raise a child. So, too, to birth a book, especially a book on community. My interest in this topic has grown through my own moments of community, learning from the resilient, kind seekers I've encountered, and from an ongoing conversation with many, including Howard Zinn, Parker Palmer, Rich Frankel, Charles Gibbs, John Paul Lederach, Sally Hare, Estrus Tucker, Sharon Parks, Arthur Zajonc, and Eileen Wilson-Oyelaran.

I'm grateful, as ever, to my talented agent, Jennifer Rudolph Walsh, for her insight and light, as well as Eve Attermann, Raffaella De Angelis, and the rest of the WME team for their skill and love. And to my editors at Atria: Sarah Pelz, for her clarity and care, and to Leslie Meredith, whose tireless precision and insight have graced all the books we've birthed together. And to my publisher, Judith Curr, for her vision and faith in the tribe of authors and readers. And to Brooke Warner for her careful read of this book in manuscript. And to Barrett Briske for her incredible research and curiosity. And to my publicist, Eileen Duhne, for representing me from the inside out. And a special bow to my friend Parker Palmer, whose vision and groundbreaking work in education and community is unparalleled in our time.

Gratitude to my dear friends who are my loving community. We are indeed more together than alone. Especially George, Don, Paul, Skip, TC, David, Kurt, Pam, Patti, Karen, Paula, Ellen, Dave, Jill, Linda, Michelle, Rich, Carolyn, Henk, Sandra, Elesa, and Joel and Sally. And to Oprah Winfrey, a consummate bridger of our times.

And to Paul Bowler for believing that friendship is the atom of community. And to Robert Mason who showed me that the Universe is the most dynamic community of all. And to my dear wife, Susan, for the intimate community that is our nest.

Permissions

Thanks for permission to excerpt the following from other previously published works:

The chapter "The Unfinished Painting" first appeared as an essay in *Parabola*, volume 36, number 4 (Winter 2011–12).

Much of the chapter "Notions of Community" is drawn from the chapters "Sympathetic Fibers" and "Trust of This Kind" in my earlier book *Finding Inner Courage* (San Francisco: Conari Press, 2011).

The poem "Don't ask the mountain . . ." by John Paul Lederach, used by permission of the author.

Part of the chapter "Hospitality" originally appeared in the chapter "Legacy" in my book *The One Life We're Given* (New York: Atria Books, 2016).

Part of the chapter "Our Struggle and Possibility" first appeared as the poem "Side by Side" in my book *The Way Under the Way* (Boulder, CO: Sounds True, 2016).

Excerpt from "Inscription on the Door," from *Roads of Bread: The Collected Poems of Eugene Ruggles*. (Bodega, CA: Petaluma River Press, 2010).

Part of the chapter "Helping Each Other Up" first appeared as my poem "Hill Where the Lord Hides" in the anthology *Blood to Remember: American Poets on the Holocaust*, revised second edition,

Notes

Epigraphs and poems without attribution are by the author.

vii *"When you have models"*: From a conversation with Howard Zinn in 2006.

We Can Find Each Other

xiii *In the Hindu Upanishads, there's a passage:* "As flowing rivers disappear into the sea, losing their names and forms, so a wise man, freed from name and form, attains the Purusha, who is greater than the Great." From the Mundaka Upanishad, III. ii. 8.

xiv *my teacher, Mary Brodbeck:* Mary is a remarkably talented woodblock printmaker and kind teacher. Since 1998, Mary has specialized in *moku hanga*. *Moku* is the Japanese word for *wood*, and *hanga* means *print*. *Moku hanga* simply translates as *wood print*, referring to woodblock printmaking using traditional Japanese methods and materials. Mary learned these techniques from Yoshisuke Funasaka in Tokyo, as a recipient of a Bunka-cho fellowship from the Japanese government. Mary exhibits her work throughout the United States, Canada, and Japan. For more about Mary and her work, please visit www.MaryBrodbeck.com.

xv *"We need to prepare the hearts of the children"*: Robert Enright is a professor and leader in forgiveness research at the University of Wisconsin, Madison. This quote is from a conversation in April 2005.

xv *"Every day the sun will rise"*: From *Hand in Hand: A Song for Peace; The Last Song of Yitzchak Rabin, an Adaptation of Shir l'shalom* by Yair Rosenblum, arranged for choir and keyboard by Michael Isaacson, text adaptation by Stanley Ralph Ross and Michael Isaacson, New York: Transcontinental Music Publications, New Jewish Music Press, 1998.

We Are They

xv Time *magazine reported:* From *Time*, June 15, 2015, p. 36.

FROM I TO WE

1 *"We must conceive of ourselves"*: From remarks by His Holiness the Dalai Lama during a round-table dialogue entitled "Balancing Educating the Mind with

Educating the Heart," held at the University of British Columbia in Vancouver, Canada, April 20, 2004. Participants included: His Holiness the Dalai Lama, Archbishop Desmond Tutu, Professor Shirin Ebadi, Rabbi Zalman Schachter-Shalomi, Dr. Jo-ann Archibald, and Bishop Michael Ingham.

3 *Diogenes*: A biographer of Greek philosophers. His major work, *Lives and Opinions of Eminent Philosophers* (c. 200 A.D.), is a key source for the history of Greek philosophy. The book has ten parts and includes the thinking of the Seven Sages of Ancient Greece, Socrates, Plato, the Stoics, Pythagoras, Empedocles, and Heraclitus. The work was first translated into Latin in the twelfth century and first into English in the seventeenth century.

3 *Rudolf Steiner*: Steiner (1861–1925) was a visionary philosopher, social reformer, and architect whose holistic thinking knit together mysticism, science, and social thought. He founded the spiritual movement anthroposophy and the Waldorf system of education. Both support direct access to spiritual experience through inner development. Steiner authored over four hundred volumes. Please see his books: *Philosophy of Freedom* (1894), *Mysticism at the Dawn of the Modern Age* (1901), and *The Renewal of the Social Organism* (1919).

3 *the old Scottish saying*: This saying is attributed to the Scottish clergyman George MacDonald (1824–1905).

Life Around the Fire

5 *"What if the healing of the world"*: From Wayne Muller, *How Then Shall We Live?: Four Simple Questions That Reveal the Beauty and Meaning of Our Lives*, New York: Bantam, 1997.

6 *Elie Wiesel recalls*: From Elie Wiesel, *Night*, a new translation by Marion Wiesel, New York: Hill & Wang, 2006, pp. 84–104. This brave, sensitive, and unflinching memoir of the concentration camps of World War II was first written in Yiddish as *And the World Remained Silent*. It was first translated into French, then into English. But so deep was the world's need to look away from the dark center of Nazism that the book was rejected by every major publisher despite the tireless support of the Nobel laureate François Mauriac. It took months of personal visits by Mauriac to finally get this book in print in 1956.

7 *On November 12, 1857*: The story of Richard Chenevix Trench and the meeting in the London Library is from a brilliant lecture by the journalist and author Simon Winchester based on his book, *The Meaning of Everything: The Story of the Oxford English Dictionary*, broadcast on the TVO program *Big Ideas*, March 25, 2007. See http://tvo.org/video/archive/big-ideas /simon-winchester.

7 *that eventually created the* Oxford English Dictionary: The first complete edition of the *OED* was finally published in ten volumes on April 19, 1928.

7 *the Indian Rebellion of 1857*: I also refer to this event in my spiritual novel, *This Strange and Blessed Humanness*, p. 274.

8 *who hanged thousands for sympathizing with the revolt*: The research in India of Dr. K. M Ashraf in "Ghalib & The Revolt of 1857," in *Rebellion 1857*, edited

by P. C. Joshi, 1957, proves that at least 27,000 people were hanged during the summer of 1857 for participating in or sympathizing with the revolt. Living in Delhi at the time, the famous Urdu poet Ghalib (1797–1869) witnessed it all, detailing the horror in his letters and in a diary he kept of the period called *Dastambo*.

9 *the Museum of Anthropology*: At the University of British Columbia in Vancouver. It houses one of the foremost First Nations collections in the world.

9 *Haida artist Bill Reid*: Bill Ronald Reid (1920–1998) was a Canadian jeweler, sculptor, and artist. Born to a father of European descent and a mother from the Haida, one of the First Nations of the Pacific coast, he developed a keen interest in Haida art while working as a radio announcer in Toronto. He also studied jewelry making, having first learned about his heritage from his maternal grandfather.

The Aspen Grove

15 *the most expansive growth of trees*: I'm indebted to the geo-chemist and geo-biologist Hope Jahren, author of *Lab Girl*, who confirmed that many trees share a common root system, including poplar, paw paw, hazel, guava, and ailanthus. Aspens are special in that their connected root system can generate a massive forest.

16 *Quaking aspen*: Details from M. Grant and J. Mitton, "Case Study: The Glorious, Golden, and Gigantic Quaking Aspen," in *Nature Education Knowledge* 1, no. 8, 2010, p. 40, http://www.nature.com/scitable/knowledge/library/case-study-the-glorious-golden-and-gigantic-13261308.

Notions of Community

18 *Notions of Community*: Much of this chapter is drawn from earlier versions of the chapters "Sympathetic Fibers" and "Trust of This Kind" in my earlier book *Finding Inner Courage*, San Francisco: Conari, 2007, pp. 73, 75–78. I began to explore the various notions of community in that book. Those beginnings led me here and so it seems worthwhile to revisit these passages as a context for the stories of community that follow.

18 *"Ubuntu is the essence of being human"*: From Archbishop Desmond Tutu's foreword to Robert D. Enright and Joanna North, eds., *Exploring Forgiveness*, Madison: University of Wisconsin Press, 1998.

18 *"Ubuntu (a Zulu word)"*: This definition is from Dirk J. Louw's article "Ubuntu: An African Assessment of the Religious Other," http://www.bu.edu/wcp/Papers/Afri/AfriLouw.htm.

19 *Consider that two living heart cells*: Please see my discussion of this in "The Fact of Our Oneness," in *The Exquisite Risk: Daring to Live an Authentic Life*, New York: Harmony Books, 2005, p. 78.

19 The Akasha Field: Please see Dr. Ervin László's book *Science and the Akashic Field: An Integral Theory of Everything*, Rochester, VT: Inner Traditions, 2004.

Bonds That Last

21 *"The essence of oneself"*: Joseph Campbell, from *The 2008 Shift Report*, Petaluma, CA: Institute of Noetic Sciences, 2008, p. 59.

22 *"All suffering recoils"*: Tiruvalluvar, in "The Hindu Ethic of Non-Violence," Subramuniyaswami, H. H. Gurudeva Sivaya. In *Hinduism Today*, Public Service Department, http://www.himalayanacademy.com/resources/pamphlets/AhimsaNonViolence.html.

23 *a commitment to nonviolence*: The Hindu scholar Raghavan Iyer said that Gandhi "regarded both Satya (truth) and Ahimsa (non-violence) as inherent in nature and in [people], underlying the constant working of a cosmic law. [Gandhi believed that] no society can survive without a measure of Satya (truth) and Ahimsa (non-violence)." From Raghavan Iyer, *The Moral and Political Thought of Mahatma Gandhi*, Santa Barbara, CA: Institute of World Culture, 2008.

23 *"I am not pleading for India"*: Gandhi, cited in Joah Valerie Bondurant, *Conquest of Violence: The Gandhian Philosophy of Conflict*, Princeton, NJ: Princeton University Press, 1988.

23 *In his* Analects ... *humaneness*: These concepts are clearly stated at http://www.britannica.com/topic/ren.

23 *Ren means ... "we would not be human"*: Mencius, from Kurtis Hagen, "Confucian Key Terms: Ren" (2007).

24 *Ren signifies*: This insight and other details about Ren are from Tu Wei-ming, the director of the Harvard-Yenching Institute, an independent institute jointly founded by Harvard University and Yenching University in 1928 for the higher education of humanity and social science of East Asia and Southeast Asia. Tu is the author of several books, including *Humanity and Self-Cultivation: Essays in Confucian Thought, The Living Tree: The Changing Meaning of Being Chinese Today*, and *Confucian Thought: Selfhood as Creative Transformation*.

24 *"The aftermath of nonviolence"*: From "The King Philosophy: The Beloved Community," the King Center, http://www.thekingcenter.org/king-philosophy.

24 *"our loyalties must"*: From Kenneth L. Mith and Ira G. Zepp, Jr., "Martin Luther King's Vision of the Beloved Community," *Christian Century*, 1974, pp. 361–63.

25 *"As I stood with them"*: From Martin Luther King, Jr., *Where Do We Go from Here: Chaos or Community?*, New York: Harper & Row, 1967, p. 9.

Little Raft, Big Raft

26 *These choices are represented by the two prominent Buddhist traditions*: I also refer to these traditions in the chapter "Sympathetic Fibers" in my book *Finding Inner Courage*, San Francisco: Conari, 2007, p. 78.

26 *"Freud argued that the self"*: Tim McKee, in "Conversations with a Remarkable Man: Honoring the Late James Hillman," a combined interview over ten years (1990, 1997, 2000) by Sy Safransky, Scott London, Genie Zeiger, from the

Sun, issue 439, July 2012, p. 6, https://www.thesunmagazine.org/issues/439/conversations-with-a-remarkable-man.

27 *"a society where men"*: From Kenneth L. Mith and Ira G. Zepp, Jr., "Martin Luther King's Vision of the Beloved Community," *Christian Century*, 1974, pp. 361–63.

Keeping Each Other Company

30 *"We must delight in each other"*: John Winthrop, cited in "A Model of Christian Charity," in *Puritan Political Ideas: 1558–1794*, Indianapolis: Bobbs Merrill, 1965, p. 93.

30 *Led by University of Michigan sociologist James S. House . . . lack of exercise*: "Dialing the Stress-Meter Down," Geoffrey Cowley, *Newsweek*, March 6, 1995, p. 62.

30 *In 1971, Hong Kong and Holland*: Rene Dubos, "The Diseases of Civilization," *Mainstreams in Medicine*, edited by Lester S. King, Austin: University of Texas Press, 1971, pp. 39–52.

31 *the Roseto effect*: B. Egolf, J. Lasker, L. Potvin, and S. Wolf, "The Roseto Effect: A 50-Year Comparison of Mortality Rates," *American Journal of Public Health* 82, no. 8, August 1992, pp. 1089–92.

31 *From 1954 to 1961*: Men in the community, fifty-five and older, enjoyed a death rate of 1 percent while the national average was 2 percent. Over a ten-year period, from 1955 to 1965, no one under sixty-five had a heart attack despite random lifestyles. From Ron Grossman and Charles Leroux, "A New Roseto Effect: People Are Nourished by Other People," *Chicago Tribune*, October 11, 1996.

31 *Stanford psychiatrist David Spiegel . . . and the dog's*: Geoffrey Cowley, "Dialing the Stress-Meter Down," *Newsweek*, March 6, 1995, p. 62.

32 *a privileged point of view*: From a conversation with Arthur Zajonc and Paul Wapner in Sausalito, California, May 1, 2010. Arthur Zajonc is a leading physicist and master educator whose latest book is *Meditation as Contemplative Inquiry: When Knowing Becomes Love*, Great Barrington, MA: Lindisfarne, 2009. Arthur is professor emeritus at Amherst College.

33 *anthropocentrism*: From a conversation with Paul Wapner and Arthur Zajonc in Sausalito, California, May 1, 2010. Paul Wapner is a leading environmentalist whose latest book (coauthored with Simon Nicholson) is *Global Environmental Politics: From Person to Planet*, New York: Paradigm, 2015. Paul is chair of the global environmental policy department at American University.

An Exercise in Faithfulness

35 *"Despite all our differences"*: Carl Jung, *The Undiscovered Self*, Boston: Little, Brown, 1957, p. 93.

35 *to engage the cynicism of our age*: From remarks by Dr. Stephen Toope, president of the University of British Columbia, to open the 2007 International Leadership Association Conference in Vancouver, B.C., October 31, 2007.

35 *the opposite of innocence is not guilt, but experience*: From a workshop led by Phil Levine at the University of Indiana Writers Conference, June 1977.

36 *"You will experience moments . . . power of angels"*: Rudolf Steiner. The physicist Arthur Zajonc reports that "the history of this citation is complex. We have it from the private notes of a Waldorf teacher who in turn got it from a colleague of Steiner's who received it from him. It is usually taken as truly being from Steiner, though we do not have it in his handwriting directly."

37 *"to 'remember itself'"*: From Jacob Needleman, *Why Can't We Be Good?* New York: Jeremy P. Tarcher/Putnam, 2007, p. 206.

Cooperation or Resistance

38 *Confucius*: The legendary Chinese philosopher Confucius (551 B.C.–479 B.C.) was born near the city of Qufu. As a young man, Confucius is reported to have worked as a shepherd, cowherd, clerk, and bookkeeper. His actual name was Kǒng Qiū. Fūzǐ means teacher. Since it was disrespectful to call a teacher by his full name, he became known as Kǒng Fūzǐ (Master Kǒng.) His philosophy known as Confucianism was first introduced to Europe in the early 1600s by the Jesuit Matteo Ricci, who first Latinized his name as "Confucius." See http://en.wikipedia.org/wiki/Confucius -_note-6.

The eleventh child of a seventy-year-old soldier, Confucius led a difficult life. He became a street sage; literate, compassionate, vocal, and at times hungry, homeless, unemployed, and subject to life-threatening violence.

The *Analects* (*Lun yü*, which means *Selected Sayings*) are considered the primary source of the words of Confucius. They were written over a period of thirty to fifty years after the great teacher's death. Much as the *Republic* is a collection of Socrates's discussions gathered by his disciple Plato, and as the *Sutras* are a collection of Buddha's Dharma talks gathered by his students, and as the Gospels are a collection of the times and words of Jesus written by his disciples, the *Analects* were almost certainly compiled by disciples and second-generation followers of Confucius.

In the *Analects*, Confucius presents himself as a "transmitter who invented nothing." It is said that when offered prayer when nearing death, Confucius summed up his life by saying, "My life has been a prayer."

38 *"We cease to play the part of the ruled"*: From *Hind Swaraj*, M. K. Gandhi, 1909, p. 100.

38 *"[our own] ability to preserve order"*: From *Young India*, M. K. Gandhi, August 4, 1920.

Just Take a Pebble

40 *"Don't ask the mountain"*: John Paul Lederach, from the Center for Mennonite Writing website's bimonthly journal, *Poetry of Peace* 3, no. 5, edited by Ann E. Hostetler and Jeff Gundy. John Paul Lederach is a leading peace builder at work

in the world. See *The Moral Imagination: The Art and Soul of Building Peace*, New York: Oxford University Press, 2005.

42 *"I believe human beings come into the world"*: S. Brian Williams, from an interview by Greg King, "We Are Not Worth More, They Are Not Worth Less: The Odyssey of S. Brian Williams," *Sun*, issue 447, March 2013, pp. 4–12, https://www.thesunmagazine.org/issues/447/we-are-not-worth-more.

42 *"Having two bathrooms"*: Margaret Mead, in "Sunbeams" (quotations), *Sun*, issue 447, March 2013, p. 48, https://www.thesunmagazine.org/issues/447/sunbeams.

ISLANDS IN TIME

47 *"The first peace"*: From *The Sacred Pipe: Black Elk's Account of the Seven Rites of the Oglala Sioux*, recorded and edited by Joseph Epes Brown, Norman, OK: University of Oklahoma Press, 1953, p. 115.

47 *"We are tied together"*: Martin Luther King, Jr., from his last sermon, Washington National Cathedral, March 31, 1968, quoted in Jon Meacham, "The American Soul," *Newsweek* (commemorative issue: "Obama's American Dream"), November 2008, p. 29.

Hospitality

53 *My grandfather*: I originally refer to this family legend in the chapter "Legacy" in my book *The One Life We're Given: Finding the Wisdom That Waits in Your Heart*, New York: Atria, 2016, p. 13.

53 *community cafés*: Please see http://paneracares.org.

54 *"Everyone needs some help"*: From an interview with Michael Meade by John Malkin, "Your Own Damn Life: Michael Meade and the Story We're Born With," *Sun*, issue 431, November 2011, p. 8, https://www.thesunmagazine.org/issues/431/your-own-damn-life.

54 *Bread for the Journey*: Please see http://breadforthejourney.org.

55 *"if we have no peace"*: Mother Teresa, in "Sunbeams" (quotations), *Sun*, issue 452, August 2013, p. 48, https://www.thesunmagazine.org/issues/452/sunbeams.

55 *"No human life"*: Hannah Arendt, in *Lapham's Quarterly: Politics* 5, no. 4, Fall 2012, p. 168, https://www.laphamsquarterly.org/contributors/arendt.

55 wampum: The term *wampum* is a shortening of the earlier word *wampumpeag*, which is derived from the Narragansett word meaning *white strings of shell beads*. Narragansett is the ancient language of the Algonquian tribe.

55 *Originating with the Algonquin tribe*: Details about the wampum custom are drawn from the exhibit "Grasping the Wampum" in the remarkable Eiteljorg Museum of American Indians and Western Art in Indianapolis, Indiana.

56 *When asked what stirred her*: Details about what shaped Elisabeth Kübler-Ross in her work are drawn from "The Final Stage," a memorial column written by Jonathan Rosen for the *New York Times Magazine*, December 26, 2004, p. 14.

57 *"If a heart could fail in its pumping"*: Caroline Kettlewell, in "Sunbeams" (quotations), *Sun,* issue 439, July 2012, p. 48, https://www.thesunmagazine.org/issues/439/sunbeams.

57 *"If we don't understand"*: From the historian Robert Bellah at a public dialogue held in San Francisco, June 8, 2006.

58 *"I can't cross a threshold"*: Pilar Gonzales is a community organizer and former president of the non-profit Changemakers. These comments are from a conversation in May 2008.

Of Two Minds

59 *"Socialism never took root"*: John Steinbeck, in "Sunbeams" (quotations) *Sun,* issue 447, March 2013, p. 48, https://www.thesunmagazine.org/issues/447/sunbeams.

59 *gifts were made of*: David Graeber, *Toward an Anthropological Theory of Value: The False Coin of Our Own Dreams,* New York: Palgrave, 2001, p. 205.

60 *"regalia was seized"*: This description is from the Mexican-Yaqui historian Richard Walker.

60 *"by far the most formidable"*: Robin Fisher, *Contact and Conflict: Indian-European Relations in British Columbia, 1774–1890,* Vancouver, BC: University of British Columbia Press, 1977, p. 207.

60 *Jesus fed the multitudes*: The feeding of the 5000 is also known as the miracle of the five loaves and two fish that were used by Jesus to feed a multitude. See John 6:5–15.

60 *The Abenaki elder Joseph Bruchac*: These notions are from a dialogue I had with Joe Bruchac in March 2007. For an invaluable introduction to the Native American worldview, please see his *Our Stories Remember: Indian History, Culture, and Values Through Storytelling,* Golden, CO: Fulcrum, 2003.

60 *potlatching was made illegal in Canada*: In 1884, the Indian Act was revised to ban the potlatch. Section 3 of the Act read: "Every Indian or other person who engages in or assists in celebrating the Indian festival known as the 'Potlatch' or the Indian dance known as the 'Tamanawas' is guilty of a misdemeanor, and shall be liable to imprisonment for a term not more than six nor less than two months in any gaol or other place of confinement."

60 *contrary to their values*: G. M. Sproat, quoted in Douglas Cole and Ira Chaikin, *An Iron Hand upon the People: The Law Against the Potlatch on the Northwest Coast,* Vancouver, B.C.: Douglas & McIntyre, 1990, p. 15.

61 *"We will dance when our laws command us to dance"*: Chief O'waxalagalis as recorded by Franz Boas in "The Indians of British Columbia," *Popular Science Monthly* 32, March 1888, p. 631.

61 *"The so-called* potlatch": Ibid. p. 636.

62 *"Power systems"*: Noam Chomsky, from an interview by David Barsamian, "Undermining Democracy," *Sun,* issue 462, June 2014, p. 6, https://www.thesun magazine.org/issues/462/undermining-democracy.

Fairness

64 *Eindhoven, in the Netherlands*: I learned of this story from Chris Grant, a gifted executive coach and consultant who lives and works in London.

65 *Primatologist Frans de Waal has seen that bonobos*: I happened on the story of bonobos while listening to the PBS show *Science Friday with Ira Flatow*, April 5, 2013. For more information, including the video, please see http://www.sciencefriday.com/segment/04/05/2013/-searching-for-the-roots-of-right-and-wrong.html.

The Migration of Care

70 *"allows anyone to enter private farmland"*: Gary Snyder, *The Practice of the Wild*, Berkeley, CA: Counterpoint, 2010, p. 35.

70 Osusu: Details about the practice of Osusu are from Oumou, "OSUSU, A Traditional Way of Saving in Africa," in *Lives of African Women*, posted Saturday, July 9, 2011, http://ritesritualsanddailylife.blogspot.com/2011/07/osusu-traditional-way-of-saving-in.html; Filomina Chioma Steady, *Women and Collective Action in Africa*, New York: Palgrave Macmillan, 2006; William R. Bascom, "The Esusu: A Credit Institution of the Yoruba," *Journal of the Royal Anthropological Institute of Great Britain and Ireland*, 1952; and Paul Alfred Barton, *Susu and Susunomics: The Theory and Practice of Pan-African Economic, Racial and Cultural Self-Preservation*, Lincoln, NE: Authors Choice, 2001.

72 *every fall, the monarch*: Details from "The Life Cycle(s) of a Monarch Butterfly," Monarch Butterfly Website, http://www.monarch-butterfly.com.

Whole-Mind Thinking

73 *"What you see and hear"*: C. S. Lewis, *The Magician's Nephew*, London: Bodley Head, 1955.

75 *Las Vegas (January 4, 2010)*: A man who lost a recent Social Security claim walked into the lobby of the Las Vegas federal courthouse, pulled a shotgun from underneath his jacket, and began shooting, killing a court security officer and injuring a deputy U.S. marshal.

Learning Together

77 *we first began to walk upright*: Details in these first two paragraphs are taken from "The Answers Issue," *Time*, July 6, 2015, p. 46.

77 *in Morocco*: The University of al-Qarawiyyin in Fes, Morocco, is the oldest degree-awarding educational institution in the world. It was founded by Fatima al-Fihri in 859 and has become one of the leading educational centers of the Muslim world.

78 *The Gandhara Empire*: Details about Gandhara from "Gandhara" in *New*

World Encyclopedia, http://www.newworldencyclopedia.org/entry/gandhara; Le Huu Phuoc, *Buddhist Architecture*, Lakeville, MN: Grafikol, 2010, p. 51; Barbara O'Brien, "The Lost World of Buddhist Gandhara: The Kushans at the Peak of Gandharan Culture," ThoughtCo., http://buddhism.about.com/od /buddhisthistory/a/gandhara_2.htm; Hub Pages, "History of Taxila University," http://dilipchandra12.hubpages.com/hub/History-of-Taxila-University; and "Takshashila—World's Oldest University," Gurudev, HitXP: A Blogzine by Guruduv, September 11, 2007, http://www.hitxp.com/articles/history /takshashila-taxila-oldest-university.

79 *from master to master*: Several of the leading teachers of the day found their way by studying with masters themselves. The great teacher Yun-Yen (d. 841) visited many teachers before settling on Yaoshan Weiyan as his master. In turn, the great teacher Tung-Shan (807–869) spent much of his early life wandering between Chan masters and hermits before settling on Yun-Yen as his master.

80 *Yeshe-Ö (c. 959–1040)*: Details about Yeshe-Ö are from O. C. Handa, *Buddhist Western Himalaya, Part 1: A Politico-Religious History*, New Delhi: Indus, 2001; O. C. Handa, *Tabo Monastery and Buddhism in the Trans-Himalaya*, Tagore Garden, New Delhi: Indus, 1994; Sonam Rinchen, *Atisha's Lamp for the Path to Enlightenment*, Ithaca, NY: Snow Lion, 1997; and Alexander Berzin, *Wise Teacher, Wise Student*, Ithaca, NY: Snow Lion, 2010.

From One to Another

82 *"What is a bee"*: Puanani Burgess is a poet, cultural translator, and developer of community-based organizations. She has extensive experience in community, family and values-based economic development, mediation, and conflict transformation through storytelling. Her stories and remarks come from a conversation in May 2008.

82 *"They came first"*: By Martin Niemöller, in the New England Holocaust Memorial in Boston.

82 What is Art?: This essay by Leo Tolstoy was originally published in 1896 and was translated into English by Aylmer Maude in 1899.

83 *"by lifting his heart"*: From William Faulkner's speech at the Nobel Prize Banquet at City Hall in Stockholm, December 10, 1950.

83 *"I work at a private park"*: From "Readers Write," *Sun*, issue 406, October 2009, pp. 31–32.

84 *the story of the Buddhist Bodhisattva*: I have long admired the life of a Bodhisattva and have explored this further in the section "Taking in a Hundred Rivers" in my book *Seven Thousands Ways to Listen: Staying Close to What Is Sacred* (reprint edition), New York: Atria, 2013, pp. 250–51.

84 *the nature of a Bodhisattva*: From Neal Pollock, *Practices Supporting Dzogchen: The Great Perfection of Tibetan Buddhism*, 2005, p. 43. Found in Ananda K. Coomaraswamy, *Buddha and the Gospel of Buddhism*, Boston: University Books, 1975, p. 225.

Entrainments of Heart

86 *"There is one soul and many tongues"*: Tertullian, from the chart "Reform Movements" in *Lapham's Quarterly: Means of Communication 5*, no. 2, Spring 2012, p. 70.

86 *"the necessity of speaking truth"*: James Fenimore Cooper, in *Lapham's Quarterly 5*, no. 4, Fall 2012, p. 19.

88 *Rabbi Zusya of Hanipol*: From Abraham Joshua Heschel, *The Earth Is the Lord's: The Inner World of the Jew in Eastern Europe*, Woodstock, VT: Jewish Lights, 2001, p. 50.

Our Struggle and Possibility

92 *"If you stick a knife"*: Malcolm X, from "TV Interview after 90-day moratorium," March 1964.

92 *Eldar Shafir, a professor at Princeton*: Eldar Shafir coauthored *Scarcity: Why Having Too Little Means So Much* (New York: Time Books/Henry Holt, 2013) with economist Sendhil Mullainathan.

93 *Until we fall . . . we really don't know*: An earlier version of this paragraph first appeared as the poem "Side by Side" in my book *The Way Under the Way: The Place of True Meeting*, Boulder, CO: Sounds True, 2016, p. 248.

CENTERS OF LIGHT

The Seeds of Our Nature

106 *Nalanda was one of the world's first residential universities*: Details of Nalanda University and its remarkable library are from http://en.wikipedia.org/wiki/Nalanda.

106 *"the birth of the winds and clouds"*: D. C. Ahir, *Buddhism Declined in India: How and Why?*, Delhi: B. R. Publishing, 2005.

106 *"if a monk did something without consent"*: Joseph Walser, *Nāgārjuna in Context: Mahāyāna Buddhism and Early Indian Culture*, New York: Columbia University Press, 2005, p. 102.

107 *Nalanda University was brutally sacked by the fanatic Turk general, Bakhtiyar Khilji*: From Sukumar Dutt, *Buddhist Monks and Monasteries of India: Their History and Contribution to Indian Culture*, London: Allen & Unwin, 1962, pp. 352–53.

107 *Thousands of monks were beheaded*: From William Dalrymple, "When Buddha Was Sacked" (book review of *The Buddha and the Sahibs* by Charles Allen, London: John Murray, 2002), *Guardian*, September 27, 2002.

107 *The library was vandalized and burned*: From Gertrude Emerson Sen, *The Story of Early Indian Civilization*, Bombay: Orient Longmans, 1964.

Seat of the Muses

113 *"History is necessarily personal"*: Lily Rothman, "The Founding of America? It's All About Us," *Time*, October 26, 2015, p. 54.

113 *From the earliest times, museums*: I've gathered many details from a fine article on the history of museums found in Wikipedia, https://en.wikipedia.org/w /index.php?title=Museum.

115 *During the French Revolution*: Details in this paragraph are from Pierre Nora and Lawrence D. Kritzman, *Realms of Memory*, New York: Columbia University Press, 1996, and Bette Wyn Oliver, *From Royal to National: The Louvre Museum and the Bibliothèque Nationale*, Lanham, MD: Lexington Books, 2007.

Clearings for Renewal

117 *into the soft and sudden company of others*: "Central Park is without a central place. It has many centers, and was meant to: the Sheep Meadow, the Mall, the Reservoir—all provide an experience of the center without actually being one... You learn how to get around Central Park by experience. There's no fixed path to take you where you want to go... [and w]e can never step into the same Park twice." Adam Gopnik, "Olmsted's Trip," *New Yorker*, May 31, 1997.

117 *Frederick Law Olmsted*: Details about Olmsted's life and the construction of Central Park are drawn from two outstanding articles in Wikipedia, https:// en.wikipedia.org/wiki/Frederick_Law_Olmsted and https://en.wikipedia.org /wiki/Central_Park.

Olmsted's mother died when he was three. But his early memory of her sitting beneath a large tree seeded his vision of creating peaceful spaces in nature where people could pause and gather. Another key experience came when he worked in the 1840s as a reporter in the South for the fledgling *New York Times*. From this work, he became an abolitionist. This experience shaped his social consciousness and formed his belief that urban parks had to be free and available to all.

118 *"An artist, he paints with lakes and wooded slopes"*: Daniel Burnham, from Erik Larson, *The Devil in the White City*, New York: Crown, 2003.

Where We Meet

121 *"Between the extremes of deep wilderness"*: Gary Snyder, *The Practice of the Wild*, Berkeley, CA: Counterpoint, 1990, pp. 32–33.

122 *"Rashi democratized Jewish education"*: Abraham Joshua Heschel, *The Earth Is the Lord's: The Inner World of the Jew in Eastern Europe*, Woodstock, VT: Jewish Lights, 2001, p. 41.

122 *In ancient Greece, Aristotle convened his students on the grounds*: I explore this more fully in the chapter "The Sacred Grove" in my book *The One Life We're Given: Finding the Wisdom That Waits in Your Heart*, New York: Atria 2016, p. 291.

122 *The European town square*: Details about the European town square from "Genius of the European Square," Suzanne H. Crowhurst Lennard, December 2004, http://www.livablecities.org/articles/genius-european-square.

123 *"There is no choice"*: Gary Snyder, *The Practice of the Wild*, Berkeley, CA: Counterpoint, 2010, p. 39.

The Forest Community

125 *the Bielski partisans*: Details and quotes about the Bielski partisans are from Peter Duffy, *The Bielski Brothers: The True Story of Three Men Who Defied the Nazis, Built a Village in the Forest, and Saved 1,200 Jews*, New York: HarperCollins, 2003, and Tec Nechama, *Defiance: The Bielski Partisans*, New York: Oxford University Press, 1993. The latter is the book the movie *Defiance* is based on.

Without Ever Pushing

128 *Without Ever Pushing*: Details and quotes have been drawn from Wim Wenders's magnificently life-sustaining film *Pina—Dance, Dance, Otherwise We Are Lost* (2011); an article "Working with Pina Bausch" by Patricia Boccadoro in *CultureKiosque*, October 16, 2007; an obituary by Judith Cruickshank that appeared in the *Independent*, July 3, 2009; and from an interview with Wim Wenders by Lisa Mullins that appeared in the *World*, December 23, 2011.

130 *decades of dance innovation and immersion began*: As Patricia Boccadoro says, "Her stunning work could include speech, social dance, repetition, dramatic, comic or surrealist situations, nudity, cross-dressing, brutality or tenderness, all adding up to an often uncomfortably perceptive commentary on the human situation. You might be annoyed, upset or even distressed by a work by Bausch. The settings are extraordinary. For her *Rite of Spring*, premiered in 1975, the entire stage is covered in peat which clings to the dancers' sweating, semi-naked bodies. *Nelken* features a stage planted with the carnations of the title which are gradually trampled by the action. And Sadler's Wells had to strengthen the stage to support the tons of earth which formed 20ft high ramparts for *Viktor*." From Patricia Boccadoro, "Working with Pina Bausch," *CultureKiosque*, October 16, 2007.

The Web of Knowing

132 *Wikipedia*: Details about Wikipedia, its history and reach are from *60 Minutes*, CBS, April 5, 2015, and Wikipedia, https://en.wikipedia.org/wiki/Wikipedia.

133 *In Egyptian mythology*: Details in the four paragraphs about the gods of knowledge and wisdom are from E. A. Wallis Budge, *The Gods of the Egyptians*, vol. 1, New York: Dover Publications, 1969 (original in 1904), p. 414; David Carrasco, *Quetzalcoatl and the Irony of Empire: Myths and Prophecies in the Aztec Tradition*, Chicago: University of Chicago Press, 1982; Michael Ashkenazi, *Handbook of Japanese Mythology*, New York: Oxford University Press, 2003; and Kathleen Herbert, *Looking for the Lost Gods of England*, Norfolk, UK: Anglo-Saxon Books, 2010.

A Common Song

135 *the program describes itself*: Please see "The Saint John's Pottery" on the Saint John's University website: http://www.csbsju.edu/saint-johns-pottery.

135 *an Anagama kiln*: Part of this paragraph originally appeared in my book *Finding Inner Courage*, San Francisco: Conari, 2007, p. 236.

136 *Occupying the same geographical areas*: Details from Adam S. Frankel, "Sound Production," in *Encyclopedia of Marine Mammals*, edited by William F. Perrin, Bernd Würsig, and J. G. M. Thewissen. San Diego: Academic Press, 2002, pp. 1126–37.

136 *strikingly similar to human musical traditions*: Details from Roger Payne, cited in Susan Milius, "Music Without Borders," *Science News* 157, no. 16, April 15, 2000, pp. 252–54.

137 *Iroquois dreamwork*: From Tracy Marks (Tika Yupanqui), "Iroquois Dreamwork and Spirituality," 1998, http://www.webwinds.com/yupanqui/iroquois dreams2.htm. Other details about dream-walking are from Robert Moss, *Conscious Dreaming: A Spiritual Path for Everyday Life*, New York: Random House Digital, 1996, and James R. Lewis and Evelyn Dorothy Oliver, *The Dream Encyclopedia*, Canton, MI: Visible Ink Press, 2009.

Larger Than Ourselves

139 *"[We have] to hang together"*: This and other quotes are from Anonymous, *Alcoholics Anonymous: The Big Book*, fourth edition, New York: Alcoholics Anonymous World Services, 2002, pp. xiii–xxiv.

With and Against Community

143 *"Since the Renaissance"*: From remarks by Rabbi Zalman Schachter-Shalomi during a roundtable dialogue entitled "Balancing Educating the Mind with Educating the Heart," held at the University of British Columbia in Vancouver, Canada, April 20, 2004. Participants included: His Holiness the Dalai Lama, Archbishop Desmond Tutu, Professor Shirin Ebadi, Rabbi Zalman Schachter-Shalomi, Dr. Jo-ann Archibald, and Bishop Michael Ingham.

Carrying the Water

148 *"The Chief of the Well"*: From *Tell These Secrets: Tales of Generosity from Around the World*, edited by Margo McLoughlin, an amazing collection of seventy-four stories gathered from twenty-three traditions.

149 *the Acequia Madre*: Details about the Acequia Madre are from Enrique Lamadrid, "Acequias," http://smithsonianeducation.org/scitech/impacto/graphic /rio/english/natural_acequias.html; Francis Quintana, "Farming Childhoods," in *When We Were Young in the West*, edited by Richard Melzer, Santa Fe, NM: Sunstone, 2003; Virginia Sanchez, *Forgotten Chuchareños of the Lower Valley*, Charleston, SC: History Press, 2010; and José A. Rivera, *Acequia Culture: Water, Land, and Community in the Southwest*, Albuquerque: University of New Mexico Press, 1998.

Unraveling the Knots

152 *"are almost universally loved and accepted"*: Annie B. White, "Wolf Behavior," http://www.graywolfconservation.com/Information/behavior.htm.

153 *The social impulse of gorillas*: There are roughly seven hundred mountain gorillas remaining on earth, and nearly half live in the forests of the Virunga Mountains in central Africa. Details from the National Geographic website ("Moun-tain Gorilla") at http://animals.nationalgeographic.com/animals/mammals/mountain-gorilla and the Gorillas-World website ("Gorilla Social Structure") at http://www.gorillas-world.com/gorilla-social-structure.

153 *The Jewish philosopher Abraham Herschel*: Abraham Heschel, *The Earth Is the Lord's: The Inner World of the Jew in Eastern Europe*, Woodstock, VT: Jewish Lights Publishing, 2001, p. 32.

153 *"Nothing anyone else can do"*: Parker J. Palmer, *Life on the Möbius Strip*, unpub-lished paper, 2001, p. 2.

153 *A recent study shows that rats*: David Brown, "A New Model of Empathy: The Rat," *Washington Post*, December 8, 2011, http://www.washingtonpost.com/national/health-science/a-new-model-of-empathy-the-rat/2011/12/08/gIQAAx0jfO_story.html (originally reported in *Science* 334, no. 6061, pp. 1427–30, http://www.sciencemag.org/content/334/6061/1427).

154 *Neuroscientists have discovered*: At the Brain Imaging Center at Wayne State University, Dr. Kit Green is studying how these neural structures impact the presence and absence of interpersonal connection.

154 *a compelling study of institutionalized infants*: From Lise Eliot, *What's Going On in There?: How the Brain and Mind Develop in the First Five Years of Life*, New York: Bantam, 2000, p. 5.

154 *how birds sing at the sign of first light*: An early exploration of this topic appears in the chapter "The Song of Relationship" in my book *The Exquisite Risk: Daring to Live an Authentic Life*, New York: Harmony Books, 2005, pp. 152–53.

155 *Kuntai Karmushu*: I met Kuntai at a remarkable seminar on environmental peace-building held at the Woodrow Wilson Center, January 10–13, 2010.

Bending or Loving the World

158 *Kegan defines centrism*: Robert Kegan, from his keynote "In Over Our Heads? The Hidden Curriculum of Adult Life" at the Uncovering the Heart of Higher Education Conference, San Francisco, February 23, 2007. Please see *In Over Our Heads*, Robert Kegan, Cambridge, MA: Harvard University Press, 1994.

159 *we see a pride of lions*: Details from Dean Tersigni, "Animal Group Names," www.thealmightyguru.com/Pointless/AnimalGroups.html.

160 *the term Powaqqatsi*: *Powaqqatsi* combines two notions, *powaq* (sorcerer) and *qatsi* (life). Please see the landmark film trilogy conceived by Godfrey Reg-gio, of which *Powaqqatsi* (1988) is the second. The first film is *Koyaanisqatsi* (1982), which is Hopi for a life out of balance. The third film is *Naqoyqatsi* (2006), which is Hopi for a life of killing each other.

161 *"Come in, there is no lock"*: Eugene Ruggles (1935–2004), excerpt from "Inscription on the Door," from *Roads of Bread: The Collected Poems of Eugene Ruggles*, Bodega, CA: Petaluma River Press, 2010.

The Courage to Take Others In

162 *Words on the Statue of Liberty*: These well-known lines are from the sonnet "The New Colossus" by Emma Lazarus (1849–1887), which she wrote to raise money for the pedestal on which the Statue of Liberty rests.

163 *more than 52,000 children*: Details about the Mexican children crisis of 2014 are from Jo Tuckman, " 'Flee or Die': Violence Drives Central America's Child Migrants to US Border," *Guardian*, July 9, 2014; Ian Gordon, "70,000 Kids Will Show Up Alone at Our Border This Year. What Happens to Them?" *Mother Jones*, July–August 2014; Dianna Hunt, "Dallas-area volunteers prepare for arrival of migrant children," *Dallas News*, July 7, 2014; and *The Rachel Maddow Show*, July 9, 2014.

163 *the Kindertransport*: An earlier version of the Kindertransport story originally appeared in the chapter "The Rhythm of Kindness" in my book *The Exquisite Risk: Daring to Live an Authentic Life*, New York: Harmony Books, 2005, p. 167.

Putting Down the Brick

165 *Putting Down the Brick*: This chapter first appeared under the title "The Loss of One Brick" in my book *The Exquisite Risk: Daring to Live an Authentic Life*, New York: Harmony Books, 2005, pp. 154–59.

168 *"The Height of Ambition"*: by James Glanz and Eric Lipton: *New York Times Magazine*, September 8, 2002.

Removing the Oldest Wall

170 *a phonetic alphabet, Hangul*: From the chart "Reform Movements," in *Lapham's Quarterly: Means of Communication* 5, no. 2, Spring 2012, p. 40. Details on the life of Sejong the Great are from Wikipedia: See http://en.wikipedia.org/wiki/Sejong_the_Great.

170 *Sejong created a farmer's handbook*: Sejong also employed Jang Yeong-sil (c. 1390–after 1442), a gifted inventor from the lower class. Despite court opposition, Sejong funded the inventor's work in creating water clocks, sundials, and the world's first rain gauge.

171 *In his introduction to Hangul, Sejong wrote*: "Because the speech of this country is different from that of China, [the spoken language] does not match the letters. Therefore, even if the ignorant want to communicate, many of them . . . cannot state their concerns. Saddened by this, I have [had] 28 letters newly made. It is my wish that all the people may easily learn these letters and that [they] be convenient for daily use." From the introduction to *Hunminjeongeum* by King Sejong the Great, offering Hangul as the new Korean language, October 9, 1446. See http://en.wikipedia.org/wiki/Hunmin_Jeongeum.

Blind Travelers

173 *"Moments of the soul"*: From Abraham Joshua Heschel, *The Earth Is the Lord's: The Inner World of the Jew in Eastern Europe*, Woodstock, VT: Jewish Lights Publishing, 2001, p. 13.

173 *As early as 1844 ... alienated individual*: Alienation is a theme that runs throughout the work of Karl Marx (1818–1883), beginning with his *Economic and Philosophic Manuscripts* of 1844.

173 *Karl Marx*: Comparative religion professor Tim Light of Western Michigan University notes that, in our haste to exile all Marxist thought, we've dropped some very important insights he had into the nature of society.

174 *These estrangements*: Many sociologists of the late nineteenth and early twentieth centuries were concerned about the alienating effects of modernization pointed to by Marx. German sociologists Georg Simmel (1858–1918) and Ferdinand Tönnies (1855–1936) wrote seminal works on individualization and urbanization. Simmel's *Philosophy of Money* (*Philosophie des Geldes*) explores how relationships become more and more diluted through money, while Tönnies's *Community and Society* (*Gemeinschaft und Gesellschaft*) describes the loss of primary relationships such as family bonds in favor of goal-oriented relationships.

About to Wake

178 *Plato's analogy of the cave*: It's worth visiting the full text of Plato's Allegory of the Cave, found in Book VII (514a–520a) of Plato's *Republic*, nested in a conversation between Socrates and his young follower, Glaucon. You can also hear my telling of this ancient story in my box set *Staying Awake: The Ordinary Art* (Sounds True, 2012), Disc 7, Track 9: "What We Know and How We Know It."

Grown over Centuries

181 *This remarkable epoch*: María Rosa Menocal (1953–2012), a Cuban-born scholar of medieval culture and history and professor of humanities at Yale University, authored a masterful book unfolding the magic of this time called *The Ornament of the World: How Muslims, Jews, and Christians Created a Culture of Tolerance in Medieval Spain*, New York: Back Bay, 2002. I have leaned heavily on Professor Menocal's work to inform what I want to explore here.

181 *Three renowned philosophers were born in Córdoba*: The magnificent city was also the home of the extraordinary Jewish physician-translator-diplomat Hasdai ibn Shaprut, who served as the doctor and minister of foreign affairs for Abd ar-Rahman III, the progressive caliph of Córdoba.

181 *"the brilliant ornament of the world"*: María Rosa Menocal, *The Ornament of the World: How Muslims, Jews, and Christians Created a Culture of Tolerance in Medieval Spain*, New York: Back Bay, 2002, pp. 32–33.

182 *"in those libraries"*: María Rosa Menocal, *The Ornament of the World: How Muslims, Jews, and Christians Created a Culture of Tolerance in Medieval Spain*, New York: Back Bay, 2002, p. 35.

Building Things Together

185 *Over a five- to seven-week life span*: Details from "The Social Lives of Bees," http://beespotter.mste.illinois.edu/topics/social.

185 *"indeed, there is no all-knowing central planner"*: Thomas D. Seeley, *Honeybee Democracy*, Princeton, NJ: Princeton University Press, 2010.

187 *"spiritual substance"*: Abraham Joshua Heschel, *The Earth Is the Lord's: The Inner World of the Jew in Eastern Europe*, Woodstock, VT: Jewish Lights Publishing, 2001, pp. 7–10.

187 *Baraza Inter-Community Forum*: Details about Baraza are from "Home Grown Mechanisms of Conflict Resolution in Africa's Great Lakes Region," Shyaka Anastase, George Mason University, 2007, http://www.globality-gmu.net/archives/893; "Baraza and Community Peace Courts," the Chirezi Foundation, http://chirezifoundation.webs.com/peacebuilding.htm; "Farmer Groups as a Way of Mobilizing Citizen Participation in Development," Catherine Wawasi Kitetu, 11th General Assembly, Maputo, 2005; and "About mikihawa, baraza, being intense and thinking of Bosnia."

188 conocimiento *means "to nurture connection . . . of each other"*: Details about conocimiento are from Roberto Vargas, "Transformative Knowledge: A Chicano Perspective," Context Institute, http://www.context.org/iclib/ic17/vargas; Frances F. Korten and Roberto Vargas, *Movement Building for Transformational Change*, Bainbridge Island, WA: Positive Futures Network, 2006, pp. 31–32; Roberto Vargas, *Family Activism: Empowering Your Community, Beginning with Family and Friends*, San Francisco: Berrett-Koehler, 2008; and Juan Cruz, "Cultural Dynamics."

188 *"The real connection occurs"*: Roberto Vargas, *Family Activism: Empowering Your Community, Beginning with Family and Friends*, San Francisco: Berrett-Koehler, 2008.

HOW WE MEET ADVERSITY

193 *"What is to give light must endure burning"*: Viktor Frankl, *Man's Search for Meaning*, Boston: Beacon Press, 2000.

Beginning Again

197 *the Pazzi conspiracy was set in motion*: I first encountered this compelling moment in Renaissance history while working on my epic poem *Fire Without Witness: Michelangelo in the Sistine Chapel*, Latham, NY: British American Publishing, 1988, in which I imagine Lorenzo de' Medici recounting his experience

to a young Michelangelo. Please see *Fire Without Witness,* p. 229. Details about the Pazzi conspiracy are from Lauro Martines, *April Blood: Florence and the Plot Against the Medici,* New York: Oxford University Press, 2003, pp. 187–96, and Nicolai Rubinstein, *The Government of Florence Under the Medici (1434–1494),* Oxford, UK: Clarendon Press, 1997, p. 223.

198 *the Medici Circle was created*: Details about the Medici Circle are from F. W. Kent, *Lorenzo de' Medici and the Art of Magnificence,* Baltimore: Johns Hopkins University Press, 2006, p. 248; Lee Hancock, *Lorenzo de' Medici: Florence's Great Leader and Patron of the Arts,* New York: Rosen, 2005, p. 57; "Lorenzo de' Medici" in *The Columbia Electronic Encyclopedia,* 6th edition, 2007, http://www .infoplease.com/ce6/people/A0832477.html; and Giorgio Vasari, *The Lives of the Artists,* translated by Julia Conway Bondanella and Peter Bondanella, New York: Oxford University Press, 1998. For a compelling documentary, please see Cassian Harrison and William M. Larkin, *Medici: Godfathers of the Renaissance,* DVD, Lion Television, PBS, and Devillier Donegan Enterprises, 2004.

199 *"Friendship is the end of all philosophy"*: Pico della Mirandella, from *Oration on the Dignity of Man* (1486), Washington State University, https://brians.wsu.edu /2016/11/14/pico-della-mirandola-oration-on-the-dignity-of-man-15th-c-ce.

The Bell of Nagasaki

200 *A week before the atomic bomb was dropped*: Details about Nagasaki and the atomic bomb are from Tom Skylark, *Final Months of the Pacific War,* Georgetown University Press, 2002, p. 178; C. V. Glines, "World War II: Second Atomic Bomb That Ended the War," in *Aviation History,* January 1997, http://www.historynet.com /world-war-ii-second-atomic-bomb-that-ended-the-war.htm; Record Group 457, Records of the National Security Agency, Central Security Service, Diplomatic Summaries, 1942–1945, box 18; "The Atomic Bomb and the End of World War II: A Collection of Primary Sources," National Security Archive, http://www .gwu.edu/~nsarchiv/NSAEBB/NSAEBB162/index.htm; and Duncan Anderson, "Nuclear Power: The End of the War Against Japan," BBC History, 2011, http://www.bbc.co.uk/history/worldwars/wwtwo/nuclear_01.shtml.

200 *One survivor*: From "When Atom Bomb Struck—Uncensored," *Life,* September 29, 1952, pp. 19–24.

The Road Before the Temple

203 *"Its root meaning is 'holding on to truth'"*: Gandhi's "Statement to Disorders Inquiry Committee," January 5, 1920, in *The Collected Works of Mahatma Gandhi,* vol. 19, p. 206.

204 *In Vykom*: My telling of this story is based on the account of the walk of the untouchables in Vykom originally published in Gene Sharp, "Creative Conflict," *The New Era,* London: Housmans, 1962, p. 4.

205 *"At the present moment . . . millions of Hindus"*: The three quotes in this para-

graph are from a verbatim report of a talk given by Gandhi to the volunteers at Vykom. From M. K. Gandhi, *Non-Violent Resistance: Satyagraha*, New York: Dover, 2001, unabridged republication of Gandhi's original, first published by the Navajivan Trust, Ahmedabad, 1951, pp. 181, 192–94.

207 *How do we begin to feel and understand such a moment?*: It is interesting how Gandhi came to understand his own moment of Satyagraha. As a young lawyer in South Africa, Gandhi experienced the dehumanization of Africans and Indians. This was to be his crucible, in which he struggled not to succumb to either violent outrage or helpless resignation. Slowly and painfully, he found his way to his lifelong quest to grasp for the truth that lives beneath imperfect laws.

In the fall of 1906, the Transvaal Assembly of South Africa introduced the Asiatic Law Amendment Ordinance, intended to reduce Indians and Chinese to a semi-criminal status. On September 11—yes, 9/11—three thousand Indians, both Hindu and Muslim, gathered at the Empire Theater in Johannesburg to voice their outrage. The outrage was leading to violence when Gandhi found himself onstage calling for the assembled to pledge their non-cooperation regardless of the consequences. It was here that the thousands fell silent. It was here that Satyagraha was born.

It is a sad irony that Gandhi was nominated for the Nobel Peace Prize five times: in 1937, 1938, 1939, 1947, and finally in 1948, a few days before his assassination. Clearly, there are many caste systems at work in the world. In a manner similar to how the orthodox Hindus blocked the temple road, the Nobel Prize was never awarded to Gandhi because he was considered "neither a real politician nor a humanitarian relief worker." To his credit, Michael Sohlam, the executive director for the Nobel Foundation, said many years later that not awarding Gandhi the Peace Prize was "a big regret."

Helping Each Other Up

208 *"Pain marks you"*: Margaret Atwood, in "Sunbeams" (quotations), *Sun*, September 2012, issue 441, p. 48, https://www.thesunmagazine.org/issues/441/sunbeams.

208 *monumental efforts to heal the wounded*: Details about healing the Civil War wounded are from Eric Foner, "Civil War Reconstruction Era and Aftermath," Thomas' Legion, http://thomaslegion.net/aftermath.html; National Museum of Civil War Medicine, http://www.civilwarmed.org/visit; "Soldiers Home History: A Summary," Milwaukee Soldiers Home Foundation, http://www.soldiershome.org/our-history; and "Health and Healing in North Carolina," http://ncmuseumofhistory.org/exhibits/healthandhealing/topic/34.

209 *Clara Barton (1821–1912)*: Details about Clara Barton are from Stephen B. Oates, *A Woman of Valor*, New York: Macmillan, 1994, pp. 58–64.

209 *Kovno, Lithuania*: Details about Kovno, Lithuania, and the Kovno Ghetto are from Dr. Joel Elkes, *Dr. Elkhanan Elkes of the Kovno Ghetto: A Son's Holocaust Memoir*, Brewster, MA: Paraclete Press, 1999; Avraham Tory, *Surviving the Ho-*

locaust: The Kovno Ghetto Diary, Cambridge, MA: Harvard University Press, 1991; Herman Kruk, *The Last Days of Jerusalem in Lithuania,* edited by Benjamin Harshav and translated by Barbara Harshav, New Haven, CT: Yale University Press, 2002; "Kaunas," Dov Levin, Yivo Encyclopedia of Jews in Eastern Europe, http://www.yivoencyclopedia.org/article.aspx/Kaunas; Jono David, "The Jews of Kovno: Text and Photographs," http://www.jewishvirtuallibrary.org/jsource/vjw/Kovno.html; and "The Kovno Ghetto," Association of Lithuanian Jews in Israel, http://www.lithuanianjews.org.il/HTMLs/article_list4.aspx?C2014=14287&BSP=14432&BSS59=14432.

209 *the Germans arrived in Kovno:* This is difficult to write about, because it's difficult to accept the depth of cruelty we're capable of. It's also difficult because, as a Jew, I've been touched by the cruelty of the Nazis. My grandmother's sister, her husband, and their son all died in Buchenwald.

209 *that summer in 1941:* An earlier treatment of this event appeared as my poem "Hill Where the Lord Hides" in the anthology *Blood to Remember: American Poets on the Holocaust,* second edition, edited by Charles Fishman, St. Louis, MO: Time Being, 2007, p. 305.

210 *"The Nazis also aimed to destroy":* Avraham Tory, *Surviving the Holocaust: The Kovno Ghetto Diary,* Cambridge: Harvard University Press, 1991.

210 *As Lenin said:* From the 2007 German film *The Lives of Others (Das Leben der Anderen)* by director Florian Henckel von Donnersmarck.

210 *tossing children . . . in potato sacks:* Aharon Barak was one of the small children tossed over the walls of the Kovno Ghetto in Lithuania in potato sacks to avoid being slaughtered by the Nazis. He was then smuggled away from the ghetto in a suitcase. He would later emigrate to Israel, where he would become the chief justice of the Israeli Supreme Court (1995–2006). His strength of character and fairness have made him legendary and controversial with many of his rulings upholding Palestinian rights in the long conflict between Israel and Palestine. Judge Barak was also instrumental in the famous Camp David Accords, which resulted in peace between Israel and Egypt.

Let the Trauma Speak

212 *"Trauma is an experience":* Pumla Gobodo-Madikizela, from her keynote, "Transcending Hatred" at the *Uncovering the Heart of Higher Education Conference,* San Francisco, February 23, 2007.

212 *This reminds me of a public learning ground in our time, South Africa:* Earlier versions of these two paragraphs first appeared in my essay "The Wisdom of an Open Heart" in *The Oprah Winfrey Show: Reflections on an American Legacy,* edited by Deborah Davis, New York: Harry N. Abrams, 2011.

213 *Pumla Gobodo-Madikizela:* Pumla is a remarkable human being. She is a clinical psychologist and associate professor of psychology at the University of Cape Town in South Africa. She was born in the Langa Township, one of the areas designated for blacks under apartheid. As mentioned above, Pumla served on the Truth and Reconciliation Commission (TRC) in 1996 as a member on the

Human Rights Violations Committee. For a compelling account of her experience, see her book *A Human Being Died That Night: A South African Story of
Forgiveness*, New York: Houghton Mifflin, 2003.

213 *Psychotherapist Edward Tick*: Ed and I have known each other for forty years.
Through his devotion to the healing of veterans, he is adding to our under-
standing of what violence does to the soul and to the society that ignores these
psycho-spiritual physics. Please see his books *War and the Soul: Healing Our
Nation's Veterans from Post-Traumatic Stress Disorder*, Wheaton, IL: Quest, 2005;
*The Practice of Dream Healing: Bringing Ancient Greek Mysteries into Modern
Medicine*, Wheaton, IL: Quest, 2001; and *Sacred Mountain: Encounters with the
Viet Nam Beast*, Santa Fe, NM: Moon Bear Press, 1989.

214 *"Indigenous cultures . . . watched over their warriors"*: Edward Tick, from an
interview, "Like Wandering Ghosts: Edward Tick on How the U.S. Fails Its
Returning Soldiers," in the journal *Sun*, issue 390, June 2008, p. 9, https://www
.thesunmagazine.org/issues/390/like-wandering-ghosts.

215 *Fambul Tok*: Details about Fambul Tok are from "What is Fambul Tok," Fambul
Tok International, http://www.fambultok.org/what-is-fambul-tok; "Fambul
Tok: A Film About the Power of Forgiveness," http://www.fambultok.com
/about/synopsis.

When to Stand Up

217 *Let's begin with Masada*: Details about Masada are from Jerome Murphy-
O'Connor, *The Holy Land*, Oxford Archaeological Guides, fifth edition, New
York: Oxford University Press, 2008, pp. 378–81; *"Masada: Legendary Strong-
hold of Judaism,"* Dabbs, The Cultured Traveler, and "The Conquering of Masada." Tog News, 2009.

217 *Flavius Josephus (37–100)*: Josephus was head of the Jewish forces in Galilee,
fighting against the Romans until surrendering in 67 A.D. Since Josephus foretold that Vespasian would become emperor of Rome, Vespasian kept Josephus
as a slave and interpreter. When Vespasian did become Emperor in 69 A.D., he
granted Josephus his freedom. In return, Josephus assumed the emperor's family name of Flavius. From that point on, Josephus fully defected to the Roman
way of life and was granted Roman citizenship. He became an advisor to Vespasian's son, Titus, serving as his translator when Titus attacked Jerusalem.

219 *at Babi Yar*: Details about Babi Yar are from Alexander V. Prusin, "A Community
of Violence: The SiPo and Its Role in the Nazi Terror System in Generalbezirk
Kiev," *Holocaust Genocide Studies* 21, no. 1, March 2007, 1–30; "Massacre at Babi
Yar," *Holocaust Chronicle*, http://www.holocaustchronicle.org/staticpages/270
.html; Victoria Khiterer, "Babi Yar: The Tragedy of Kiev's Jews," *Brandeis
Graduate Journal* 2, 2004, 1–16, http://www.berdichev.org/khiterer2004.pdf;
Abram L. Sachar, *The Redemption of the Unwanted*, New York: St. Martin's/
Marek, 1983; "The Einsatzgruppen: Babi Yar," Jewish Virtual Library, http://
www.jewishvirtuallibrary.org/jsource/Holocaust/babiyar.html; Michael Ber-
enbaum, *The World Must Know: The History of the Holocaust as Told in the United*

States Holocaust Museum, United States Holocaust Memorial Museum, 2006, pp. 97–98; and Jennifer Rosenberg, "Babi Yar: Mass Murder at the Babi Yar Ravine During the Holocaust," ThoughtCo., http://history1900s.about.com /od/holocaust/a/babiyar.htm.

219 *Anatoly Kuznetsov*: Kuznetsov described his experiences in German-occupied Kiev during World War II in his internationally acclaimed novel *Babi Yar: A Document in the Form of a Novel*, New York: Farrar, Straus and Giroux, 1970.

Facing Evil

222 *Facing Evil*: Details about the Warsaw Ghetto Uprising are from "Voices from the Inferno: Holocaust Survivors Describe the Last Months in the Warsaw Ghetto—January 1943: The First Armed Resistance in the Ghetto," an online exhibition by Yad Vashem, http://www.yadvashem.org/yv/en/exhibitions /warsaw_ghetto_testimonies/resistance.asp?WT.mc_id=wiki; Hanna Krall, *Shielding the Flame: An Intimate Conversation with Dr. Marek Edelman, the Last Surviving Leader of the Warsaw Ghetto Uprising*, translated by Joanna Stasinska Weschler and Lawrence Weschler, New York: Henry Holt, 1986, p. 95; Hanna Krall, *To Outwit God*, translated by Joanna Stasinska Weschler and Lawrence Weschler, Chicago: Northwestern University Press, p. 218; and Shmuel Krakowski, *War of the Doomed: Jewish Armed Resistance in Poland, 1942–1944*, New York: Holmes & Meier, 1984, pp. 213–14.

226 *"I don't think there's any real need to analyze the Uprising"*: Antony Polonsky, *The Jews in Poland and Russia: Volume III, 1914 to 2008*, Oxford, UK: Littman Library of Jewish Civilization, 2012, p. 537.

227 *the web page Voices from the Inferno: Holocaust Survivors Describe the Last Months in the Warsaw Ghetto*: This is an invaluable resource of history created by Yad Vashem, the world center for documentation, research, education and commemoration of the Holocaust, established in Israel in 1953. See http://www .yadvashem.org/yv/en/exhibitions/warsaw_ghetto_testimonies/resistance.asp.

In the Middle of the Storm

228 *persecuted for centuries*: Details about the history of homosexuality and the LGBT movement are from https://en.wikipedia.org/wiki/History_of_homo sexuality and https://en.wikipedia.org/wiki/Timeline_of_LGBT_history.

228 *the Etoro and Marind-anim tribes*: From *Ritualized Homosexuality in Melanesia*, edited by Gilbert H. Herdt, Berkeley and Los Angeles: University of California Press, 1984, pp. 128–36.

228 *the indigenous peoples of the Americas*: From Stephen Murray, "Mexico," in *GLBTQ: An Encyclopedia of Gay, Lesbian, Bisexual, Transgender, and Queer Culture*, edited by Claude J. Summers, Chicago: GLBTQ.com, 2004.

228 *the Spanish explorer Balboa*: Pedro Mártir de Anglería (1530), cited by Alexandre Coello de la Rosa, "The Dark Side of the New World," *Delaware Review of Latin American Studies* 3, no. 2, August 2002.

229 *And though same-sex marriage is now legal*: Same-sex marriage dates back to 54 A.D. when Nero, as emperor as Rome, married two men, Pythagoras and Sporus, in a legal ceremony to the disapproval of more conservative factions. Yet it wasn't until 1889 that homosexuality was legalized in Europe (in Italy).

229 *"The gay ghetto was a tinderbox"*: David France, "Pictures from a Battlefield," *New York Times*, March 25, 2012.

230 *fighting for their lives with dignity*: For a remarkable and heartfelt account of this time, please see the Oscar-nominated documentary *How to Survive a Plague* by David France, http://surviveaplague.com, and the history of ACT UP at https://en.wikipedia.org/wiki/ACT_UP; http://www.actuporalhistory .org/interviews/index.html; and http://actupny.com/actions/index.php/the -community.

230 *ACT UP organized protests and demonstrations*: At the initial protest in March 1987, 250 ACT UP members demonstrated on Wall Street and Broadway to demand greater access to experimental AIDS drugs and for a coordinated national policy to fight the disease. A year later, on March 24, 1988, ACT UP returned to Wall Street for a larger demonstration in which more than a hundred people were arrested simply for asking for help. See https://en.wikipedia.org/wiki /ACT_UP and http://www.actuporalhistory.org/interviews/index.html.

Turning Fire into Light

233 *In the 1830s . . . peanuts, and cotton*: Nick Mathiason, *Observer*, July 3, 2005.

234 *Williams was brought . . . while he burned*: These two paragraphs are from a compelling book, *Crimes of Hate*, edited by Phyllis B. Gerstenfeld and Diana R. Grant, Thousand Oaks, CA: Sage, 2003, pp. 8–9.

Reclaiming Our Humanity

237 *"Some day man will see"*: León Felipe, *Roots & Wings: Poetry from Spain 1900– 1975*, edited by Hardie St. Martin, New York: White Pine, 2005, p. 3.

237 *one of his Tutsi sisters had been murdered*: From conversations with Dr. Hagengimana in December 2005. A native of Rwanda, Dr. Hagengimana has worked in Kenya, Sierra Leone, and Liberia and has been a research fellow at Harvard Medical School in war-related mental health.

OUR INTERESTS ARE THE SAME

245 *"Man did not weave the web of life"*: Chief Seattle, from *Words of Power: Voices from Indian America*, edited by Norbert S. Hill Jr. (Oneida), Golden, CO: Fulcrum, 1994, p. 36.

247 *Martina Whelsula*: Please see *Living a Generous Life: Reflections on Giving and Receiving* at www.LearningtoGive.org/materials/folktales. This reference is from p. 36. These interviews were conducted and edited by Megan Scribner.

Megan is a gifted editor and dear friend. Her books include *Teaching with Fire* and *Leading from Within*.

When We Understand

249 *"When you understand"*: From "Bells and Robes," in "The Gateless Gate," in *Zen Flesh, Zen Bones*, compiled by Paul Reps and Nyogen Senzaki, Boston: Shambhala, 1994, p. 189.

249 *his response*: From Mark Nepo, "The Common Cradle of Concern: An Interview with Howard Zinn," *Essays on Deepening the American Dream* 11, Fall 2006.

250 *When the Paris Commune*: Details about the Paris Commune of 1871 are from Donny Gluckstein, *The Paris Commune: A Revolution in Democracy*, Chicago: Haymarket, 2011.

250 *social anarchists*: Details about the anarchists of Catalonia are from George Orwell, *Homage to Catalonia*, New York: Mariner, 1980; an eight-minute film called "Anarchists in the 1936 Spanish Civil War," http://www.youtube.com /watch?v=VUig0lFHDDw; and the website Spanish Revolution (1936).

251 *and shopping was done with vouchers*: Jack White, one of the founders of the Irish Citizen Army, found himself in Barcelona in 1936 during the uprising against Franco. He was there as an administrator for a British Red Cross unit. He was looking to set up a field hospital when his unit was canceled because the ambulances were redirected elsewhere. He was left to wander for days in Barcelona and recorded these impressions: "My first and deepest impression is that of the natural nobility of the Catalan people. I got that impression early, when we had to spend six hours waiting for the Barcelona train. A bright sun was shining which tempted me to bathe in the bay. After undressing I left my coat, with some 80 English pounds in the pocket, on the rocks close to a frequented path with a sense of its perfect safety. Half an hour in Catalonia and a few conversations in my faulty Spanish made me feel I was among friends.

"This impression of revolutionary honor has been maintained by all I have seen and experienced. It is [also] a fact that many of [the burnt churches] are used to house medical stores. The destruction of the churches has not destroyed love and honesty in Spain. If they are not based on the love of God, they are based on brotherliness, selflessness and self-respect, which have to be experienced to be believed."

252 *"Right from the moment of our birth"*: The Dalai Lama, in "Sunbeams" (quotations), *Sun*, issue 433, January 2012, p. 48, https://www.thesunmagazine.org /issues/433/sunbeams.

252 *to care for the soul of the Earth*: From the chapter by Bill Plotkin, "Care of the Soul of the World," in *Spiritual Ecology: The Cry of the Earth*, edited by Llewellyn Vaughan-Lee, Point Reyes, CA: Golden Sufi Center, 2013, pp. 224–25.

Our Global Body

254 World Report on Violence and Health: World Health Organization, Geneva, 2002, p. 8.

255 "What would a vaccine for violence look like?": Frances Henry, from Vaccines for Violence, Cummington, MA: East Branch, 2008, pp. 5–6.

If Another World Is Possible

257 Vincent Harding: Vincent Harding (1931–2014) was an elder in the civil rights movement who became an African-American historian and scholar. He founded the Veterans of Hope Project.

257 Cynthia Cherry: Cynthia Cherry is the president and CEO of the groundbreaking International Leadership Association.

257 "When we stay together, we can't be broken": In "Sunbeams" (quotations), Sun, February 2006, issue 362, p. 48, https://www.thesunmagazine.org/issues/362/sunbeams.

258 "Each leaf-carrying ant": Dr. Barbara Royal, Huffington Post, http://www.huffingtonpost.com/barbara-e-royal-dvm/new-year_b_2386424.html and http://www.royaltreatmentveterinarycenter.com.

258 Next to humans: Details from "Leafcutter ants," http://en.wikipedia.org/wiki/Leafcutter_ant.

259 the Roman Seneca's: Seneca (4–65 A.D.) was a Roman philosopher and statesman. Born in Córdoba, Spain, he made his way to Rome where he became a tutor and advisor to the emperor Nero.

259 "In Tibet": Sun, issue 443, November 2012, p. 14. Originally published in Shambhala: The Sacred Path of the Warrior, Chögyam Trungpa. Boston: Shambhala Publications, 1984.

260 the Sahtu Got'ine tribe: The account of this pilgrimage was told by As Be'sha Blondin, an elder of the tribe, at the 2015 Parliament of the World's Religions held in Salt Lake City. Cited by Trebbe Johnson in "How Do We Reclaim the Heart of Humanity?" in Parabola, Spring 2016, p. 106.

260 "It Is I Who Must Begin": Václav Havel, excerpt from Letters to Olga, translated by Paul Winston, New York: Alfred A. Knopf, 1988.

The Seeing Place

262 Larry Braskamp: Please see his book Putting Students First: How Colleges Develop Students Purposefully, Bolton, MA: Anker, 2006.

262 "Our call is to appreciate, not classify": From Raimon Panikkar's talk at the 2004 Parliament of the World's Religions in Barcelona, Spain, July 7–13, 2004. In the lineage of the Hindu spiritual leader, Ramakrishna (see the chapter "The Swan and the Tailor" in Finding Inner Courage, San Francisco: Conari, 2007), Raimon Panikkar (1918–2010) was one of the world's leading exemplars of interfaith practice and dialogue. Please see his books The Vedic Experience Mantraman-

jari: *An Anthology of the Vedas for Modern Man and Contemporary Celebration,* new edition, Delhi: Motilal Banarsidass, 2016, and *The Unknown Christ of Hinduism: Toward an Ecumenical Christophany,* London: Darton, Longman & Todd, 1981.

264 *Lo-Sun, a blind boy*: From *Tell These Secrets: Tales of Generosity from Around the World,* an amazing collection of seventy-four stories gathered from twenty-three traditions, edited by Margo McLoughlin and Ian Simmons. Many of these stories are available as a teaching resource at www.LearningtoGive.org.

The Peacemakers

267 *"I do not want"*: Helen Keller, in "Sunbeams" (quotations), *Sun,* issue 462, June 2014, p. 48, https://www.thesunmagazine.org/issues/462/sunbeams-462.

267 *Legend has it*: Details about the League of the Iroquois Nations are from "The Peacemaker and the Tree of Peace" in First People: The Legends, http://www.firstpeople.us/FP-Html-Legends/ThePeacemakerAndTheTreeOfPeace-Iroquois.html; "The Birth of Frontier Democracy from an Eagle's Eye View: The Great Law of Peace to The Constitution of the United States of America." Statement given by Gregory Schaaf before the Select Committee on Indian Affairs United States Senate (One Hundredth Congress, First Session on S. Con Res. 76), Washington, D.C., December 2, 1987; and David Yarrow, "The Great Law of Peace: New World Roots of American Democracy," September 1987.

269 *The Iroquois tribal system involved three councils*: This paragraph is from James Mencarelli and Steve Severin, *Protest 3: Red, Black, Brown Experience in America,* Grand Rapids, MI: William B. Eerdmans, 1975, pp. 173–74.

Eight Worldviews and Practices

272 *The Lebanese greeting, "Ya Ayuni!"*: I'm indebted to my friend, the wonderful poet Naomi Shihab Nye, for introducing me to this joyous custom.

272 *an Infinite Wheel*: An earlier treatment of this metaphor appears in my book *The Book of Awakening: Having the Life You Want by Being Present in the Life You Have,* San Francisco: Conari, 2000, entry on January 6.

273 *"a form of everyday togetherness"*: From "Interweavings: A cultural phenomenology of everyday consumption and social atmosphere within Danish middle-class families," Jeppe Trolle Linnet, University of Southern Denmark, 2010.

273 *a greeting offered by African Bushmen*: An earlier treatment of this metaphor appears in my book *The Book of Awakening: Having the Life You Want by Being Present in the Life You Have,* San Francisco: Conari, 2000, entry on December 31.

The Highest Ethic

276 *In Chicago*: Details about the foreclosure of homes in Chicago are from an article by John Leland, "Sheriff in Chicago Ends Evictions in Foreclosures," *New York Times,* October 8, 2008.

277 *John Bryan... Alliance for African Assistance*: From a presentation by John Bryan at the 2007 International Leadership Association Conference in Vancouver, British Columbia, November 1, 2007.

A Small Boy

280 *Chim*: The American photojournalist David Seymour was born in Warsaw, Poland, in 1911 as David Szymin. With heart and determination, he chronicled the rawness of the human spirit meeting the rawness of the world. He died while on assignment in Suez in 1956. The photo mentioned appeared in the exhibit "Chim" at the International Center for Photography in New York City, August 28, 2007. His photo-essay, *Children of Europe*, was published by UNESCO in 1949.

281 *Blind, Armless Boy Reading with His Lips, Italy, 1948, Chim*: Photograph from *Children of Europe*, UNESCO, 1949, http://blindflaneur.com/2008/02/19/curiosity-the-blind-photographer-2-david-seymour.

Index

About the Author

MARK NEPO moved and inspired readers and seekers all over the world with his #1 *New York Times* bestseller *The Book of Awakening*. Beloved as a poet, teacher, and storyteller, Mark has been called "one of the finest spiritual guides of our time," "a consummate storyteller," and "an eloquent spiritual teacher." His work is widely accessible and used by many, and his books have been translated into more than twenty languages. A bestselling author, he has published twenty books and recorded fourteen audio projects. In 2015, he was given a Life Achievement Award by AgeNation. And in 2016, he was named by *Watkins: Mind Body Spirit* as one of the 100 Most Spiritually Influential Living People, and was also chosen as one of OWN's *SuperSoul 100*, a group of inspired leaders using their gifts and voices to elevate humanity. In 2017, Mark became a regular columnist for *Spirituality & Health* magazine.

Recent work includes *Things That Join the Sea and the Sky* (Sounds True, 2017); *The Way Under the Way: The Place of True Meeting* (Sounds True, 2016), a Nautilus Book Award Winner; *The One Life We're Given* (Atria), cited by *Spirituality & Practice* as one of the Best Spiritual Books of 2016; *Inside the Miracle* (Sounds True), selected by *Spirituality & Health* magazine as one of the top ten best books of 2015; *The Endless Practice* (Atria), cited by *Spirituality & Practice* as one of the Best Spiritual Books of 2014; his book of poems, *Reduced to Joy* (Viva Editions), named by *Spirituality & Practice* as one of the Best Spiritual Books of 2013; a six-CD box set of teaching conversations based on the poems in *Reduced to Joy* (Sounds True, 2014); and *Seven Thousand Ways to Listen* (Atria), which won the 2012 Books for a Better Life Award.

Mark was part of Oprah Winfrey's "The Life You Want" tour in 2014 and has appeared on her *Super Soul Sunday* program on

OWN TV several times. He has also been interviewed by Robin Roberts on *Good Morning America*. *The Exquisite Risk* was listed by *Spirituality & Practice* as one of the Best Spiritual Books of 2005, calling it "one of the best books we've ever read on what it takes to live an authentic life." Mark devotes his writing and teaching to the journey of inner transformation and the life of relationship. He continues to offer readings, lectures, and retreats. Please visit Mark at: www.MarkNepo.com, threeintentions.com, and wmespeakers.com/speaker/mark-nepo.